MODELS AND CONTACTS

BRILL'S SERIES IN JEWISH STUDIES

VOL. 25

TUTA SUB AEGIDE PALLAS · 1683 ·

MODELS AND CONTACTS

Arabic Literature and its Impact on Medieval Jewish Culture

BY

RINA DRORY

BRILL
LEIDEN · BOSTON · KÖLN
2000

This book is printed on acid-free paper.

Library of Congress Cataloging-in-Publication Data

Drory, Rina.
Models and contacts : Arabic literature and its impact on medieval Jewish culture / by Rina Drory.
p. cm. — (Brill's series in Jewish studies, ISSN 0926-2261 ; vol. 25)
Includes bibliographical references and index.
ISBN 9004117385 (cloth : alk. paper)
1. Arabic literature—750-1258—History and criticism. 2. Hebrew literature—Arab influences. 3. Hebrew literature, Medieval—History and criticism. I. Title. II. Series.
PJ7530.D76 2000
892.7'09003—dc21 00-039777
CIP

Die Deutsche Bibliothek – CIP-Einheitsaufnahme

Drory, Rina:
Models and contacts : Arabic literature and its impact on medieval Jewish culture / by Rina Drory. – Leiden ; Boston ; Köln : Brill, 2000
(Brill's series in Jewish studies ; Vol. 25)
ISBN 90-04-11738-5

ISSN 0926-2261
ISBN 90 04 11738 5

PRINTED IN THE NETHERLANDS

For Yossi and Yoel

TABLE OF CONTENTS

ACKNOWLEDGMENTS

I wish to express my warmest thanks to all the people who have given me support of various kinds during the development of this book. First of all, to Itamar Even-Zohar, who has been a constant source of inspiration for me during the many years we have been working together. I owe the very possibility of developing my own research on the Arabic-Jewish context to the conceptual framework he has established for working on the dynamics of heterogeneous bodies of literature, and recently, of complex cultural entities. Nearly every section of this book has benefited from his unfailingly generous attention and skillful advice. To Gadi Algazi I owe a special debt for reading the entire manuscript and for offering many valuable comments. His suggestions and remarks through long hours of conversation have greatly shaped my thinking; while his fresh outlook and remarkable talents as both historian and culture researcher have added significant value to this work. His support in countless ways during the long process of preparing the book for publication has been a source of renewed encouragement. Chapter four of this volume originated as an MA thesis written under the supervision of Benjamin Harshav (Hrushovski). I would like to extend my gratitude to him not only for providing me with the theoretical framework for studying rhyme, but also for his invaluable remarks and continuous encouragement to publish the study on the Arabic rhyme in English.

I am grateful to Raymond Scheindlin for his assistance in rendering into English difficult medieval Hebrew and Judeo-Arabic. His precise and refined understanding of both languages and obvious love for the intertwined relationships between Hebrew and Arabic was brought to bear upon the English, to which he willingly devoted precious time. With Ella Almagor I spent most enjoyable time working on the English translation of Abū Nuwās's wine-poems. Her meticulous scholarship in Arabic and great attention to the English product are evident in the translation.

A veritable team of editors has also dealt with this work over the years of preparation. I express my special appreciation to Larry Lester for the devoted editing and copyediting of chapter four, and to Dahlia Scheindlin, who handled the final version of rest of the book, for her professional editing, careful attention and generous readiness to always be there for me, regardless of time or other constraints.

Thanks are owed to the institutions that gave me the academic framework for advancing this research. A Charter Fellowship in Oriental Studies at Wolfson College, Oxford, has enabled the research on which Chapter Ten of this volume is based; a semester with a research group on Saʿadiya Gaon at the Institute for Advanced Studies at the Hebrew University of Jerusalem produced Chapter Eight. I thank all the publications where the previously published chapters here first appeared, for allowing me to published the revised versions: The Porter Institute for Poetics and Semiotics, Tel Aviv University, *Jerusalem Studies in Arabic and Islam*, *Dappim* (Research in Literature), *Geniza Research After Ninety Years: The Case of Judaeo-Arabic*, *Israel Oriental Studies*, *Jerusalem Studies in Hebrew Literature*.

The fact that so many of the people who have assisted me in this book are also dear friends is what makes this laborious project so worthy and rewarding. But more than anything else, the love and support of my husband, Yossi, and my son, Yoel, provided me with the emotional basis for completing this project during a most trying period in life.

INTRODUCTION

This volume examines the historical poetics of medieval Arabic literature and its contacts with contemporary Jewish literature. While connected by a clear strand of development, the diverse works collected here, partly published and revised and partly unpublished, clearly reflect an evolving research trajectory regarding various aspects of medieval Arabic literature, as fresh questions suggest the adoption of new perspectives and theoretical approaches, and these, in turn, bring new material into view. From an initial focus on the literary text as an autonomous—even privileged—piece of artistic work, this research moves to view "literature" as a cultural institution, a function of socio-cultural relations. Eventually, it attempts to investigate the complex modes in which textual activities model reality and provide people with paradigms of conduct and perception.

My work in classical Arabic literature started with the study of classical Arabic rhyme (chapter four of this volume). It was strongly motivated by the rejection of a then-powerful orientalist paradigm, which, captivated by the Western image of belles lettres, refused to recognize the "literariness" of Classical Arabic texts. The orientalist disregard for the "genuine" literary qualities in Arabic literary (and even poetic) texts created an impression that they merited only historical-philological reading. Following Roman Jakobson's emphasis on the role played by the organization of a text's non-semantic aspects in constituting its "literariness," I focused on the institution of rhyme, traditionally considered by Arabic literary criticism to be a hallmark of "literariness." Unlike Arabic meter, which seems to have received generous scholarly attention, consistently stimulating new hypotheses and speculations, very little research has actually been done on rhyme. Received knowledge of classical Arabic rhyme systems consisted basically of the re-assembly, re-phrasing, re-classification and re-interpretation by modern scholarship of the conclusions reached by medieval Arab prosodists.

My study of rhyme is an attempt at a functionalist analysis of the conspicuous and well-established institution of rhyme in classical Arabic literature, which so far has only been considered within a taxonomic approach. Working with a theoretical framework for analyzing prosody developed by Benjamin Harshav, I was able to establish an underlying rhyming-system regulating rhyming in classical Arabic texts, having examined a corpus of rhymed texts in both poetry and prose.

I would like to emphasize two of the major conclusions of this study at the outset:

(a) Contrary to the common impression (often considered an established fact in modern scholarship), classical Arabic rhyme is *not* founded solely (or even mainly) on the last root-consonant in the line (*rawiyy*), but rather on a basic tri-syllabic phonological pattern, which determines, in several optional ways, the possible range of repeating sound-elements in the rhyme. The Arabic rhyme is sound-poor, often based on only one consonant. Aesthetic effect is thus achieved by the repetition of fixed morphological patterns, rather than by an impressive abundance of consonants. Nevertheless, this scheme was supple enough to produce a range of variants to accommodate tastes and preferences throughout the classical period, from a minimum of only one terminal rhyming consonant to a maximum of sound repetition of all elements, identical in sound and distinguishable only on the semantic level.

(b) Semantic considerations indeed played a major role in the rhyming system of classical Arabic rhymed prose. Unlike poetry, which retains a uniform rhymeme throughout the whole poem (for the concept, see chapter four, sections 1.1-4), rhymed prose is characterized by multiple rhymemes within one text. The question of what determines the alternation of the rhymemes was one of my main concerns in this study. In Western poetic traditions an arbitrary alternation pattern is imposed on rhyme alternation. Arabic rhymed prose is different. What at a first glance seems to be an inconsistent chain of rhymed phrases and unpredictable rhymemes, actually constitutes a highly elaborate sequence, carefully arranged according to two semantic principles: repetition and complementarity. These are analogous to Roman Jakobson's distinction between the metaphoric and the metonymic principles governing textual organization. Each of the two determined, respectively, either the number of rhyme members sharing the same rhymeme, or the alternation of the rhymemes. Rhyme alternation is thus governed by the same semantic principles that structured the sequencing of text segments. Different authors of rhymed prose, in particular the *maqāmāt* authors al-Hamad̲ānī and al-Ḥarīrī, employed these two principles with varying intensity on different levels of textual organization, creating not only different rhyme alternation patterns, but also distinct stylistic and narrative models. Rhyme analysis thus yields new perspectives on prose narrative structures for both medieval Arabic and Hebrew literatures, since the *maqāmāt* genre was successfully adopted by medieval Hebrew authors (chapter ten).

This stage of my work exemplifies what a functionalist approach can achieve. It permitted going beyond codified poetics as formulated by medieval and modern scholars, to discern underlying regularities where randomness had seemed to reign. A specific rhyme system emerged, manifest on different levels of textual organization and over a wide range of literary texts, both prose and poetry. However, this was achieved at the cost of ignoring many non-formal aspects of literary production less capable of formalization.

The shift in my research to the semantic dimensions of literature and the production of meaning is evinced in the first section of this volume (chapters one to three). Dedicated to the problem of fictionality in classical Arabic literature, chapters one and three explore the fictional models which developed; chapters one and two investigate the status and legitimation of fiction. While still working with a corpus of texts considered "literary" in a narrow sense (*adab* and *maqāmāt*), my actual concern in this section is with the classical Arabic repertoire of models for representing, or rather, constructing "reality." As fiction does not reside solely in literary texts, it seemed necessary to explore its role in other domains of classical Arabic literature, like *ḥadīṯ* and historical writings.

The first chapter in this section deals with the emergence of the *maqāma* genre at the end of the tenth century. Relying heavily on existing literary materials and forms, notably those gathered in *adab* collections, the *maqāma* nevertheless molded them into a distinct new literary model. For example, pieces of descriptions cited as samples of eloquence in *adab* collections, complete with transmission chains attributing them to their presumed enunciators, were deployed in the *maqāma* as text segments and integrated in a narrative, thereby assuming a new function and status. But the main innovation introduced by the *maqāma* was its overt fictional character.

Fiction was generally rejected in classical Arabic culture, especially as far as prose texts were concerned. Governed by powerful religio-poetic norms, literary texts maintained a strict distinction between "truth" and "falsehood." Almost no legitimacy was extended to texts considered both *fictional* and *meaningful.* Texts not claiming to purport "truth" were tolerated only if deemed "not serious," possessing solely entertainment value. The introduction of the *maqāma* as an overtly declared fictional genre should be assessed against this background. The chapter discusses both the initial difficulty of introducing fiction into classical Arabic literature, and the subsequent adjustment of the *maqāma* to the dominant poetic norms. While previous works introduced as meaningful fiction remained peripheral or were marked as "non-Arabic", the *maqāma* was actually accepted and celebrated. Yet this was achieved at a dear price: its declared fictionality was blurred through marginalization of plot, dialogue and fictional characters, and a preeminent place was accorded to feats of eloquence and to edifying subject matter. Plot was reduced to a mere prop for traditional *adab* materials.

Whereas chapter two focuses on the problematization of fictionality in the *maqāma*, chapter three discusses the specific techniques in classical Arabic texts for creating a sense of reality, an *effet du réel.* I try to demonstrate the achievement of this effect in a particular group of poems by Abū Nuwās, dedicated to drinking scenes in Abbasid wine-taverns. One might expect a realistic effect to be simulated by cataloguing reality-items of wine culture. However, while most of Abū Nuwās's wine poetry is indeed rife with reality-items connected to the drinking culture of the time, these reality-items are not used to convey realism so much as to support an extremely elaborate imagery, in accordance with the norms of descriptive poetry (*waṣf*). It is not immediate recognition of the "real world" that is sought here, but attention to the linguistic encoding and verbal artistry. In the group of poems examined, such reality-items are, however, conspicuously absent; the poems mainly consist of a dialogue between the wine vendor and his customer-guests. Nearly devoid of description, an unmistakable "realistic" effect is nonetheless created, as the vivid bohemian and humorous atmosphere of the tavern drinking sessions is conveyed. This "lifelike" impression could not have been achieved by cataloguing reality-items, for their use was reserved for figurative functions. Though Arabic poets were familiar with dialogue from its prominence in *ḥadīṯ*, where it was associated with an immanent claim for authenticity, dialogue was rarely employed in poetry. Not overdetermined by prior poetic conventions, yet bearing the "authenticity" of Islamic tradition, Abū Nuwās found dialogue a suitable vehicle for creating a sense of "reality" in some of his wine poems. Future study might assess whether dialogue performs the function of realism elsewhere in classical Arabic literature.

Attitudes towards the status of fiction and fictional texts within the classical Arabic literary system can be inferred from the occasional attempts to legitimize fiction, which are discussed mainly in chapter two. An apparent attempt to legitimize the *ḵurāfāt* genre by employing *ḥadīṯ* techniques is found in a tradition called *ḥadīṯ ḵurāfa*. It explains, on the authority of the Prophet, the origin of the word *ḵurāfa* as a name of a person ravished by demons in Ǧāhiliyya times who, upon returning to the human world, recounted his adventures. The Prophet emphasizes that his stories were true. Through his authority, legitimate status was accorded to stories both "true" and fantastic. Although such stories circulated in respected *adab* symposia, they were often regarded as particularly appealing to women and younger adults, and thus were relegated to a low status.

Another strategy to legitimize fiction endeavored to affiliate the *maqāma* with animal fables, and in particular with *Kalīla wadimna*. Here, animals assumed the capacity of human speech, serving as protagonists based on a poetic convention quite remote from official *ḥadīṯ* and *adab*. Although the semi-allegory of this Indian-Persian import was indeed very different from the prevalent "realistic" prose models of classical Arabic literature, the book itself attained high status and considerable popularity in court circles and became one of the most famous works of Arabic literature. While obviously regarded as fiction, animal fables were acknowledged to embody profound wisdom relevant to real life. Considered alien yet highly appreciated, necessarily fictional yet deeply meaningful, *Kalīla wadimna* was thus a particularly suitable banner under which to promote the legitimacy of prose fiction.

Another attempt to legitimize the *maqāma*'s fictionality involved the tradition of love poetry (*tašbīb*). That classical Arabic poetry did not convey "reality" was granted by both poets and critics throughout the classical period (suffice it to mention here the famous apothegm *aḥsanu al-šiʿri akḏabuhu*: "falsehood makes for the best poetry"). At the same time, the social function of love poetry and its thematic conventions demanded that poets include pseudo-autobiographical accounts of love in their poems. They did this by incorporating "true" details into love poems, such as the name (or nickname) of the poet's beloved and allusions to their supposed amorous encounters. Contriving a realistic impression on one hand, while renouncing any commitment to "truth" on the other, *tašbīb* poetry embodied an uneasy conflation of poetry and life. This constitutive ambiguity of fictional and realistic status served as a common denominator between love poetry and the *maqāmāt*.

Providing protagonists with real names and places of birth was a significant and controversial step. Whereas *ḵurāfāt* tales were situated in a remote and fantastic reality, and animal fables were overtly fictional in their use of animals as protagonists, the *maqāma* presented fictional protagonists as "real" figures located in familiar settings. Such an ambiguous attempt at fictionality *and* a certain verisimilitude could perhaps be tolerated in poetry, but certainly not in prose. We might conclude that in classical Arabic literature the major *functional* distinction between prose and poetry resides first and foremost in their respective associations with specific modes of representation, rather than in formal attributes such as meter and rhyme. While prose is committed to representing "reality", poetry is not necessarily consigned to that role.

The examination of fictionality in classical Arabic literature proved that the issue cannot be properly addressed so long as its research remains compartmentalized into the rigid, traditional divisions of poetry, *adab*, *ḥadīṯ*, Koranic exegesis, historical chronicles, and so on. Research on fictionality in classical texts requires an integrated consideration of the heterogeneous corpus, in order to identify the repertoire of literary models, the range of options, their interrelations and possible transformations.

This conviction informs the topic to which the last section of this volume is devoted, namely, Jewish literary contacts with medieval Arabic literature. Building on my previous work on Arabic literature, chapters five to ten explore the role of Arabic literature in the reconstitution of Jewish (both Hebrew and Judeo-Arabic) literature between the tenth and the thirteenth centuries. The methodological framework for studying the dynamics of literatures in contact and of cultural interference proposed by Itamar Even-Zohar in his works on Polysystem Theory proved to be extremely fruitful here. Although space constraints prohibit a summary of the complex issues involved in contact between Jewish and Arabic literatures, I would nonetheless like to point out some implications of my work for general processes of literary contact and cultural interference.

First, literary contacts are not necessarily manifest in recognized, readily identifiable textual elements, such as particular motifs, metaphors, etc. Such elements can be totally ignored when borrowing, or can be adopted without significant impact on the dynamics of the borrowing system. Even finalized texts produced via literary contact do not necessarily bear traces of that process. Instead, literary contact is often manifest in the adoption of productive models and organizing principles for literary activity. From the tenth century onwards, the organizing principle of the Arabic hierarchy of literary genres (with the Koran at its summit) is introduced into Jewish literature, with such results as the configuration of new literary activities around the Bible (chapter five); the emergence of a new division of functions between the written languages (chapter seven); and the adoption of new Arabic literary models in Jewish literature, reshaping the repertoire of models for writing in Hebrew and in Judeo-Arabic (chapters five and six). A case study (chapter five, section three) reveals how a Jewish grammarian follows an Arabic precedent to establish linguistic standards for Hebrew: as Arabic grammarians looked to Bedouins as speakers of pure, uncorrupted Arabic, he ascribes a similar function to the speech of the people of Tiberias, projecting analogous attributes onto them.

Second, the study of literary contacts is often reduced to the detection of borrowed elements, and retracing them back to an assumed origin in some foreign literature. This can be a misleading strategy, as isolated elements may well acquire new significance, function or status when inserted into a new context. Rather than concentrate on isolated elements and apparent similarities, it would be more productive, therefore, to endeavor to reconstruct the *contexts* for borrowing and assimilating; where borrowing is conceived not as a by-product of casual proximity, but as an active process of selection and transformation. Apparent borrowing may well conceal an entire network of transformations of the borrowed element, as demonstrated by Dunaš Ben Labraṭ's introduction of syllabic metre into Hebrew poetry in tenth-century Andalus. Contrary to the accepted view that Dunaš Ben Labraṭ adopted Arabic metre in its entirety, I contend that he only adopted its structural principle (my description of which differs from the accepted one), adjusting it to Hebrew morphology (chapter nine).

Third, contacts do not necessarily take place where communities actually meet. Physical or social propinquity is not enough in itself to induce actual borrowing. Models must be available to their prospective borrowers, and, more importantly, they should serve the borrowers better than existing options within their own system. An analysis of the borrowers' literary system becomes essential for understanding literary contacts. This is demonstrated in the case of the Jewish adoption of Arabic literary models that took place outside the Jewish-Islamic arena, in northern Spain and Provence, where Jewish emigrants from Andalusi Spain (like Moses Ibn Ezra) sought to establish themselves in their host communities on the basis of Arabic cultural prestige. In a similar fashion, al-Ḥarīzī's Hebrew adaptation of al-Ḥarīrī's Arabic *maqāmāt* was not simply the product of a Jewish encounter with Arabic literature, but rather that of a Provençal Jew encountering Arabized Jewish communities of the East (chapter ten).

Fourth, the question of what language to choose for the borrowed writing models has proven to be far from a simple, neutral decision, made according to convenience considerations, or one done solely on the linguistic level. Every language maintains its own repertoire of culturally constructed images and conceptions of "life." The choice of a language has therefore far-reaching implications for the basic cultural assumptions through which the writer delineates the cultural identity of his reading public and of himself as author. Writing in Hebrew or in Arabic suggested wholly different models of reality, and Saʿadya Gaon took full advantage of these options in the two introductions he wrote to his book *Sefer ha-egron* (chapter eight).

No valid account of the dynamics of Jewish literature in the Islamic world can dispense with a serious consideration of Arabic culture, as some adherents of a purified national history maintain. On the other hand, Arabic literature does not provide a ready explanation for shifts in Jewish literature; its proximity alone does not make it a relevant context, as some romanticized versions of the Jewish-Arabic cultural encounter would have us believe. The impingement of Arabic literature was always mediated by the inner dynamics of Jewish literature, and it is in this perspective that the contact should be considered and evaluated.

In turn, insights procured through the study of contacts between Jewish and Arabic literature have modified my views of classical Arabic literature. Certain traits of Arabic literature acquire their significance when set against the background of contemporary Hebrew literature. I have argued, for example, that organizing principles borrowed from Arabic influenced the elevation of the Bible to its supreme status in tenth-century Eastern Jewish literature. Yet its position in medieval Jewish literature as a productive model for style and narrative makes the limited role played by the Koran in Arabic literature all the more intriguing, revered as the zenith of Arabic eloquence without having developed into a model for actual literary production.

Analysis of literary contacts focuses attention on competition and conflict within borrowing communities and on literary strategies pursued by participating agents. Emphasis that had once shifted from final texts to productive models, now shifts again to the agents manipulating these models in fluctuating circumstances. Hence, my later work will concentrate on agents and their strategies for modifying not only literary models, but their own cultural roles and self-images.

An early version of the first chapter was published in Hebrew under the title: "Libeʿayat hitqabluta shel ha-maqāma ba-sifrut ha-ʿaravit ha-qlasit." *Ha-Sifrut* 32 (1982): 15-26. Chapter Two is based on my paper "Three Attempts to Legitimize Fiction in Classical Arabic Literature," published in *Jerusalem Studies in Arabic and Islam* 18 (1994), 146-164. An earlier version of Chapter Four was published in Hebrew under the title: *Ha-Poetika shel ha-ḥariza basifrut ha-arvit ha-klasit* (Tel Aviv: The Porter Institute for Poetics and Semiotics, Tel Aviv University and ha-kibuz ha-Meukhad, 1980). Chapter Five offers a synthesis based on some of the main arguments presented in my Hebrew book, *The Emergence of Jewish-Arabic Literary Contacts at the Beginning of the Tenth Century* (Tel Aviv: The Porter Institute for Poetics and Semiotics, Tel Aviv University and Hakibuz Haneukhad, 1988). Chapter Six is based on a Hebrew paper originally published in *Dappim (Research in Literature)* 9 (1994), 101-110. An earlier version of Chapter Seven was first published in the volume *Geniza research after ninety years: the case of Judaeo-Arabic.* Joshua Blau and Stefan Reif eds. (Cambridge: Cambridge University Press, 1992). First version of Chapter Eight was published in *Israel Oriental Studies* 15 (1995), 11-23. Chapter Nine is a revised version of my Hebrew paper published in *Jerusalem Studies in Hebrew Literature* 10-11 (1987-1988) (=Essays in Memory of Dan Pagis, part II), 483-499. Chapter Ten is based on my Hebrew paper, *Peʿamim* 47-48 (Spring 1991): 9-28, revised and amplified in *Poetics Today* 14:2 (Summer 1993): 277-302.

CHAPTER ONE

INTRODUCING FICTIONALITY INTO CLASSICAL ARABIC LITERATURE: THE *MAQĀMA*

1. *The Arabic literary system when the* maqāma *was introduced*

The *maqāma* first appeared in Arabic literature at eve of the eleventh century CE, when the canonized Arabic literary system was in its final stages of institutionalization. The position and status of the genres within the system as well as their inter-relations were set and established. The literature was governed by rigid didactic norms, which assigned to it educational, religious and informative functions, and dictated the character of its genres and the structure and development of the system as a whole. Scholarly, administrative and social needs of the Islamic élite were met by abundant literary output that comprised religious, historical, biographical and linguistic genres, as well as poetry and *adab* literature. Together, all of these genres constitute what can be regarded as the canonized Arabic literary system.

One of the symptoms of canonization was the development of a normative poetics, that is, the literature's official ideology, whose function was to preserve the status quo and secure the system against innovation. In various formulations, this ideology claimed that contemporary writers were inferior to the writers of earlier generations in both wisdom and knowledge and, consequently, the only legitimate literary activity was to copy, imitate or anthologize the works of preceding generations.[1] As a result, a considerable part of the literary activity of the period was primarily dedicated to the production of various collections and anthologies.

Of all the other classical Arabic disciplines, *adab* is mostly characterised by its reliance upon the other genres in the literary system as a reservoir of materials. *Adab* works actually compiled a melange of quotations from poetry, historical tales (*akbār*), anecdotes, proverbs, Koranic verses and exegeses, *ḥadīṯ*, and so on. The quotations were presented as though they had been handed down by reliable transmitters. The bulk of the *adab* writer's task was to edit a selection of

---

[1] For early formulations of this ideology, see Ibn al-Muqaffa' 1913:*5-6* (*Adab Ṣaġīr*); *ibid.*:40-41 (*Adab Kabīr*). For later formulations, see, for example, Ibn 'Abd Rabbihi 1965:1, 2-3; Ḥuṣrī 1953:1, 33-35.

existing literary material on the basis of certain principles established for the *adab* genre. There was no intention of blurring or disguising the fact that the material had been collected from existing sources. On the contrary, the material is explicitly presented as quoted, preceded by a transmission chain of at least one person who is usually mentioned by name. Even original material is presented as quoted, lending to it the legitimacy of a "text".

The transmission chain is one of the techniques applied for creating credibility. It was intended to persuade the reader that the texts deal with actual historical reality. Similar to other literatures that developed out of religious motivations (such as ancient literatures, especially ancient Hebrew literature), classical Arabic literature claims to make absolute, definitive statements about the course of history, and to derive from them mandatory behavioral edicts. Hence, a great deal of effort is made to persuade the reader of the veracity of the texts, by appending a transmission chain (in *ḥadīṯ* texts by developing a full-fledged apparatus for checking the credibility of the transmission chain), and by incorporating historical figures as well as the names of real people and places. The major poetic claim of classical Arabic literature is its historicity; the claim is so authoritative that it is made in all the prose genres, even in those that have no direct association with religion. There is hardly a story in classical Arabic literature, not in the *adab* and certainly not in other genres, that does not claim that its events were actual and not invented. Fiction obviously exists—and in many cases can be clearly demonstrated—but it fosters the validity of historical truth; and it does so by using the above-mentioned *ḥadīṯ* techniques for creating credibility. It should be emphasized, however, that the model discussed here is not a model that purports to present reality "as it is" for the mere sake of realism, but one that claims to present reality as it is in its most correct and desired form. The problems that this creates for the study of ancient Muslim history is familiar to every scholar in the field.

It is at this point, when the system is governed by these rigid poetic norms, that the *maqāma* first appears. The first *maqāmāt* were written at the beginning of the eleventh century, when, according to al-Ṯaʿālibī (1956:4, 257), al-Hamaḏānī reached Nishapur in 997. But they hovered on the periphery of the canonized system for about a hundred years, until the *maqāmāt* of al-Ḥarīrī (d. 1122) appeared on the scene. Although al-Hamaḏānī's *Maqāmāt* were widely dispersed and well appreciated, they provided little stimulation for the writing of similar compositions on a larger scale (see note 5). The *Maqāmāt* of al-Ḥarīrī, in contrast, captured the literary taste of the period within a short time. The explicit praise of literary critics,[2] the many commentaries written on his *Maqāmāt* almost from the time they were first published,[3] and the testimonies of learned men who came from distant places, including Spain, to hear the authorized version of al-Ḥarīrī's *Maqāmāt* from his own mouth[4] all provide ample evidence of a near-immediate popularity. Al-Ḥarīrī's model, which is explicitly built upon al-Hamaḏānī's, became the representative model of the *maqāmāt* to such an extent that it pushed aside other models of the *maqāma* (albeit a small number), which were neglected and forgotten.[5]

One hundred years were required for this genre to enter the centre of Arabic literary system and be accepted into it. This is a rather long time, even in terms of the period, compared to the amount of time it took for other genres to become accepted, and especially considering the rapid canonization of al-Ḥarīrī's *Maqāmāt*. Part of the reason for this is that al-Hamaḏānī's *Maqāmāt* offered a new poetics for prose writing which contrasted too sharply with the rigid contemporary poetic norms. This study deals with the innovative poetics of *maqāmāt* and with the reaction of the canonized literary system towards it.[6]

---

[2] For Yāqūt's enthusiastic declaration, see Yāqūt 1936-38:16, 262, 267. For others, see *ibid.*:268-276. For al-Zamakhšarī's, see Ḥāǧī Ḵalīfa 1941-43::2, 1787. For al-Muṭṭarizī's, see *ibid.*:1789, note.

[3] A detailed list can be found in Ḥāǧī Ḵalīfa 1941-43:2, 1787-1791.

[4] Ample evidence for this can be found in various biographies. Al-Ḥarīrī himself testifies, according to one tradition, that he authorized seven hundred versions that were read to him in 1120 (Yāqūt 1936-38:16, 266-267). On a scholar from Spain who heard al-Ḥarīrī recite his *maqāmāt* in Baghdad, see Maqqarī 1968::2, 509 (n. 193). Cf. MacKay 1971.

[5] Cf. Al-Qalqašandī's unique observation in this respect (1913-19:14, 110). Of the *maqāmāt* composed between the time of al-Hamaḏānī and that of al-Ḥarīrī, the following are known: one by Ibn Nubāta (938-1014) (Berlin Ms. no. 7425, 39a-35b); ten by Ibn Nāqiyā (1020-1092), (Huart 1908; Ibn Nāqiyā 1912: 123-153; 1988); two by Ibn Šaraf al-Qayrawānī (ca. 1000-1067), (Ibn Šaraf 1953, 1983[2]); extracts from a *maqāma* by Ṭalḥa b. Aḥmad al-Nuʿmānī, a contemporary of al-Ḥarīrī's (d. ca. 1126) (Iṣbhānī 1955:2, 3-16). Ibn Buṭlān's *Risālat daʿwat al-aṭibbāʾ* (Ibn Buṭlān 1985), composed in 1054, could also be included in this corpus of early *maqāmāt*. These *maqāmāt* and the optional models they present deserve a separate discussion.

[6] Some of the issues discussed here, especially that of fictionality, have already been touched upon by Beeston 1971; 1990; Kilito 1976; 1983:125-142, 155-169; Monroe 1983: 25; Pellat 1986; Bonebakker 1992 (for discussion of theological stands towards fiction). Their respective discussions displays, however, theoretical per-

2. *The new poetics of the* maqāmāt

2.1. *Al-Ḥuṣrī on al-Hamadhānī's* maqāmāt

In one of the most discussed passages in the history of the *maqāma*,[7] the writer al-Ḥuṣrī, a young contemporary (d. 1022) of al-Hamadānī's, asserts that al-Hamadānī wrote his *maqāmāt* as a response to Ibn Durayd's *Arbaʿūna ḥadīdan*, "Forty Tales" (Ḥuṣrī 1953:1, 261). Al-Ḥuṣrī says that Ibn Durayd "created (the Forty Tales) from the springs of his heart and quarried them from the quarry of his mind," and that he strays from the accepted literary code in both theme and language, and in directing their style and narration according to his own will. In reaction, al-Ḥuṣrī goes on to explain, al-Hamadānī wrote four hundred *maqāmāt* on the same theme—mendicancy—but in a language that conformed to the accepted literary code. He describes al-Hamadānī's stories as entertaining and notes that they are recounted by two alternating figures to whom al-Hamadānī himself gave the names—that is, in a more modern formulation, two invented personae. What al-Ḥuṣrī's account tells us, in fact, is that al-Hamadānī succeeded in shaping material that was alien to the normative literary taste in such a way as to make it acceptable. He accomplished this by changing some stylistic features of the material while retaining the "creation from the heart" and "the method of talking through the mouths of people"; in other words, its fictional character.

2.2. *The authors on their* maqāmāt

Apart from very brief and incidental comments, we have no statemant made by al-Hamadānī himself about this new genre, of which

spectives different from my own, even though some of our conclusions may seem similar. The main difference lies in the fact that whereas most of these works mention the fictionality of the *maqāma* (or rather of its two protagonists) as a simple, even obvious, fact, my study is concerned with fiction as an optional mode of expression and with its *function*, set against that of the non-fictional mode of expression within Arabic literature.

[7] See Prendergast 1915 (1973²):16-19; Margoliouh 1927; Mubārak 1931:86-88; 1934:1, 199-200; Blachère et Masnou 1957:13-15; Beeston 1971:1-2, 9; Kilito 1976; 43; Bosworth 1976:1, 98; Pellat 1986:108; Malti-Douglas 1985:247-251, and recently Richards 1991:90. See also Appendix: al-Ḥuṣrī's speculation on the birth of the *maqāmāt*.

he is thought to be the creator. Al-Hamaḏānī did not edit his own collection of *maqāmāt*,[8] And, apparently, for a long time there was no agreed upon version of it.[9] We do, however, have remarks by other

[8] This is evident from the short introductory passage that opens the 1880 Constantinople edition, which served as a basis for all later editions: "The respected Teacher, Abū al-Faḍl Aḥmad b. al-Ḥusayn al-Hamaḏānī, reader of the Quran and *ḥadīth*, wonder of all time, would recite at the end of his public assemblies *maqāmāt* which he improvised. He attributed the *maqāmāt* to a narrator who told them to him, whom he called ʿĪsā b. Hišām and whom he claimed had recounted them from the lips of an eloquent man whom he called Abū al-Fatḥ al-Iskandarī; he called his *maqāmāt* 'The Mendicancy *Maqāmāt*'" [*kāna 'l-ustāḏu 'l-ǧalīlu abū 'l-faḍli aḥmadu bnu 'l-ḥusayni 'l-hamaḏāniyyu 'l-ḥāfiẓu badīʿu 'l-zamāni yumlī fī awāḵiri maǧālisihi fī 'l-ǧamʿi maqāmātin yunšiʾuhā badīhan wayuzawwiruhā ʿalā lisāni rāwiyatin rawāhā lahu yusammīhi ʿīsā bna hišāmin yazʿumu annahu ḥaddaṯahu ʿan balīġin yusammīhi abā 'l-fatḥi 'l-iskandariyya wasammāhā maqāmāti 'l-kudyati*] (al-Hamaḏānī 1880:2). This is not the statement of a man presenting his own work to the reader, but of someone who heard al-Hamaḏānī's *Maqāmāt*, either from the author himself or from someone else, collected them and committed them to writing. Nor are the titles of the *Maqāmāt* original; rather they were coined by the editor of this edition, as he himself states in the colophon, most likely following the model of the titles in al-Ḥarīrī's *Maqāmāt*, which were composed after al-Hamaḏānī's. Prior to the Constantinople edition, we find *maqāmāt* titles such as *Maqāmat al-dīnār*, *Maqāmat al-ṣūfī*, and an untitled *maqāma* (Grangeret de Lagrange 1828:153-163); *Maqāmat al-faras*, *al-Maqāma al-iskandariyya*, probably named after Abū al-Fatḥ al-Iskandarī (Ahlwardt 1895:7, 529, no. 8535); *Maqāmat al-šuʿarāʾ* (De Sacy 1826:200); *Maqāmat al-ġāzī*, *Maqāmat al-qarrād*, *Maqāmat al-mayyit*, *Maqāmat al-sāʾil bi-aḏarbiǧān*, *Maqāmat al-imām* and an untitled *maqāma* (*ibid.*: 78-94, Arabic text). Ms. Bibliothèque Nationale 3923 (which was most probably the source for these French editions) has, in addition to the titles mentioned, *Maqāmat al-walīma*, *Maqāmat al-saḥāb*, *Maqāmat al-asad*, as well as some other untitled *maqāmāt*. Richards (1991:97-98) discusses several of these issues. Although he had not seen my Hebrew article of 1980, he bases himself on similar materials and comes to similar conclusions.

[9] On the problems related to the time and circumstances under which the *maqāmāt* were composed, see Blachère and Mansou 1957:29-30. The various manuscripts of al-Hamaḏānī's *maqāmāt* which have been preserved do not all contain the same number of *maqāmāt* (for a list of manuscripts, see Brockelmann 1909:1, 95; Sup. 1937:1, 152). Yūsuf al-Nabhānī, who edited the 1880 Constantinopole edition, which is the most complete of all the editions (the publisher of the Beirut edition, Muḥammad ʿAbduh, took the liberty of omitting an entire *maqāma* and passages from another *maqāma* that he regarded as obscene; later publishers followed suit) testifies in the colophon (*ibid.*: 100) that he compiled the edition out of two manuscripts, one of which (no. 4270 in the Nūr ʿUṯmāniyya library, including 50 *maqāmāt*; Rescher 1913:113) contained *maqāmāt* which were absent in the other (no. 4283 in the Aya Sofia library, including 30 *maqāmāt*; Rescher 1912:95). Ibn Šaraf al-Qayrawānī, a disciple of al-Ḥuṣrī, states in the preface to his *Masāʾil al-intiqād* that the number of al-Hamaḏānī's *maqāmāt* "is twenty, according to those who transmitted them, but this number has not reached us [that is, Spain]" (Ibn Šaraf 1953:4). In his anthology, al-Ḥuṣrī himself presents nineteen full *maqāmāt* by al-Hamaḏānī of which eighteen are also the first eighteen *maqāmāt* in the collection we have of al-Hamaḏānī. This, of course, does not mean that al-Ḥuṣrī was

maqāmāt authors on the genre, as well as comments by contemporary literary critics. During the stage in which the *maqāmāt* were first becoming established, most of the authors refer in their *maqāmāt* preface to the poetic innovation of the new genre. Their comments are generally formulated in a moderate and highly cautious fashion, which seems to reveal an intention to obscure the innovation rather than declare it. Although we do not find any unequivocal critique on the established *adab* literature, the authors were clearly sensitive to its poetic norms. A careful reading of the prefaces reveals that most of the *maqāmāt* authors focus on the fictionality of the *maqāmāt*, both as a problem in itself and as an innovative departure from *adab* poetic norms. Notwithstanding the fact that an explicit terminology identifying fiction was lacking, these authors discuss three characteristics of the *maqāmāt* which, jointly, illustrate their conception of fiction.

2.2.1. *"Creation from the heart"*

In the passage mentioned above, al-Ḥuṣrī indicates that the "creation from the heart" is a characteristic of the *maqāma*. A number of authorial statements relating to the fact that their stories are entirely invented, with nothing borrowed, also appear in the prefaces to the *maqāmāt* compilations. Al-Ḥarīrī states:

> I did not include [in my composition] any verses from other poems, with the exception of two, on which I constructed the *Maqāma al-ḥulwāniyya*, and one other pair of verses which I included at the end of the *Maqāma al-karağiyya*; to everything else, my own thoughts gave birth and created for good or for bad (Ḥarīrī 1929:7).

---

not familiar with other *maqāmāt* by al-Hamaḏānī, but it is likely that in an earlier period, in the generation following al-Hamaḏānī's death, only a small collection of twenty of his *maqāmāt* was known in the Maghreb. On the other hand, about a hundred years later the Sevillian al-Kalāʿī writes in his *Iḥkām ṣanʿat al-kalām* that "al-Hamaḏānī had composed 400 *maqāmāt*, of which about 40 have reached me" (al-Kalāʿī 1985:196); while his apparent contemporary al-Ḥanafī emphasizes in the preface to his own *maqāmāt* that there were in fact thirty of them, "unlike the *maqāmāt* of the two masters of eloquence, al-Hamaḏānī and al-Ḥarīrī, which numbered fifty or twenty" (Ḥanafī 1912: 4). De Sacy, however, mentions a manuscript that was in the possession of Scheid, which contained fifty *maqāmāt* (De Sacy 1826:261) and Rescher describes three manuscripts in Constantinople containing fifty *maqāmāt* each (Rescher 1912:112-116). Despite Brockelmann's opinion (Sup. 1937:1, 151), it may well be that the collection of fifty-one *maqāmāt* that we have today is the product of subsequent editing, which was influenced by the model of the fifty *maqāmāt* in al-Ḥarīrī's collection. Cf. Richards 1991:92-96 and end of note 8.

Ibn Šaraf al-Qayrawānī, who preceded al-Ḥarīrī (d. 1067 in Seville), issues an even more detailed statement, in what was an exceptionally acute declaration:

> I looked through works on various subjects, and I found nothing but what was passed down from father to son or presented as ancient tradition; you hardly find a story, however rare or special, that is not presented as something handed down, that "so and so told me" or that "I heard from so and so". The authors recount by their pens [that is, they copy] instead of by their own words. Their compositions are repeated over and over again, and everything that is repeated becomes boring, as everyone knows, while the soul longs for marvellous words... But there seem to be many barriers between the original invention and the ability. I tried to compose something for which there was no precedent and for which only my thoughts would come to my assistance. And I wrote a book called *Virgin thoughts*, ... and there is not a single story in it that I recounted as one that was passed down, whether by an ancient or a contemporary, or as something that was told to me by someone near or remote (Ibn Bassām 1979:7, 179-180).[10]

The "creation from the heart" stands in opposition not only to the borrowing and quotation from the existing literary reservoir (as is the case in *adab* literature),[11] but also, and perhaps mainly, to the entire set of techniques used to present the story as historical truth, as real events which have been accounted for and transmitted by reliable transmitters. Behind the terms that speak of "creation" and "the original thought of the author," there is actually a rebellion against the entire poetics of presenting literary reality as actual and uninvented.[12]

---

[10] According to Ibn Bassām, this is a passage from Ibn Šaraf's introduction to his *Aʿlām al-kalām*. The book itself, which was apparently a collection of twenty *maqāmāt*, or "dialogues" (*aḥādīṯ*), has been lost. We do have two *maqāmāt* and a preface called *Masāʾil al-intiqād* which, there is reason to believe, were part of *Aʿlām al-kalām* (see Pellat's argument, Ibn Šaraf 1953:23, introduction). This preface does not include the passage presented by Ibn Bassām; but apparently Ibn Bassām does not quote from the preface to the book, rather, from the dedication to the King of Seville, al-Muʿtaḍid (ruled 1042-1068). As is well known, these prefaces would often be individually adapted to each patron they addressed. Ibn Bassām also quotes a passage from a dedication in another work by Ibn Šaraf, *Abkār al-afkār*, to the rival of al-Muʿtaḍid, Bādīs b. Ḥabbūs the king of Granada (ruled 1038-1073), and here too the inventiveness and originality of the stories are emphasized (*ibid.*:177).

[11] Criticism of the traditional *adab* are also to be found in this period in other contexts. See, for example, the comments of al-Tanūḵī (d. 994), a contemporary of al-Hamaḏānī's, in his preface to the first (Tanūḵī 1971) and second (Tanūḵī 1930) parts of *Nišwār al-muḥāḍara*. He explains that the book is unique in that it contains no material that is found in the existing *adab* literature, but only material that he actually heard. Obviously, he values the latter literary material more than the traditional material of the established *adab* literature. Ibn Ḥazm (d. 1064) expresses a similar sentiment in the preface to his *Ṭawq al-ḥamāma* (Ibn Ḥazm 1992:76).

[12] It is interesting to compare these declarations with declarations of "creation

2.2.2. *Naming the hero and the narrator*

Of all the functions in a literary work, persona, or "character," is perhaps the most powerful creator of "real world" effect, and therefore the most important factor of reality representation. In classical Arabic literature, whereby reality representation was a major issue, this function was fulfilled by resorting to historical figures as literary characters, both in the narration and in the transmission chain. Hence, when the *maqāmāt* authors wanted to declare the fictionality of their works, they did so by repeatedly proclaiming that they themselves named their characters. This was meant to assert that they invented their own personae, rather than resorting to historical figures.

Al-Ḥuṣrī's unique statement, which seems to reflect his personal attempt to understand al-Hamad̲ānī's *maqāmāt*, emphasizes quite clearly al-Hamad̲ānī's poetic innovation in naming a fictional hero and narrator. According to al-Ḥuṣrī:

> Al-Hamad̲ānī ceated an exchange in the *maqāma* between two characters, one of whom he called ʿĪsā b. Hišām and the other, Abū al-Fatḥ al-Iskandarī, and had them exchange pearls of wisdom ... and witty, charming phrases on amusing matters, so as to make the sad

from the heart" in the Hebrew *maqāmāt*. Let me briefly present two examples: (a) The *maqāma* of Solomon Ibn Ṣaqbel (Muslim Spain, first half of 12th century) ends with these words: "Be aware, my friends, of the sweetness and beauty of my words, and take care not to let them trap you, for they are only the palaver of lovers courting and words that your friend, the author, invented from his heart" (Schirmann 1961[2] :2, 565). I believe that the concept of fiction implied here is quite different from that implied in the Arabic *maqāmāt*. The concept of fiction in the Arabic *maqāmāt* demands that the reader accept it within the framework of mimetic norms. In contrast, the concept of fiction expressed here aims to prevent the audience from reading the story as an account of something that could reasonably be expected to happen in reality. It intentionally exposes the fact that words create an illusion. The declaration of "invention from the heart" clearly assumes two opposite functions when appearing in Hebrew or in Arabic contexts, which is very significant for understanding the process of Hebrew appropriation from Arabic literature. (b) Al-Ḥarīzī's famous declaration in the preface to *Sefer Taḥkemonī*: "but all the themes of this book were created out of my own mind, new, recently come up, issued from the fountain of Judah" (al-Ḥarīzi 1952:14; English trans.: al-Ḥarīzi 1965-73:1, 38)—may be reinterpreted in light of the poetics of the Arabic *maqāmāt* presented here. It seems that Schirmann's astonishment at the contradiction between this declaration and the fact that some of the Arabic sources of the *Sefer Taḥkemonī* can be identified (Schirman 1961[2] :1, 369) is somewhat misguided. Al-Ḥarīzī is actually following here the manner of the Arabic *maqāmāt* writers, especially that of al-Ḥarīrī, in overtly declaring "invention from the heart" in their prefaces. Al-Ḥarīzī's lines above intend to point to the poetic principle of fiction; they do not constitue a feigned innocent claim that no other sources were used.

> person laugh and arouse the complacent ... and sometimes assigned the action to one and the narration to the other (Ḥuṣrī 1953:*ibid.*).

Ibn Šaraf al-Qayrawānī described what al-Hamaḏānī did in his *maqāmāt* in similar terms:

> al-Hamaḏānī also fabricated (*zawwara*) highly ornamental *maqāmāt*, improvising [the stories] at the end of his literary sessions. He would ascribe them to a narrator who had told him the story and whom he called ʿIsā b. Hišām, and would claim that this narrator had heard the tale from a man of eloquence whom he (al-Hamaḏānī) called Abū al-Fatḥ al-Iskandarī (Ibn Šaraf 1953:4. Cf. also note 9).

Al-Ḥarīrī also focuses on the naming of the narrator and the hero when, in the preface to his *maqāmāt*, he describes al-Hamaḏānī's *maqāmāt* as a model for his own:

> al-Hamaḏānī attributed the action to Abū al-Fatḥ al-Iskandarī and the narration to ʿĪsā b. Hišām, both of whom are anonymous. (al-Ḥarīrī 1929:5)

These comments contain terms and concepts taken from *ḥadīṯ* scholarship, in which they were used to verify the transmission chain. Terms that had negative connotations in *ḥadīṯ* scholarship—*nasaba*, *ʿazā*, *zawwara*, *zaʿama annahu ḥaddaṯahu bihā*, *maǧhūl*, *nakira* ("attributed," "falsified," "[falsely] claimed [that *ḥadīṯ*] passed on to him," "an unknown personality")—appear here in a new, positive context in the description of the new poetics represented by al-Hamaḏānī. They legitimize the fictional hero and narrator as products of the author's imagination, personae who exist only within the context of a literary work.

Other *maqāmāt* authors also declare that they put their own words into the mouths of fictional characters, attribute the events to characters, or call their characters by one name or another. In his preface to *Masāʾil al-Intiqād*, Ibn Šaraf writes: "I ascribed [the stories] to Abū al-Rayyān al-Ṣalt b. al-Sakan b. Sulaymān" (Ibn Šaraf 1953:2). He then outlines a sort of biography of Abū al-Rayyān, which, lacking any identifying characteristics, seems to be imaginary.[13] Ibn Mārī writes in the preface to his *Maqāmāt*: "I called the narrator Abū al-

---

[13] But see Pellat in Ibn Šaraf 1953:115, note 1; Kilito 1983:130, note 82; Richards 1991:90. Richards similarly says that "ʿĪsā b. Hišām bears the same name as a *ḥadīṯ* scholar who taught al-Hamaḏānī in his home town" [*ibid.*], but presents no evidence for that.

K̲ayr b. al-Ḥārit̲, and the person who [the story] is about Abū al-Faḍl b. al-Wārit̲."[14] Ibn al-Ǧawzī states in the preface to his *Maqāmāt:*

> "So that he should be known by name, I called him Abū al-Qawīm (that is, a righteous man), because I discovered that he received inspiration from Abū al-Taqwīn (he who has ability to lead people on the right way, that is the way of Allah), for those who have the knowledge are distinguished by their ability to create parables, and only the knowledgeable understand them".[15]

Having become a standard part of *maqāmāt*'s prefaces, this declaration found its way into the prefaces of Hebrew *maqāmāt* (founded upon Arabic borrowed model) as well. Here are the words of al-Ḥarīzī in his preface to *Sefer Taḥkemonī*:

> All the words of this book I have put upon the tongue of Heman, the Ezrahite, and in the name of Ḥeber, the Kenite, I have founded and built them, although neither of them live in our generation; and all that I have mentioned in their name never was and never been happened, but only fiction (al-Ḥarīzī 1965-73:1, 40).[16]

All these declarations signify the official introduction of unabashed fiction into the world of classical Arabic prose.[17] At the same time, the principle of selecting names for the heroes and narrators in the *maqāmāt* clearly illustrates the limits of fiction of this genre. Begin-

---

[14] *wasammaytu 'l-rāwiya abā 'l-k̲ayri bni 'l-ḥārit̲i wa'l-marwiyya anhu abā 'l-faḍli bni 'l-wārit̲i* (Wien Ms. 384, 2b).

[15] *waqad kanaytuhu liyata'arrafa abā 'l-qawīmi li'anni ra'aytnhu qad talaṭṭafa min abī 'l-taqwīmi wa'annahu tafāwata fī ḍarbi 'l-amt̲āli 'l-'ālimūna wamā ya'qiluhā illā 'l-'ālimūna* (Ibn al-Ǧawzī 1980:6). The last words refer to Koran 29:43).

[16] וכל דברי הספר הזה בלשון הימן האזרחי עשיתים. ועל שם חבר הקיני יסדתים ובניתים. ואף על פי שאחר בדורנו לא היה. וכל אשר דברתי בשמם לא היה ולא נברא אלא משל היה. al-Ḥarīzī 1952:15. Cf. also the words of Jacob Ben Ele'azar in the preface to his *Love stories*: ושמי במשלַי לא כִּניתי. והסבותיו ללמואל בן איתיאל ואותו שִׁנִּיתִי. כי כן חֻקות ישמעאלים. להָסֵב שמותם במשלים. אך עתה אגידנו כי אני יעקב בן אלעזר. למען אשר לא יקרב איש זר. "Rather than lend my name to the stories, I narrated them instead in the name of Lemuel ben Itiel; and thus I concealed my own. This I did in the manner of the Ishmaelites, whose habit is to disguise their names in their stories. Nevertheless, I declare now that I am indeed Jacob Ben Ele'azar, in order that 'no stranger shall draw near' [a reference to Num 17:5]" (Ben Ele'azar 1992-93:14).

[17] This was first acknowledged by Beeston (1971), and again in 1990 he says: "[al-Hamad̲ānī] consistently throughout the work gives each episode on the authority of the same manifestly fictional narrator, whom he names 'Īsā b. Hišām. In this way he frankly acknowledged the fictional character of the narratives, and is the first Arabic author to compose a confessedly fictional prose work" (Beeston 1990:127).

ning with al-Ḥarīrī's *maqāmāt*, the names of the heroes and narrators are modelled on actual names, but at the same time they indicate, in one way or another, that they are indeed fictional by alluding to the names of former *maqāmāt* heroes, or by having an allegorical meaning. Al-Ḥarīrī founded the principle of choosing names for the protagonists in the *maqāmāt* when he selected for his two protagonists names that the reader could identify as fictional. The name of the narrator, al-Ḥāriṯ b. Hammām is based on a well-known *ḥadīṯ* of the Prophet:

> Call yourselves by names of the prophets; the names best liked by Allah are ʿAbd Allah and ʿAbd al-Raḥmān, the truest names are al-Ḥāriṯ ("one who works hard for his bread") and Hammām ("one who has a goal and persists to attain it"); the ugliest names are Ḥarb and Murra.[18]

These two names suited al-Ḥarīrī's purpose both because they suggest positive characteristics and because they are defined as the most proper and truest names—for what the *maqāmāt* critics judged as a totally "false," non-existent protagonist![19] The name of the hero, Abū Zayd al-Sarūǧī, is clearly constructed on the name of al-Hamaḏānī's hero, Abū al-Fatḥ al-Iskandarī, and this allusion refers openly to a literary model, rather than to historical reality. These two principles of choosing names, the allegorical principle, and the reference to a literary model, were both adopted by the *maqāamāt* writers following al-Ḥarīrī.

In the *maqāmāt* modelled upon al-Ḥarīrī's, the names of the narrator and hero usually allude openly to al-Ḥarīrī's names. Ibn Mārī calls his narrator Abū al-Ḵayr b. al-Ḥāriṯ and his hero Abū al-Faḍl b. al-Wāriṯ; in *al-Maqāmāt al-luzūmiyya* of al-Saraqustī the narrator is called al-Sāʾib b. Tammām (occasionaly the name of a second narrator, al-Munḏir b. Ḥumām is added to create the rhyme) and the hero is named Abū Ḥabīb al-Sadūsī; in al-Ḥanafī's *Maqāmāt*, the narrator is al-Fāris b. Bassām, and the hero, Abū ʿAmr al-Tanūḵī; in *al-Maqāmāt al-zīniyya* by Ibn al-Ṣayqal al-Ǧazarī the narrator is

---

[18] *tasammaw biʾasmāʾi ʾl-anbiyāʾi waʾaḥabbu ʾl-asmāʾi ilā ʾllahi ʿabdu ʾllahi waʿabdu ʾl-raḥmāni waʾaṣdaquhā ʾl-ḥāriṯu wahammāmun waʾaqbaḥuhā ḥarbun wamurratun.* Šarīšī 1952:1, 27; Abū Dawūd 1950-51:4, 394; Ibn Ḥanbal 1969:4, 345; Ibn Qutayba 1963a:61. Cf. also Kister's discussion of this ḥadīṯ (1975:7, 12, 15, 19), which presents numerous other sources.

[19] Cf. Ibn al-Khaššāb 1929.

al-Qāsim b. Ḥiryāl al-Dimašqī, and the hero Abū Naṣr al-Misrī (see Ḥāǧī Kalīfa 1941-43:2, 1785).

In the *maqāmāt* that are more removed from al-Ḥarīrī's model, especially those that developed along an allegorical-didactic line, such pseudo-realistic names are entirely abandoned in favor of the elaboration of long allegorical transmission chains, in a way borders on parody. For example, this transmission chain appears in al-Suyūṭī's allegorical *maqāmāt*: "... Fresh [Flower] told us, as had been passed down by his Fragrant Father from the Father of the Rose Aban (first name) from Singer of the Branches from Eyelid from Star of the Garden from the Sprinkling Shower."[20]

But there are also more modest transmission chains: "Desirous Lover recounted as has been passed down by Honest Lover"[21] and: "Told Blaze, Son of Flame, as he heard from Son of Spark, Father of Flintstone, who said...";[22] or: "The Horned One (also the epithet for Alexander the Great), the one who brings friends together, related...";[23] al-Qalqašandī has in a *maqāma* dedicated to the art of epistolography: "the Prose Composer, son of the Poetry Composer, related and said",[24] which apart from being overtly fictional, also clearly alludes to al-Ḥarīrī's al-Ḥāriṯ b. Hammām.

2.2.3. *Relating the* maqāmāt *to established literary tradition*

In an attempt to underplay their departure from the established literature, the authors of the *maqāmāt* claim that their works are in keeping with some of the traditional genres whose status within the system is undisputed. Upon examining the common basis they establish between the *maqāmāt* and these genres, we find, again, the issue to be that of fictionality.

Thus, for example, Ibn Nāqiyā states:

> I have assigned to [my stories], (*ḥikāyāt*, and further on in this passage, *maqāmāt*) a "borrowed" [e.g. fictional] name (*ism musta'ār*) as is

[20] *ḥaddaṯanā 'l-rayyān 'an abī 'l-rayḥān 'an abī 'l-wardi abān 'an bulbuli 'l-aġsān 'an nāẓiri 'l-insān 'an kawkabi 'l-bustān 'an wābili 'l-hattān qāla* (Suyūṭī 1986:81 [1988:39])

[21] *ḥakā 'l-muǧramu 'l-'āšiqu 'ani 'l-muḥibbi 'l-ṣādiqi* (Berlin Ms. 8592; Ahlwardt 1895:7, 554).

[22] *ḥakā ša'latu bnu abī 'l-lahab 'an abī 'l-zinād šihāb annahu qāla* (Escorial Ms. 524; Derenbourg 1884:352).

[23] *akbaranā ḏū 'l-qarnayn 'l-mu'allifu bayna 'l-qarīnayn* (Muḥammad b. 'Afīf al-Dīn al-Tilmisānī, *al-Maqāma al-haytiyya wa'l-šīrāziyya*. Berlin Ms. 8549, 6b).

[24] *ḥakā 'l-nāṯiru bnu naẓẓām qāla* (al-Qalqašandī 1913-19:14, 112).

> the custom of the poets in their love poems (*tašbīb*), and as the wise men place words of wisdom in the mouths of animals...The fables of the Arabs also contain things that cannot possibly occur in reality in the way that they describe, yet they are not called lies because of this (Ibn Nāqiyā 1912:123 [1988:63]).

Ibn Nāqiyā associates the *maqāmāt* here with both love poetry and fables (*amṯāl*), and more specifically, with animal fables. An examination of the poetic grounds upon which this association is based would prove most instructive to our understanding of the prevailing attitude towards fiction in classical Arabic literature.

2.2.3.1. "The custom of the poets in their love poems"

The first reference here is to the *tašbīb* of the ancient love poetry.[25] The social function of this kind of courting poetry and its thematic conventions required a pseudo-autobiographical description of love. This requirement was met by incorporating into the love poem "true" details, such as the name of the poet's beloved and of her tribe, and allusions to amorous encounters that supposedly occurred between the poet and his beloved.[26] Verses of *tašbīb* were supposed to pretend to account for real life events, and at the same time to be accepted as disclaiming any commitment to reality, as can be discerned from the following anecdote:

> Al-Ḥāriṯ b. K̲ālid was one of the best at composing courting poems, which he did without really intending what they meant. He only did this out of chivalry and indecency. His love poems were about ʿĀʾiša bint Ṭalḥa, the wife of Muṣʿab b. al-Zubayr. When asked why he did not propose to her after her husband was killed, he answered: "I don't want people to think that I really meant what I said about her [in my poems]!"[27]

The world represented in the love poems is thus a fiction that explicitly proclaims itself to be such. Not only does it avoid the pretense of being historical reality, as is the case with *ḥadīṯ* prose, but it also declares that it is in no way committed to faithfully conveying reality.[28] This open declaration of fictional status was, then, the

---

[25] On *tašbīb*, see Vadet 1968:102-158.

[26] But see Ibn Rašīq 1972:2, 121-122; ʿAskarī 1952:158; Ǧāḥiẓ 1932:1, 232.

[27] *wakāna 'l-ḥāriṯu bnu k̲ālidin aḥada 'l-muǧīdīna fī 'l-tašbībi walam yakun yaʿtaqidu šayan min ḏālika wa'innamā yaqūluhu taẓarrufan watak̲alluʿan. wakāna šiʿruhu fī ʿāʾišati binti ṭalḥata. falammā qutila ʿanhā muṣʿabu bnu 'l-zubayri qīla lahu law k̲aṭabtahā, qāla innī la'akrahu an yatawahhama 'l-nāsu ʿalayya anni kuntu muʿtaqidan limā aqūlu fīhā* (Ḥuṣrī 1953:1, 243).

[28] The social context of the *tašbīb* is actually more intricate than that. The ways

common denominator of the love poetry and the *maqāmāt*. It was this common denominator that was called upon to legitimize the *maqāmāt*'s new poetics. If we were now to reexamine our traditional definitions of poetry and prose, we would be unable to avoid the conclusion that the fundamental distinction between these two major modes of expression in classical Arabic literature lies mainly in the conveying of reality in a fictional or a non-fictional way, rather than in formal constraints such as meter and rhyme.[29]

2.2.3.2. "Words of wisdom in the mouths of animals"

Ibn Nāqiyā, Ibn Šaraf al-Qayrawānī and al-Ḥarīrī all ask their readers to regard their *maqāmāt* in the same way they regard fables and stories told by animals or inanimate objects.[30] The representative example that they choose is the fables of *Kalīla wadimna*.[31] In *Kalīla wadimna*, animals talk and behave like human beings, telling stories and fables about the human world and relationships. Choosing

---

people employed *tašbīb* or reacted to it display an ambivalent attitude towards the relation between poetry and reality. *Tašbīb* verses could work for or against the woman for whom they were composed, they could bring her fame or insinuate that she was not of the best moral behavior; and the poet could either be praised for his talent, or chased by angry husbands, as we are able to discern from the many *tašbīb* anecdotes in Arabic literature. Two famous examples: al-Muḥallaq managed to marry off his daughters, thanks to the *tašbīb* of the poet al-Aʿšā (al-Iṣbahānī 1963:9, 118); While Waḍḍāḥ al-Yaman lost his life for his *tašbīb* to the wife of the caliph al-Walīd b. ʿAbd al-Malik (al-Iṣbahānī 1963:6, 209-241); See also Ibn Rašīq 1972:2, 121-122; Ǧāḥiẓ 1932:1, 232. The subject deserves a separate discussion.

[29] Cf. Ibn Kaṯīr 1966:5, 217 (for *Sūrat al-šuʿarā'*, vv. 224-226). The famous saying in medieval Arabic poetics, *aḥsanu 'l-šiʿri akḏabuhu* ("what is best in the poem is its falsehood") can thus be understood in the context of unabashed fiction, which does not declare itself committed to "reality", rather than in the context of rhetoric, as is usually the case (Cf. Jacobi 1972; Bürgel 1974).

[30] Ibn Šaraf 1983[2] :19-21; al-Ḥarīrī 1929:9; al-Šarīšī 1952:2, 25.

[31] Ibn Šaraf al-Qayrawānī gives as an example also *al-Nimr wa'l-ṯaʿlab* ("The Tiger and the Fox") by Sahl b. Hārūn, who lived at the beginning of the ninth century (see Ibn Hārūn 1973); Al-Ǧāḥiẓ mentions a book named *Ṯaʿla waʿafra* and says that Sahl b. Hārūn wrote it in an attempt to compete with (*mūāraḍa*) *Kalīla wadimna* by Ibn al-Muqaffaʿ (Ǧāḥiẓ 1932:1, 59-60; see also Ḥuṣrī 1953:1, 577; Ibn al-Nadīm 1964:120); Al-Ḥarīrī does not explicitly mention any particular book, but in his commentary al-Šarīšī mentions *Kalīla wadimna* and other compilations, "written from the mouth of those who have neither brain nor soul." (Šarīšī 1952:1, 25); Ibn al-Kaššāb mentions *Kalīla wadimna* and *The Stories of Sindibād* (Ibn al-Kaššāb 1929:5); Al-Kalāʿī (1985:208) mentions *Kalīla wadinma*, and Abū al-Alā' al-Maʿarrī's *Kitāb al-fā'iq*; Ibn Buṭlān entitles his *maqāma*-styled composition, *Risālat daʿwat al-aṭibbā' ʿalā maḏhab kalīla wadimna* (Ibn Buṭlān 1985:3). Cf. Bonebakker 1992: 7-10 for futher material.

animals for human roles was a poetic decision rooted in a literary tradition quite remote from that of the official *ḥadīṯ* and *adab*. Yet although the semi-allegorical model represented in this imported work was in many respects actually very different from the prevalent "realistic" prose models of classical Arabic literature, the book itself acquired a high status and considerable popularity in court circles, and became one of the most famous works of classical Arabic literature.[32] Its dual status in the Arabic literary system, of representing alien poetic norms, yet being a recognized and highly appreciated literary work, made this book a perfect banner for promoting new literary initiatives. *Maqāmāt* authors turned to it in order to gain recognition for their literary innovation precisely because of the fundamental poetic basis of evident fictionality they felt was common to both *Kalīla wadimna* and their compositions.

2.2.3.3. "The fables of the Arab"

The same status is given to fables and verses of poetry of Arab-Bedouin origin which were told by animals (*amṯāl al-ʿarab*). Ibn Nāqiyā cites as an example three verses (taken from al-Mubarrad's *Kitāb al-kāmil*) in which the lizard son addresses its father; Ibn al-Ǧawzī presents several examples of such animal tales, recounted with detailed transmission chains in the *ḥadīṯ* manner. Al-Šarīšī, too, in his commentary on al-Ḥarīrī's *maqāmāt*, presents similar material.[33] As in the animal fables such as *Kalīla wadimna*, here, too, the animals speak like human beings. There is, however, one difference, which is reflected in the previously quoted preface of Ibn Nāqiyā to his *Maqāmāt*: Since these *amṯāl* were regarded as "Arabic in their origins," greater adherence to "reality" was demanded of them than of those of the *Kalīla wadimna* type, which were felt to be "foreign" long after the book itself had been accepted into Arabic literature.[34] Hence, while Ibn Nāqiyā dismisses the animal fables with the brief comment that, like the love poems, they make use of "fictional names," he judges "fables of the Arabs" against a more severe realistic norm,

[32] The fascinating subject of *Kalīla wadimna*'s course in Arabic literature deserves a separate discussion.

[33] Ibn Nāqiyā 1912:123-124; al-Šarīšī 1952:1, 15; Ibn Ǧawzī 1980:2-6; see also Ibn Qutayba 1904:73; al-Iṣbahānī, 1963:20, 85, 93-94; al-Suyūṭī 1970:1, 465-466. On *akāḏīb al-aʿrāb* see al-Ǧāḥiẓ 1943:6, 239-240, 251-256.

[34] On the function of status in the historical dynamics of literature cf. Yahalom 1980.

when claiming that "[although] they contain things which cannot possibly occur in reality in the way they describe, yet they are not called lies because of this." Nevertheless, as *adab* literati were familiar with both types of *amṯāl*, and their fictional character was neither denied nor condemned, they could very well have served as a proper basis for legitimizing the fiction of the *maqāmāt*.

Lastly, it should be mentioned that *Kalīla wadimna* and other similar works "'*alā alsinati 'l-nāsi wa-'l-ṭayri wa-'l-bahā'imi*" were listed among the *asmār wa-ḵurāfāt* in Ibn al-Nadīm's *Fihrist* (see chapter two).

3. *Reaction of the established literary system*

3.1. *The argument against relating the* maqāmāt *to the tradition of the animal fable*

Evident fictionality was clearly a sensitive issue, for of all the formulations of the new poetics of fiction, it was precisely this attempt to place the *maqāmāt* in the allegorical tradition, especially that of the animal fable, that enraged the adherents of the old poetics. In an essay called *A Refutation of al-Ḥarīrī's Maqāmāt*, Ibn al-Ḵaššāb al-Baġdādī (d. 1172) argues that this claim is based on a fundamental error, since in fables such as *Kalīla wadimna* there is no confusion between truth and falsehood. It is obvious to everyone that the lion does not really talk with the fox or the tiger with the tree, the monkey with the turtle, or doves with sheep; and everyone who hears the stories realizes their allegorical intention immediately and intuitively. In contrast, the stories of Abū Zayd al-Sarūǧī (the hero of al-Ḥarīrī's *Maqāmāt*) do not make the same clear distinction between truth and falsehood, for it is not impossible to find in reality an eloquent schemer named Abū Zayd from the city of Sarūǧ. Nor is it any less likely that a man like al-Ḥāriṯ could meet Abū Zayd, as al-Ḥarīrī describes. Such stories are lies that sound like the truth, where the author does not even claim that they are true. This is not the case with the animal fables, which bear no resemblance to reality (Ibn al-Ḵaššāb 1929:4-5).

Speaking again in terms of truth and falsehood, Ibn al-Ḵaššāb views literary models according to how they present reality. The animal fables, he argues, can be understood according to an allegorical key precisely because they employ a clearly non-realistic model, so there is no problem of deception in this case, or of any conflict with the norms of presenting reality in *adab* literature. The *maqāmāt*, in contrast, represent a very problematic model of "reality" which, although declared by the authors to be "invented" (that is, fictional), does not seem implausible enough to be conceived as a renunciation of any claim to represent reality. It is both realistic and non-realistic at the same time, and thus necessarily declares itself to be "a lie": although using the standard realistic model of classical prose, it nevertheless exempts itself from conveying, or pretending to convey, "real life," and is thus in complete opposition to the basic poetic principle of *adab* literature.

Given the sharp conflict between the poetics of the *maqāma* and that of *adab* literature, it becomes quite clear that the *maqāma* could not have been easily admitted into the established literature of the period. The *maqāma* did eventually succeed in securing a prestigious position in the literary system, yet not without undergoing a process of adjustment which changed its own poetics sufficiently in order that the governing literary taste would accept it.

3.2. *The invention of a biography for the hero of al-Ḥarīrī's* maqāmāt

Ibn al-K̲aššāb's *A Refutation of al-Ḥarīrī's Maqāmāt* did not remain unanswered. One of al-Ḥarīrī's adherents, Ibn Barrī (d. 1187), wrote an essay in response to Ibn al-K̲aššāb defending al-Ḥarīrī's *Maqāmāt*. He makes the following remarks regarding Ibn al-K̲aššāb's distinction between the animal fables and the *maqāma*:

> Ibn al-K̲aššāb's argument against al-Ḥarīrī's protagonists Abū Zayd al-Sarūǧī and al-Ḥārit̲ b. Hammām bears no relevance here, since there existed in reality such a man as Abū Zayd. Tāǧ al-Dīn related and said: I heard the faithful transmitter Abū Bakr, a worshipper of Allah, son of Muḥammad b. Aḥmad, a Baghdad fabric merchant, tell: I heard al-Ḥarīrī, the author of the *maqāmāt*, tell: Abū Zayd al-Sarūǧī was a beggar with a gift for words who made his rounds of the gates most eloquently. He showed up at Basra, and one day he stood at the mosque of Banū Ḥarām and talked and asked for alms [using eloquent language]. One of the governors was present, and the mosque was full of worthy people. Abū Zayd made them marvel at the eloquence of his language and the fine way he formulated his statements and at his wit, and recounted that the Byzantines took his daughter prisoner, just as was told in *al-Maqāma al-ḥarāmiyya*, the *maqāma* number 48. [Al-Ḥarīrī] continued: That same evening the dignitaries and scholars of Basra gathered at my home, and I told them about the beggar and his tremendous talent for getting what he wanted by the

> skill of his tongue. Every one of the guests told that he saw the same beggar at his own mosque, and had heard him speak even more beautifully than I had, and that at every mosque he would change his clothes and appearance and prove his talent at scheming. Each one was amazed at his expertise in his field, and I composed *al-Maqāma al-ḥarāmiyya* [named after the mosque in the Basrian suburb Banū Ḥarām], and afterwards modelled the other *maqāmāt* on it, and it was the first *maqāma* that I wrote (Ibn Barrī, in: Ibn al-K̲aššāb 1929:5-6).

With this story Ibn Barrī attempts to refute the argument that the *maqāmāt* are lies that pretend to be truth. The *maqāmāt* tell of an actual reality: Abū Zayd, the hero of the *maqāmāt*, is a real historical figure whom al-Ḥarīrī met one day in the Banū Ḥarām Mosque, as he himself testifies. The famous technique of the *ḥadīṯ* is once again exploited here in order to verify that this is not fiction but an historical account, conforming to the highest requirements of *adab* poetics, and that the *maqāma* should thereby be considered a literary form legitimate in every respect.

This story also appears in al-Ḥarīrī's biography, where Yāqūt (1936-38:16, 262-263) recounts it in a similar way, while Ibn al-Ǧawzī and Ibn K̲alikān present slightly different versions, on the authority of al-Ḥarīrī's son. The following is Ibn K̲alikān's version:

> One day my father was at the mosque in Banū Ḥarām, and an old man wearing a pair of travel-worn, tattered old rags, looking worn out and speaking eloquently with fine expressions, entered. And people asked him: 'Where are you from?' He answered, 'from Sarūǧ'. They asked: 'What is your name (*Kuniya*)?' And he answered, 'Abū Zayd'. And [then] my father composed the *maqāma* known by the name of *al-Ḥarāmiyya* which is the 48th *maqāma*, and he attributed it to the mentioned Abū Zayd. (Ibn K̲alikān 1968-71:4, 63; Ibn al-Ǧawzī 1940:10, 77).

Both versions of the story of al-Ḥarīrī's encounter with Abū Zayd al-Sarūǧī at the mosque are told to prove that Abū Zayd was not a fictional character. The information given about him in these transmissions appears, however, to be exclusively derived from the 48th *maqāma* itself. This *maqāma* includes a supposedly "autobiographical" poem by Abū Zayd, in which he introduces himself and relates misfortunes from the time when the Byzantines conquered his city. He lost everything he had, and the Byzantines took his daughter. Other than what is told in this *maqāma*, we have no further information from other sources about the life of Abū Zayd.

The same data which served the hero to introduce himself in the 48th *maqāma* were then used to construct the historical biography of Abū Zayd al-Sarūǧī. But even within the fictional framework of the *maqāma*, this autobiography is declared to be false: Abū Zayd relates his allegedly life story here as part of his scheme. He offers a person who wishes to repent for breaking the wine-abstention vow, the opportunity to do so by helping to finance the retrieval of Abū Zayd's daughter from Byzantine captivity. At the end of the *maqāma* he even explicitly admits to the narrator that he had invented his autobiographical poem in order to take an easy opportunity to earn a living.

It seems that the supposedly autobiographical information in this *maqāma* is what initiated the claim that this *maqāma* was the first that al-Ḥarīrī composed. If so, why did al-Ḥarīrī, who arranged the collection himself, place it towards the end of the collection rather than at the beginning?[35] One should also regard in this context al-Ḥarīrī's explicit declaration in the preface to his *Maqāmāt* that he has composed them as an imitation of al-Hamadānī's *maqāmāt* (i.e., not on the basis of any personal experience), and that he moulded his characters on the model provided by al-Hamadānī. The names of al-Ḥarīrī's protagonists are evidently built on al-Hamadānī's model, as Sadan has shown (1975:8): al-Ḥarīrī's "Abū Zayd al-Sarūǧī" imitates al-Hamadānī's "Abū al-Fatḥ al-Iskandarī." Both Iskandarun and al-Sarūǧ were northern Syrian cities located on the Byzantine border. The conclusion that the forty-eighth *maqāma* was actually the source for the story of the encounter between al-Ḥarīrī and Abū Zayd at the mosque, and not the other way around, thus seems unavoidable, as was previously suspected by several scholars (see Margolioth 1927: s.v. al-Ḥarīrī; Kilito 1976:50; Sadan 1975:*ibid.*; cf. Zakharia 1994).

My purpose here, however, is not to disprove the story, but rather to discuss its function. The story provides evidence of an acceptance process—well anchored in the Arabic literary tradition—which operated on the *maqāma* in order to adjust it to the strict poetic norms of the *adab*. According to these norms, Abū Zayd could only have been accepted as a legitimate hero by being a genuine historical figure. Even the author's unabashed admittance of Abū Zayd's fic-

---

[35] Cf. now Zakharia's discussion of the evidence, and her claim that *al-Maqāma al-ṣanʿāniyya* (the first in al-Ḥarīrī's book) rather than *al-Maqāma al-Ḥarāmiyya* in fact holds an inaugural function (Zakharia 1994).

tionality could not prevent him from being regarded by the following generations as someone who once existed.

The same function can be observed in another tradition that Ibn K̲alikān relates in the biography of al-Ḥarīrī. The tradition is taken from the biographical dictionary of grammarians, *Inbāh al-ruwāt ʿalā anbāʾ al-nuḥāt* by Ibn al-Qifṭī:

> The mentioned Abū Zayd is a man by the name of al-Muṭahhar b. Salām or Salār, [see Yāqūt 1936-38:16, 272] and was a Basrian grammarian and lexicographer; he was friendly with the mentioned al-Ḥarīrī, studied and specialized under him in Basra (Ibn Khalikān 1968-71:4, 64; cf. Ibn al-Qifṭī 1955:3, 276).

We have here a more moderate attempt to show that while Abū Zayd is a literary name, the known historical figure of a Basrian grammarian stands behind it.

The following statement about Abū Zayd, which appears in one of the commentaries on al-Ḥarīrī's *maqāmāt* should also be noted:

> I found this in the hand-writing of al-Waraqustī: I asked the Sun of the Poets, Ṭalḥa al-Nuʿmānī[36] what al-Ḥarīrī, the author of the *maqāmāt*, looked like. He described al-Ḥarīrī's appearance to me ..., and stated that he used to live in the Banū Ḥarām vicinity at Basra. Then he said: As for Abū Zayd al-Sarūǧī, he was tall, had a goat-like beard, and was of Syrian origin. He used to buy oil for lighting (?), and give it to the people.[37]

Along with biographical and physical data on al-Ḥarīrī, similar data on Abū Zayd al-Sarūǧī are also presented here. On the other hand, al-Šarīšī, while discussing the shape of Abū Zayd's beard in his commentary to *al-maqāma al-Ḥulwāniyya*, states: "every description al-Ḥarīrī ascribed to al-Sarūǧī was actually taken from his own appearance."[38]

In a later biography of al-Ḥarīrī, written about 250 years after his death, Ibn Kaṯīr summarizes the dispute on the historical existence of the *maqāmāt* hero thusly:

---

36 Cf. note 5.

37 *waǧadtu bik̲aṭṭ ʾl-waraqustī: saʾaltu šamsa ʾl-šuʿarāʾi ṭalḥata ʾl-nuʿmāniyya ʿan hayʾati ʾl-ḥarīrī ṣāḥibi ʾl-maqāmāti faqāla: kāna rabʿa ʾl-qāmati naḥīfa ʾl-badani fī ʿainihi ʾl-yusrā ḥawaṣun yūlaʿu binatfi d̲aqanihi wakāna yanzilu biʾl-basrati bibanī ḥarāmin waʾammā abū zaydim ʾl-sarūǧyyu faqad kāna ṭawīlan kawsaǧan šāmiyyan yabīʿu ʾl-midāda wayahdīhi ilā ʾl-nāsi* (al-Ṭarāʾifī, *Kitāb al-ṭawḍīḥ fī šarḥ al-maqāmāt al-ḥarīriyya*, Berlin Ms. 8540, 28a).

38 *wakullu ṣifatin yaṣifu bihā ʾl-sarūǧiyya fī al-maqāmāt fatilka kānat ṣifata ʾl-ḥarīriyyi* (Šarīšī 1952:1, 46).

> There are those who claimed that Abū Zayd and al-Ḥārit̲ b. Hammām al-Muṭahhar [*sic*!] never existed, and [that al-Ḥarīrī] composed these *maqāmāt* in the manner of the fables; and there are others who said that Abū Zayd b. Salām al-Sarūǧī did exist and was a virtuous man and a scholar of language. God only knows. (Ibn Kat̲īr 1932-37:12, 192).

This later source clearly confirms the fact that at an earlier stage there were indeed disagreements as to the historical veracity of Abū Zayd al-Sarūǧī and not everyone agreed that there had actually been such a person. Such disagreements represent a stage of indecision towards the recognition of the *maqāma* by normative literary agents of the period.

3.3. *The ascription of al-Ḥarīrī's* maqāmāt *to a Magrebi origin*

Another strategy for absorbing the innovation of al-Ḥarīrī's *maqāmāt* can be identifed in the attempt to relocate its origins. It is found in a tradition also from al-Ḥarīrī's biography, which is transmitted in two versions. Yāqūt's version recounts:

> [al-Ḥarīrī] presented his *maqāmāt* to the minister Anūšiwān [b. K̲ālid], and he liked them. The people passed them around among themselves, and [then] those who envied al-Ḥarīrī accused him by saying: these are not his own because they are not consistent with his virtues [as a writer] and do not match his style. They are the work of a man who was a guest at his house and died there, and al-Ḥarīrī deceptively attributed them to himself. And others said, 'No, the Arabs [Bedouins] rather attacked a caravan, and among their spoils was a leather saddlebag that belonged to a Maghrebian. The Bedouins sold it in Basra, and al-Ḥarīrī bought it and fraudulently claimed it was his own (Yāqūt 1936-38:16, 265).

Ibn K̲alikān's version recounts:

> I saw in one of the collections that al-Ḥarīrī at first wrote (only) forty *maqāmāt*, and he brought them to Baghdad and claimed they were his. A group of Baghdad *adab* literati did not believe him, saying that he did not compose them, but someone from Maghreb did, a man of eloquence who died in Basra and whose writings found their way to al-Ḥarīrī, and he fraudulently ascribed them to himself (Ibn K̲alikān 1968-71:4, 65).

Despite the difference in details, the two versions both describe the immediate reaction towards al-Ḥarīrī's new creation. The *maqāmāt* are enjoyed by the ruler, who can be regarded as representing a suitable audience for this type of new literature—the governing circles and local bourgeoisie. But by al-Ḥarīrī's own circle of *adab* literati and scholars which represents the traditional literary taste and authoritative poetics, they are met with suspicion. The authoritative poetics is also responsible for the rather odd claim as to the true origin of the *maqāmāt*—in Magreb of all places—without any mention of al-Hamadānī, or of the literary centres in Persia where he composed his *maqāmāt*. This claim is indicative of the established position regarding the *maqāmāt*'s new and unfamiliar poetics. The semiotic opposition of "belonging to the literary system," "being structured according to its poetics," versus "being alien to the system," "not structured according to its poetics," and, therefore "unstructured" and "chaotic" (see Lotman 1976) is identified as an opposition between "centre" and "periphery"; in this case the opposition is between the literary centres of Baghdad and the Maghreb. From the point of view of the Baghdadian literary centre, the *maqāma* was created in a remote peripheral place where the cultural rules did not apply. Baghdad therefore could not be held responsible for its peculiarities. The new poetics of the *maqāmāt*, supposedly originated from the periphery, comprised essentially a non-poetics, lacking the fitting literary structure of the establishment.

4. *Conclusion: The Acceptance of the* maqāma *into the literary system*

All of the above arguments and claims, along with declarations that the *maqāmāt* are didactic works that teach both lessons in life and the art of writing (see Šarīšī 1952:1, 25), are mobilized to camouflage the *maqāma*'s revolutionary poetic innovation and to present it as consistent with the official poetics of the prevailing literary system. The acceptance of the *maqāma* into the Arabic literary system was accompanied by an extensive blurring of the genre's self-proclaimed fictionality. Emphasis was shifted from its fictional characteristics to its language, style and edifying subject matter. Its fictional world was gradually reduced to a mere skeleton, with its plot serving to connect now larger and more important presentations of information on a wide range of subjects.

As a new literary genre with a new poetics, the *maqāma* might have altered and revitalized the canonized literary system. But this potential was never actualized. In order to gain acceptance, the *maqāma* had to adjust to the normative classical poetics, thus rapidly losing its potential for making a significant impact on the established system. Despite the considerable prestige the *maqāma* had won for itself, it failed ultimately to become a fertile and productive literary model.

Appendix: al-Ḥuṣrī's speculation on the birth of the maqāmāt

Al-Ḥuṣrī's assertion that al-Hamaḏānī wrote his *maqāmāt* upon the inspiration of Ibn Durayd's *Arbʿūna Ḥadīṯan* ("Forty Tales"; Ḥuṣrī 1953:1, 261) provoked what today seems a rather naive scholarly debate on the question of whether al-Hamaḏānī or Ibn Durayd is the initiator of the *maqāma*. Margoliouth (1927) and Mubārak (1931, 1934) claimed that, in light of al-Ḥuṣrī's statement, Ibn Durayd should be credited with the title "originator of the *maqāma*," rather than al-Hamaḏānī. Mubārak further attempted to identify the *Forty Tales*—which has not survived—in literary material transmitted under the authority of Ibn Durayd in *al-Amālī* by al-Qālī, a disciple of Ibn Durayd.

Others, mainly Blachère and Masnou, rejected this idea outright, claiming that there is no proof whatsoever that a work bearing that title, or a similar one, by Ibn Durayd actually existed, or what its contents were (Blachère and Masnou 1957:13-15). As Bosworth concluded, "since no biographer of Ibn Durayd's mentions these tales, and since we know nothing to connect Ibn Durayd with the themes of *muǧūn* and *kudya*, it seems best to regard Ḥuṣrī's information as suspect" (Bosworth 1976:1, 98).

I would like to present here al-Ḥuṣrī's statement in a different light. It must be remembered that al-Ḥuṣrī was a critic and scholar who lived in a local literary centre of Kayrawān, peripheral to the main literary centres which were, at that time, in Baghdad and Basra, as well as in the satellite centres in Persia: Hamaḏān, Ray, Nishapur, Herat. Mendicant-poets gained high status in the Eastern courts at the time, and anecdotes about all sorts of beggars (*mukaddūn*) were favourable there precisely in the period that al-Hamaḏānī composed his *maqāmāt*.[39]

Of all the numerous types of "mendicancy" described in Arabic literature,[40] al-Hamaḏānī chose to build the hero of his *maqāmāt* on the very specific Eastern paradigm of a *mukaddi* who attempts to

[39] On the status of Abū Dulaf al-Ḵazraǧī in the court of al-Ṣāḥib b. ʿAbbād, and on other mendicant-poets, see Bosworth 1976:1, 48-80.
[40] See, for example, Ǧāḥiẓ 1938:1, 85-100 [1990⁵ :46-53]; Bayhaqī 1902:622-624 [1970:582-584].

arouse pity as a victim of the holy wars on the Byzantine borders. The tales of such *mukaddūn* exploit the sympathy and respect that the people who lived in the Eastern provinces of the Muslim empire (which were quite remote from the Byzantine borders) held for the fighters and victims of those wars. Al-Hamaḏānī thus acted within literary trends that were fashionable in the East, and anchored in a socio-cultural phenomenon that had special impact there.

Al-Ḥuṣrī was asked by Abū al-Faḍl al-ʿAbbās b. Sulaymān, a local senior official and patron of *adab*, to compile an anthology from his most recent literary acquisitions of contemporary writers, which he had brought back from a journey to the East.[41] In this way, al-Hamaḏānī's *maqāmāt* reached al-Ḥuṣrī along with the comment that al-Hamaḏānī had composed four hundred such *maqāmāt* "on mendicancy" (*fī al-kudya*—a word of Persian origin!)[42] In the anthology al-Ḥuṣrī inserted some excerpts from al-Hamaḏānī's *rasāʾil*, as well as seventeen *maqāmāt*, together with a note explaining their inception (cf. section 2.1). Al-Ḥuṣrī was a local man of letters, quite removed from the literary fashions of the Eastern centers in which al-Hamaḏanī was active, but well acquainted with canonized classical literature; he could only interpret the new model of the *maqāma* in light of the established literary models familiar to him. He read the theme of mendicancy (*kudya*) as referring to the many anecdotes about Bedouins (*aʿrāb*) begging eloquently in city markets, which are dispersed throughout *adab* literature.[43] This was not on the whole a misreading of al-Hamaḏanī's *Maqāmāt*; after all, they do draw heavily on the *adab* repertoire, as was described. These anecdotes were highly regarded by Arab grammarians, who collected them in the course of their research on "pure," "correct" Arabic, i.e., the language of

---

[41] See al-Ḥuṣrī 1953:1, 2. The names of al-Hamaḏānī, al-Mikālī, Abū Bakr al-Kawārizmī, al-Ṣāḥib b. ʿAbbād and others are mentioned in *Zahr al-ādāb*.

[42] Interestingly enough, al-Ḥuṣrī's words in the passage under discussion bear a remarkable resemblance to al-Hamaḏānī's own words, in the introduction to a collection of his writings (including nineteen *maqāmāt*), found in the Biblioth?que Nationale Ms. 3923, in which he boasts of composing four hundred *maqāmāt* on mendicancy with not one resembling the other, neither in content, nor in style (*ibid.*:2b-3a). One cannot avoid the impression that al-Ḥuṣrī had been familiar with this text when speculating on the birth of the *maqāmāt* in his *Zahr al-Ādāb* (cf. Prendersast 1915 [1973[2]]:18-19).

[43] Many examples of this type were collected by al-Waššāʾ in his *Kitāb al-fāḍil fī funūn al-balāġa* (al-Waššāʾ 1991: 161ff., esp. 173-179). I thank Professor M. Kister who brought my attention to this work many years before it was published, and allowed me to consult his copy of the manuscript (British Museum Ms. Or. 6499).

the Koran and of ancient poetry, of which they believed the Bedouins to be the trusted guardians. Consequently, many of the anecdotes are conveyed by grammarians, such as al-Aṣmaʿī, Ibn Durayd and others (Blachère 1950). Although al-Ḥuṣrī makes no explicit reference in this passage to the content of Ibn Durayd's *Forty Tales*, it is quite plausible that he was referring to this sort of literary material, as this was the kind Ibn Durayd dealt with. Examples of similar anecdotes by Ibn Durayd himself were preserved, in the abovementioned book by his disciple al-Qālī.

It should also be noted that al-Šarīšī (d. 1222), who wrote a commentary in Spain on al-Ḥarīrī's *maqāmāt*, quotes this passage by al-Ḥuṣrī, and after the words *maʿādin fikrihi* he adds *ʿalā ṭabʿ al-ʿarab al-ǧāhiliyya*: "in the style of the Jahili Arabs" (al-Šarīšī 1952:8). This addition explicitly testifies to the type of material under discussion. Even if this is a later interpretative addition to al-Ḥuṣrī's text, it still indicates the way in which al-Ḥuṣrī's words were understood, at least in medieval Spain.

Al-Ḥuṣrī's general claim in this passage is that al-Hamaḏānī took a known model from Ibn Durayd, reshaped it and was extraordinarily successful with it. In order to prove that al-Hamaḏānī was more successful than Ibn Durayd, al-Ḥuṣrī uses the numbers argument. Beeston has already observed that the numbers "forty" and "four hundred" signify "a large amount" rather than an exact quantity (Beeston 1971:12); in addition, al-Hamaḏānī himself speaks of "four hundred types of epistles" (al-Āḥdab:74), or of "four hundred *maqāmāt* on mendicancy" (see note 42), in the sense of "a very large number". Since we have no literary work by the title of *Arbaʿūna Ḥadīṯan* ("Forty Tales") by Ibn Durayd, we can infer that the expression "forty tales," which is also formulaic in several *ḥadīṯ* works (see Karahan 1955 and Vajda 1957), perhaps may not refer to the title of a specific work by Ibn Durayd but to a symbolic number that was reduced, for its stylistic effect, from the number "four hundred" of al-Hamaḏānī's *maqāmāt*. Al-Ḥuṣrī's statement offers a personal view of the *maqāma*'s inception, and represents an interesting testimony as to how a new literary fashion was accepted in an epigonic centre—by being conceptualized in terms of familiar, conventional literary traditions.

CHAPTER TWO

LEGITIMIZING FICTION IN CLASSICAL ARABIC LITERATURE: *ḤADĪṮ ḪURĀFA*

1. *The status of fiction in classical Arabic literature*

Anyone well-versed in classical Arabic literature knows what a great effort it makes to persuade the reader (or listener) that it is telling us nothing but authentic facts. Having developed primarily out of religious motivations, classical Arabic prose is very much occupied with the "truth" or "falsehood" of its texts. Every *ḥadīṯ* and *ḫabar*, be it a saying of the Prophet, a report on an historical event, a tale from Ǧāhilī times, an anecdote or even a joke—each claims to be "true"; that is, to speak of things that were not "invented" by the author, but actually happened in reality. This is, as argued in the previous chapter, the central poetic claim of classical Arabic prose, and so fundamental that it is made in all the prose genres, even in those that have no association at all with religion.

From such a poetic claim, an entire set of operative poetic norms and literary techniques is derived. Two of the major poetic techniques which serve to create credibility for the texts should be mentioned here again:

First, a text is not considered legitimate, and has absolutely no literary status, unless it is presented as having originated with a speaker (who should be a reliable one), and having been handed down through a chain of reliable transmitters (*isnād*). It is almost superfluous to mention, in this connection, the full-fledged apparatus developed in *ḥadīṯ* literature for establishing or denying the credibility of the *isnād*.

Second, as argued previously (ch. 1, 2.2.2), because of the recognized power of the literary "persona" to create a realistic effect, classical Arabic prose almost always employs historical (rather than fictional) figures as its personae, both in the narrative and in the transmission chain. In the same way, it chooses the names of real places as settings for its scenes, and many reality-items are inserted into the narrative.

These techniques and others are part of a model representative of reality employed in classical Arabic prose which is designed to create the impression of "actual" reality and to convince the reader of the historicity of its texts.

Obviously, such a strict and powerful literary model would not permit the introduction into classical Arabic prose, certainly not into its canonized genres, of any kind of fiction that declared itself to be such.[1] Any such attempt would be condemned as a lie (*kiḏb*, or *bāṭil*), and would result in a total theological prohibition against employing such a model in literature. Consequently, theoretical discussions on the subject seem to be quite rare, and interestingly enough, even Aristotle's discussion of *mimesis* in his *Poetics* (known to the Arabs at least by 940 from Mattā b. Yūnus's translation from Syriac) did not seem to arouse interest outside philosophical circles, or prompt the Arab literati to deal with fiction as a literary problem. Nevertheless, there have been a few attempts to legitimize fiction in the history of classical Arabic literature (Bonebakker 1992). Some of these, as, for instance, the association of fiction with courting poetry (*tašbīb*), or with animal fables of the kind of *Kalīla wadimna*—discussed in chapter one (2.2.3) in connection with the *maqāma*—represent a significant turning point in its development. Another interesting attempt to legitimize fiction, which has to do with the manipulation of a fundumental paradigm in Classical Arbic culture—that of *ḥadīṯ*—is the subject of this chapter. It is the case of *Ḥadīṯ Ḵurāfa*,[2] which concerns the *ḵurāfāt* genre, or rather the concept of *ḵurāfa*.

2. *The content and function of* ḥadīṯ ḵurāfa

It is quite plausible to presume that as early as the time of the Prophet, the phrase *ḥadīṯ ḵurāfa* denoted talk that was worthless, not-serious, even if it was humorous. *Adab* works quote a verse by Ibn

[1] cf. Perry 1960:7-8.

[2] I would like to extend my gratitude to Prof. M. Kister, who first drew my attention to the issue of *Ḥadīṯ Ḵurāfa*, and to al-Nahrawānī's important discussion on it in his *al-Ǧalīs al-ṣāliḥ* (al-Nahrawānī 1981:1, 273-279). I would also like to acknowledge my colleagues: Prof. Joseph Sadan, for providing me with important references on research concerning fantastic literature in Arabic; Prof. Uri Rubin, for his references to *ḥadīṯ* sources; and Dr. Gadi Algazi, whose comments on the draft of this study were invaluable.

al-Zabʿarā, a poet who refused to accept Muḥammad's mission, in which the phrase means exactly this:

> *ḥayātun ṯumma mawtun ṯumma našrun ḥadīṯu ḵurāfatin yā umma ʿamrī*
> Life, then death, then resurrection—that is such unbelievable nonsense, Umm ʿAmr![3]

Also quoted are a verse by Abū Nuwās and one by Abū al-ʿAtāhiyya with the same meaning.[4] However, it seems that *ḥadīṯ ḵurāfa* became the subject of a literary-theological debate which extended (but also defined) its meaning far beyond that of "nonsense." Several traditions concerning this concept can be found in *ḥadīṯ* literature, but most are found in *adab* compilations.[5] One tradition handed down in several versions, usually on the authority of Anas b. Mālik or ʿĀʾiša, is as follows:

> One night, the Prophet was relating a story to his wives, and one of them said: "Oh, Messenger of God, isn't this story a *ḵurāfa* [that is, fictitious, something that cannot be true]?" The Prophet then said: "Do you know what *ḵurāfa* is? Ḵurāfa was a man from ʿUḏra, who was carried off by the *ǧinn* in Ǧāhilī times. He stayed with them a while, then after they returned him to human society, he would tell the people incredible stories about what had happened to him with the *ǧinn*. Afterwards people called stories of this kind [after him] '*ḥadīṯ ḵurāfa*'" (Ibn Ḥanbal 1969:6, 157).

Al-Maydānī, relating this tradition in his *Maǧmaʿ al-amṯāl* as an explanation for the saying *ḥadīṯ ḵurāfa*, puts it even more bluntly:

> The Arabs claim that [Ḵurāfa] was a man from ʿUḏra who was ravished by the *ǧinn* and stayed with them a while. When he came back, he told the people what he had seen in the world of the *ǧinn*, and they considered his tales to be such lies, that they began to call [every story about] what could not happen in reality a "*ḥadīṯ ḵurāfa*" (al-Maydānī 1955:1, 195).

---

[3] al-Ṯaʿālibī 1965:130 [no. 185]; al-Nahrawānī 1981:1, 275.

[4] al-Ṯaʿālibī, op. cit. See also Abū Nuwās 1958-88:1, 23.

[5] See Aḥmad b. Ḥanbal 1969:6, 157; Abū Yaʿlā 1986:7, 419-420; Ibn al-Aṯīr 1963:2, 52; al-ʿAǧlūnī 1974:1, 452 (no. 1207); al-Hayṯamī 1967:7, 315; al-Tirmiḏī 1925: 148; al-Ǧāḥiẓ 1943:1, 301; 6, 210; Ibn Ḥaǧar 1972:2, 270-271 (I thank M. Lecker for this reference); Ibn Qutayba 1970:264; Ibn ʿAbd Rabbihi 1965:3,75; al-Nahrawānī 1981:1, 273-274; al-ʿAskarī 1988:2, 237; al-Maydānī 1955:1, 195 (No. 1028); al-Zamaḵšarī 1987:1, 361 (No. 1553); al-Ṯaʿālibī 1965:130 (no. 185); Ḥamza al-Iṣbahānī 1971:2, 389; al-Yūsī 1981:2, 100-102; al-Šarīšī 1952:1, 56-57; *Lisān al-ʿArab*: s.v. *Ḵurāfa*. For an elaborated version see al-Mufaḍḍal b. Salama 1960:168-171, cited also in al-Šarīšī, op. cit., and discussed further on in this chapter.

What, indeed, is meant by *ḥadīṯ ḵurāfa*? It seems that this tradition, with its differing versions scattered mainly within *adab* literature, teaches us several things about the meaning and the literary and social context of this phrase. First of all, we learn about the nature, and perhaps content, of the *ḵurāfa*-tales: they are stories of a fantastic nature, most likely dealing with wonders and bizarre events (the sources use the words *ʿaǧāʾib*, *ṭuraf al-aḵbār*). Although the connection to the world of the *ǧinn* is made in the Prophet's eponymous use of the word *ḵurāfa*, and in additional references to it in some of the versions of *ḥadīṯ ḵurāfa*,[6] the stories were not necessarily only about the *ǧinn*. They were obviously regarded not as "truth," but as "lies" describing incredible occurrences that could never have happened in reality (as can be inferred from Muḥammad's wife's reaction upon hearing them). Nonetheless, these stories were enjoyed by their audience.[7] We can also discern the status of these stories within the Arabic literary system. Ibn Ḥanbal's version informs us that the Prophet was talking to, or rather chatting with, his wives when the phrase *ḥadīṯ ḵurāfa* came up;[8] al-Nahrawānī's version says: "he was talking in the way a man talks at home, to his family [or to his wife]."[9] Al-Ṭabarānī, on the other hand, introduces a more intimate version, which states that ʿĀʾiša and the Prophet were together with a cloth, or a blanket, wrapped around them when the subject arose.[10] Most of the versions state that the

[6] One version of *ḥadīṯ ḵurāfa* states that the relationship of Ḵurāfa with the *ǧinn* was such that whenever they eavesdropped on heavenly talk and discovered some information, they would disclose it to him; Ḵurāfa would then disperse it to his fellow human-beings, and they would find it to be true (Ibn Qutayba 1970: 264; al-Ṯaʿālibī 1965:130 [no. 185]). This is another way of understanding the Prophet's words "*wa-Ḵurāfatu ḥaqqun*," discussed further on (see al-Maydānī 1955:1, 195 [no. 1028]: *Ḵurāfatu ḥaqqun, yaʿnī mā taḥaddaṯa bihi ʿani 'l-ǧinni ḥaqqun*). But cf. Ibn Kaṯīr 1966:5, 216 (*Sūrat al-šuʿraʾ* [26], v. 223: *yulqawna 'l-samʿa wa-akṯaruhum kāḏibūna*).

[7] *waʾaǧrawhu ... ʿalā kulli mā yustamlaḥu wayutaʿaǧǧabu minhu* (Ibn al-Aṯīr 1963:2, 25).

[8] So also al-Mufaḍḍal b. Salama, who presents the most detailed, as well as interesting, version of *ḥadīṯ ḵurāfa*. He is not only informing us that the Prophet was talking to his wives (*kāna yuḥaddiṯu nisāʾahu*, that is, by way of relating to them a *ḥadīṯ*), but is also telling us what exactly the content of that *ḥadīṯ* was. This was obviously a tale bearing a moral concerning the wife's position and good conduct within the family, especially with regard to her mother-in-law (1960:168-169).

[9] *fa-ǧaʿala yaqūlu 'l-kalimata kamā yaqūlu 'l-raǧulu ʿinda ahlihi* (al-Nahrawānī 1981:1, 274).

[10] *ḥaddaṯahā biḥadīṯin wahuwa maʿahā fī liḥāfin* (al-Haytamī 1967:7, 315).

event took place at night, this being the time dedicated to entertainment and activities of an informal character.[11] In other words, the implication here is that these stories were circulating primarily among women and young people, often in an unofficial setting, and were meant for entertainment rather than instruction or learning; that is, they were regarded as successfully consumed by an audience of inferior social status. In all probability men, who had a higher social status, also enjoyed the *ḵurāfa*-tales. Nevertheless, the fact that these tales were regarded as fit for a socially inferior audience of women and young people, is a clear indication of their non-canonized status within the literary system, certainly with regard to the canonized *adab*.

Although these stories are obviously fictitious, they were not totally condemned by the *adab* authorities, or by representatives of the official literary norms. They must have been very popular and well received by their audience, for we have yet another tradition which says:

> The Prophet said: "Ḵurāfa was a man from ʿUḏra who was ravished by the demons (*šayāṭīn*)." One day the Prophet was relating a *ḥadīṯ*, and one of his wives said: "that is a *ḵurāfa* story" [meaning something like "this is really an incredible one!"]. The Prophet answered: "No, Ḵurāfa is true! (*lā, wa-ḵurāfatu ḥaqqun*)" (al-Ǧāḥiẓ, *Ḥayawān*:6, 210).[12]

We have here an example of an attempt to legitimize literary material of a clearly fictional character (as it was regarded, apparently, by the contemporary audience) in order that it might conform to the governing poetic norm formulated in terms of the religious opposition of "truth" vs. "lie." *Ḵurāfa*-tales are not only permitted by the Prophet, according to this tradition, but have the same status as any other true *ḥadīṯ* (*wa-ḵurāfatu ḥaqqun*) and therefore, there should be no reservations about listening to these tales or passing them on. The *ḥadīṯ ḵurāfa* acquires the status of being true not only through an explicit statement by the Prophet, but also through the way in which the word *ḵurāfa* is explained: not as a *word* designating untrue speech, or nonsense, but as the *name* of an

[11] Cf. *Lisān al-ʿarab*: s.v. *ḵurāfa*: *yurīdu bihi 'l-ḵurāfāti 'l-mawḍūʿata min ḥadīṯ 'l-layli.*

[12] See also al-Ǧāḥiẓ 1943:1, 301; Maydānī 1955:1, 195; Ibn al-Aṯīr 1963:2, 25.

existing person,[13] who told people what he himself had actually witnessed! And what could testify more to the authenticity of a *ḥadīṯ* than a reliable speaker (whose reliability was affirmed by the Prophet himself) who reported from his own experiences?[14] Such a *ḥadīṯ* would be judged as sound according to any criterion of *ḥadīṯ* criticism.

3. *Fantastic fiction: the world of the* ǧinn

It is easy to understand why a connection was made between the *ḥadīṯ ḵurāfa* and the world of the *ǧinn*, as this was probably the most available (as well as acknowledged)[15] literary option for unealistic, even fantastic stories in the literary repertoire which was regarded as representing "authentic Arab-Bedouin culture" of pre-Persian influence. Here again, it was al-Muffaḍal b. Salama who, wishing to satisfy his readers' curiosity about gaps in the often-quoted version of *ḥadīṯ ḵurāfa*, was determined to tell them exactly what Ḵurāfa's adventures were in the land of the *ǧinn*, thus providing an illustrative example of the fantastic nature of *ǧinn*'s tales. In a unique version presented in his book *al-Fāḵir*, Ḵurāfa tells the

---

[13] We quite often find medieval agents of Ǧāhilī culture (like *aḵbāriyyūn*, philologists, collectors of ancient poetry and proverbs) explaining eponymously the meaning of a proverb, a saying or a calque. Cf., for instance: *ʿiṭr manšim* (Ibn al-Anbārī 1963:261, explaining verse 19 of Zuhayr b. Abī Sulmā's *Muʿallaqa*; Ibn Qutayba 1970: 260); *ǧawf ḥimār* (Ibn al-Anbārī 1963:80-81, explaining verse 50 of Imru' al-Qays's *Muʿallqa*; al-Mufaḍḍal b. Salama 1960:14-15). In both cases the eponymous explanation is presented on the authority of Ibn al-Kalbī; *way-lun li-'l-šaǧiyyi mina 'l-ḵaliyyi* (al-Mufaḍḍal b. Salama 1960:250; (pseudo-)al-Ǧāḥiẓ 1991:309), to mention but few of the numerous examples scattered in *adab* and especially in *amṯāl* literature (e.g., Ibn ʿAbd Rabbihi 1965:3, 74-76). It should be noted, however, that the eponymous explanation is not the only one given for each of these sayings; an alternative, philological explanation is provided as well. It should also be noted that Ibn Ḥaǧar al-ʿAsqalānī apparently regards Ḵurāfa as a real companion of the Prophet, for he includes a profile of him in his lexicon of *ḥadiṯ* transmitters (see note 5).

[14] In al-Muffaḍal b. Salama's version of *ḥadīṯ Ḵurāfa* (1960:169), Ḵurāfa is relating his incredible adventures with the *ǧinn* to the Prophet himself!

[15] If we are to judge from the numerous *ǧinn* anecdotes which can be found in almost every genre of classical Arabic literature. Cf. for example al-Qurašī 1963:40-55; al-Ǧāḥiẓ 1943:1, 301-302; 6, 200-225; Ibn Qutayba 1963b:2, 109-114; al-Maṣūdī 1964:2, 157-164; al-Maṣūdī 1978:33-40; Yaqūt 1923:6, 121-122; al-Bāqillānī 1981:38-41; al-Iṣbhānīi 1963:6, 294-295; al-Marzūbānī 1965:553, 557, to mention only few random examples.

Prophet that one night while away on business he was taken prisoner by three *ǧinn*. As they were discussing whether to kill, release or enslave him, another person appeared. Upon hearing of their dilemma he suggested sharing the prisoner with them, in return for which he would tell them an extraordinary story (*ḥadīṯ ʿaǧab*). He then told them how, while on the run from a debt, he was caught inside a well, where a spell was cast upon him, turning him into a woman. He came to a town,[16] married a man and gave birth to two children. After some time he felt homesick, went back to the same well, became a man again and returned home. He married a woman and had two other children, this time as a man. Upon hearing this tale, the *ǧinn* admitted that it was indeed an extraordinary story and agreed to share their prisoner. While they were discussing the prisoner's fate, a bull flew through the air, followed by a man chasing it with a stick. By the same procedure the bull-chaser promised to tell the group an even more bizarre story. He told them that he and his six brothers were competing for the hand of their rich uncle's beautiful daughter, who was already betrothed to another man. One day this man's beloved calf ran away, and he promised the hand of his fiancée to whomever captured the lost calf. The bull-chaser continued: "I took my stick, put on my belt and began running after the calf. This all happened when I was a young boy; now I am old, and I am still running after the bull without my getting any closer, or it stumbling." This time, too, they admitted how truly incredible the story was, and accepted the second storyteller as another partner. Yet a third person, riding a mare and accompanied by a servant riding a beautiful horse, arrived and offered his even more incredible story in return for a share in the prisoner. He began "I had a wicked maid," then turned to the mare and asked "Isn't it so?" The mare affirmed by nodding its head. "I suspected her of having an affair with this slave." He pointed towards the horse on which his servant rode, and said: "Isn't it so?," and the horse nodded its affirmation. "Then one day I sent

[16] Ismāʿīl b. Abān al-Warrāq, from whom the entire version is quoted, remarks at this point: "The first transmitter did mention the name of that town; however, Ziyād [meaning Ziyād b. ʿAbd Allah al-Bakkāʾī, his previous link in the transmission chain] has forgotten it"—a remark which would certainly not support the credibility of any decent tradition, or of its transmitters, in the eyes of *ḥadīṯ* scholars. It seems that the strict norms regarding the *ḥadīṯ* transmission had less power over such *ḵurāfāt*-tales. On the role of the ninth-century *warrāqūn* in producing and distributing fictitious works, see Ghazi 1957:169.

this servant of mine to the maid with some business and she captured him there. He fell asleep and had a dream. In his dream he heard her shouting, and a rat suddenly appeared. 'Plough!' she ordered the rat, and he ploughed. 'Sow!' she ordered, and he sowed. 'Reap!' she ordered, and he reaped. 'Tread!' she ordered, and he trod. She then ordered a handmill and prepared a bowl of barley-nectar. The servant awoke in horror, and the maid ordered him to take the nectar to me, his master, and trick me into drinking it. My servant returned and informed me of what was happening, so, I tricked the two of them into drinking from the bowl, whereupon they turned into a mare and a horse. Isn't it so?" They both nodded. Everybody admitted that this was certainly the most extraordinary story of all, and accepted him as a partner. They decided to release K̲urāfa, and he came to the Prophet and told him what he had experienced (al-Muffaḍal b. Salama 1960:169-171).[17]

Anyone acquainted with classical Arabic prose, especially with *adab* literature, will agree that this story stands out as most uncommon precisely because of its fantastic characteristics and the lack of any historical setting. It is not often that we encounter in classical Arabic prose legendary motifs like magical sex-transformation, a flying bull taking a lifetime to catch, or a witch preparing a magic potion with the assistance of a rat.[18] But is it the adventures of K̲urāfa himself in the land of the *ğinn*, mentioned in almost all the other versions of *ḥadīṯ kurāfa*, which are expounded here? As a matter of fact, no. K̲urāfa is not really the hero of this legend; he is only a listener and a transmitter, a means to present three distinct fantastic tales. If we expected this manifestly fictional text to unfold the adventures of a "real," historical figure before its audience, we were mistaken. This apparently daring version of *ḥadīṯ kurāfa* is, in one respect, quite conservative, as it retains the very fundamental characteristic of the *ḥadīṯ* discourse, that of the text being a *qawl*, a report or narration presented as originating with a certain speaker. There is no break through the solidified literary framework of *ḥadīṯ* and *adab* in this case, and K̲urāfa is promoting tales rather than

[17] For an earlier English translation of this story and a discussion of its possible sources and connections with the *1001 Nights* see MacDonald 1924:371-379.

[18] But see, for instance, *maṯalu 'l-mar'ati 'l-sū'i*, Ibn Qutayba 1963b:4, 117. On fantastic genres in classical Arabic literature see Arkoun et al. 1978; K̲awam 1981: 7-11; Sadan, forthcoming.

"real" adventures. Furthermore, as a mere transmitter of tales, rather than a reporter of his own experiences, Ḵurāfa is not, in a sense, really held responsible for their fantastic content. The overall realistic setting of the text is thus also retained, in complete accordance with the strict norms of the *ḥadīṯ* discourse.

It is highly significant in another, even contrasting, respect as well that Ḵurāfa relates tales rather than reporting on his own experiences. The tales are recounted as part of a story-for-a-life bargain: an incredible story in return for a share in a prisoner, that is, in having a say in deciding his fate. Only if the storyteller succeeds in impressing his audience will he be able to influence "real life" events. The message conveyed here is that, as in *Thousand and One Nights*, a fictional narration is not merely entertainment without any implications for "life." It does have power over reality, and can function as an active agent in it. The power to fascinate by narrating can be transformed into a power to influence the course of real events. This message, it should be noted, was strongly rejected by the diverse, canonized Arabic prose genres, which constantly insisted that fiction was appropriate, if at all, for entertainment alone.[19]

4. *The* ḵurāfāt *genre and its Persian origin*

It was not, however, until Arabic literature was initially exposed to Persian literary models, from the beginning of the Abbasid period onward, that the whole concept of *ḵurāfa* acquired a new meaning. Ibn al-Nadīm dedicates an entire chapter in his *Fihrist* to a literary genre which he refers to as *al-asmār wa-'l-ḵurāfāt*,[20] which was initially based on translations from Persian (also mentioned are "Indian books" and "Greek book"), and later, on Arabic adaptations of Persian models, in addition to original Arabic works.[21] Both al-Masʿūdī and Ibn al-Nadīm mention as a representative exam-

[19] Like fiction, humor was also associated with "lie" in classical Arabic litarary theory (Sadan 1983:56-71).

[20] *al-fannu 'l-awwalu fī aḵbārī 'l-musāmirīna wa-'l-muḵarrifīna wa-asmā'i 'l-kutubi 'l-muṣannafati fī 'l-asmār wa-'l-ḵurāfātī*. Ibn al-Nadīm:422-428. Cf. Perry 1960:18-27.

[21] Ibn al-Nadīm (422-428) lists about 200 book titles for this genre. For a concise list of fictitious genres see Ghazi 1957.

ple of the genre the book *Hazār afsān* ("A Thousand Fables"), the title of which they translate as *Alf ḵurāfa*. People refer to this book as *Alf layla walayla*, says al-Masʿūdī, and the identification is confirmed by both synopses of the frame-story of this book. We also learn from their accounts that the *ḵurāfāt* genre was popular in the royal court (especially in al-Muqtadir's day [908-932], according to Ibn al-Nadīm:428). Indeed, it was so well enjoyed by the Abbasid caliphs that al-Ǧahšiyārī, an official Abbasid clerk (d. 942), prepared a book that was intended to contain thousand tales (*samar*), and collected the materials from professional storytellers and existing books of *asmār wa-ḵurāfāt*. Al-Ǧahšiyārī died before completing the book, but he did complete "480 'nights', each of which held an entire *samar* of about 50 pages!"[22] The popularity of the genre in court circles is affirmed by additional references to it in tenth-century Arabic sources.[23] It is evident from these that the genre was regarded as purely entertaining and not instructive, which could also explain why it was considered suitable mainly for women and young people.[24]

It is highly likely that al-Nahrawānī (d. 999) is referring in particular to this genre when he says in *al-Ǧalīs al-ṣāliḥ* that people usually understand the word *ḵurāfa*

> ... to mean a story (*ḥadīṯ*) which has no truth to it, such as those recounted at nighttime gatherings for entertainment. Stories of this kind contain wonders and bizarre events which are arranged in a way that pleases the people who are assembled together. They enjoy engaging in such storytelling, and spend their time together passing these tales around. These stories, or rather most of them, have absolutely no basis at all (*lā aṣla lahu*; al-Nahrawānī 1981:1, 274).

Phrases like "*ḥadīṯun lā ḥaqīqata lahu*" and "*lā aṣla lahu*," which appear

[22] Ibn al-Nadīm:423.

[23] Macdonald 1924; Abbot 1949:149-164.

[24] See al-Tawḥīdī 1953:1, 23: *wa'l-ḥadīṯu maʿšūqu 'l-ḥissi bimaʿūnati 'l-ʿaqli walihāḏā yūlaʿu bihi 'l-ṣibyānu wa'l-nisā'u*. Later in this passage, al-Tawḥīdī makes it clear that by the word "*ḥadīṯ*," the *ḵurāfāt* genre is meant: *walifarṭi 'l-ḥāǧati ilā 'l-ḥadīṯ mā wuḍiʿa fihi 'l-bāṭilu waḵuliṭa bi'l-muḥāli wawuṣila bimā yuʿǧibu wayuḍḥiku walā ya'ūlu ilā taḥṣīlin wataḥqīqin, miṯla hazār afsan wakulli mā daḵala fī ǧinsihi min ḍurūbi 'l-ḵurāfāti*. See also the interesting incident between the son of the caliph al-Muqtadir (d. 932) and messengers from the palace of his grandmother, Šaġab, reported by al-Ṣūlī, where it is implied that books belonging to the *ḵurāfāt* genre were widely read in the palace (Abbot 1949:155). Cf. also al-Sayyid 1978:39; Mez 1937:253-254, with additional references.

in this passage, as well as "*aḵbārun mawḍūʿatun min ḵurāfātin maṣnūʿatin*" (al-Masʿūdī 1964:2, 259); "*faṣannafa 'l-warrāqūna ['l-asmāra wa'l-ḵurāfāti] wakaḏḏabū*" (Ibn al-Nadīm:428); "*aḥādīṯ muḥāliyya*" (al-Šarīšī 1952:1, 57); and "*yurīdu bihi 'l-ḵurāfāti 'l-mawḍuʿata min ḥadīṯi 'l-layli, aǧrawhu ʿalā kulli mā yukaḏḏibūnahu mina 'l-aḥādīṯi, waʿalā kulli mā yustamlaḥu wayutaʿaǧǧabu minhu*" (*Lisān al-ʿarab*: s.v. *ḵurāfa*), all associate *ḵurāfa* with "lie." In other words, they point specifically to the fact that the *ḵurāfāt* genre is fictional both in the sense of being "invented" rather than "historical," and of being governed by a fantastic rather than realistic model of reality. It seems that the *ḥadīṯ ḵurāfa* reflects, therefore, an attempt to legitimize the type of fiction represented in the *ḵurāfāt* genre.

CHAPTER THREE

CREATING A SENSE OF "REALITY" IN CLASSICAL ARABIC LITERATURE: THE CASE OF ABŪ NUWĀS

1. *Reality in classical Arabic wine-poetry*

Wine-poetry (*k̲amriyyāt*) is one of the most famous, as well as well-documented, genres of classical Arabic verse. It captured the attention of scholars almost from the first appearance of wine poems in print (Ahlwardt published part of Abū Nuwās's *k̲amriyyāt* as early as 1861),[1] and many studies took interest in it.[2] Scholarly interest in wine-poetry tended to be twofold: first, a literary interest was focussed upon the poetic repertoire of motifs and images of the Bacchic genre. Following to a certain extent the example of the medieval collections of *maʿānī*, much effort was dedicated to surveying and summing up the various topoi which constitute that repertoire (Bencheik̲ 1963-4; Ḥāwī 1970:275-98); second, there was a more socio-cultural concern with learning about the actual wine-culture, as part of medieval Islamic civilization (Sadan 1977). This interest in Islamic wine-culture could not of course confine itself to poetry alone, or even to written texts; naturally it had to consider other cultural products as well, those of everyday life, and of art. Literary texts had to be read in light of archaeological findings, and often enough a line of poetry would support an understanding of a certain archaeological item, or a piece of art help to clarify the meaning of some awkward metaphor (Rice 1958).

This procedure is so familiar that we rarely stop to consider its theoretical premises. Is it really so obvious that poetry—especially this kind of *waṣf* poetry—should supply evidence concerning everyday life? Has it not been said that poets are liars (*yaqūlūna mā lā yafʿalūna*), and has not poetry always been associated with lie—*kid̲b*, or *bāṭil*—in theological as well as poetic thinking of the period, giving rise to the idea that the more remote poetry is from reality, the better

---

[1] See Abū Nuwās 1861. For other editions of his *Dīwān* see Abū Nuwās 1898; 1932; 1953; 1958-88; 1962; 1980.

[2] See Ingrams 1933; Farūkh 1946; Gabrieli 1953; Wagner 1965; Arazi 1979; Schoeler 1990; Kennedy 1997, to mention but few.

it is (as in the famous saying: "*aḥsanu al-šiʿri akḏabuhu*")? The association of poetry with lie, apart from being an accusation from the theological point of view, is meant to say something very serious about the poetic basis of poetry: that it does not commit itself in any way to describing reality "as it is," that is, to being elaborated according to any sort of "realistic" norms (ch. 1, 2.2.3.1). Poetry does not wish to describe "how things really are"; rather, it takes "reality" as a point of departure, and tells whatever it likes about it. This is, of course, in clear opposition to religious literature like the Koran and the *ḥadīṯ*, which always claims to convey some sort of "true reality." If "falsity" is the nature of poetry, on what grounds can it be taken as a stock of "facts" about reality?

The chief concern of poetry is not to convey reality, but something else. Particularly, the more descriptive genres of Arabic poetry—those that should by definition deal with reality (like *ḵamriyyāt*, *ṭardiyyāt*, *ġazal*, and mainly *waṣf* which is *the* descriptive genre of medieval Arabic poetry)—give us quite a clear picture of the actual concerns of descriptive poetry: these are, as we all know, the words, the poetic images, the figurative language, the creation of metaphoric worlds (Hamori 1969). To understand reality by means of such texts is thus no easy task, as it goes against their very poetic foundations.[3]

It was no easier for the medieval scholars and experts on Arabic poetry either, as can be discerned from the following anecdote, which ʿAbd Allah b. al-Muʿtazz relates in his wine anthology *Fuṣūl al-tamāṯīl fī tabāšīr al-surūr*. The Caliph al-Muʿtaḍid (d. 901) asked a group of scholars (among them Ibn al-Muʿtazz himself) about the meaning of a line by Abū Nuwās, in which he refers to wine as "a virgin veiled in a scarf of white locks while still in the womb." Every scholar in turn gives his explanation to this metaphor. The last explanation, offered by al-Muʿtaḍid himself on the authority of the Caliph al-Maʾmūn (d. 833), is written down by all the attendants as the right one (Ibn al-Muʿtazz 1989: 124-126). His explanation is obviously not correct, nor is it more persuasive than the other explanations offered; nevertheless it is accepted as the right one because of the authority of the Caliph, rather than any expertise opinion. Interestingly, only about eighty years after the death of Abū Nuwās scholars can no longer agree on the correct meaning of a verse of his.

[3] For a discussion of the presence of reality in animal descriptions of ancient Arabic poetry see Arazi 1989:107-150.

And yet, even those who have had limited experience with Arabic descriptive poetry would feel the presence of "reality" in it. It is practically quite impossible to understand wine-poetry, for instance, without knowing a great deal about the process of the preparation of the wine, the vessels served for this process, the circumstances of drinking, the pouring of the wine, the look of the cups, who serves the wine, etc. Descriptive poetry is not interested in conveying reality, and yet, reality is there, very strongly, and a line of verse can in fact contribute a lot to an understanding of contemporary reality, as was so successfully shown by Rice, Sadan and others.[4]

How can we account for it? On what literary basis is this "presence of reality" constructed, within a poetic framework that strives so much to move away from reality? Let us take a closer look at some examples from Abū Nuwās's wine poetry.

2. *Four wine-poems by Abū Nuwās*

1. *ʿAfā ʾl-Muṣallā* (Arabic text: Abū Nuwās 1958-88:3, 29-35)[5]

(1) The Muṣallā (prayer-site) has been erased, and the hills are devoid of me and so are the two markets of Mirbad, and Labab

(2) [and so is] the Great Mosque in which chivalry and glory (or: religion)[6] commingle, and so are the courtyards and grounds.

(3) Places of gathering which I inhabited as a youth until my whiskers turned gray.

(4) With other youths sharp as swords that have been brandished by the prime of life, and beautified by culture

(5) Then times changed and they dispersed forever and split apart

(6) Fate will never replace them for me, indeed, how wondrous they are.

(7) When I realized that their departure will not be reversed for as long as I live

[4] For a different insight regarding the reality in Abū Nuwās's poetry see Mattock 1987-8.

[5] For an alternate translation see Kennedy 1997:265-266. Cf. also Wagner's German translation and notes (1965:292).

[6] The 1958-88 edition has *maǧd*, whereas the 1962 edition has *dīn*.

(8) I was torn apart between many aspirations
(9) So it is; whenever I am struck by the loss of a brother there is no more kinship between us
(10) My springtime abode is Qutrubbūl, my summer places are the villages of al-Kark̲ and the vine is my mother
(11) She nurses me with her milk and covers me in the shade, when the noontime sun is ablaze
(12) When the branches twist to create it [the shade] I am enfolded by its luxuriant foliage which has no gaps
(13) The doves inhabiting it are likened to women mourning their loved ones
(14) My yearning flares up along with theirs, as though we are swept away by their sweet song
(15) And so I crawled to be nursed, as a baby staggers [to the breast] when seized by hunger
(16) Until I selected a tavern's daughter [i.e., wine] tested by the years and long periods of time
(17) And so, in the dark night, I rent its loosely woven hemless veil,
(18) Made by an unskilled weaver [i.e. a spider], for whom it is futile to set up a loom on the ground[7]
(19) And then I pierced its waist with the point of an awl and it gushed forth like fire
(20) And drinking became possible to the boon-companions. [The wine] was made to flow on us by [cups of] silver and gold
(21) The golden wine and the cups so resembled each other in likeness that I ask: which of them is the gold?
(22) They are both equal, only one is solid and the other is liquid
(23) Some [cups] are plain, others engraved with images of priests and crosses
(24) [The priests] are reciting their Gospel, while above them lies a firmament of wine whose stars are bubbles

[7] Philip Kennedy's translation of this line: "a skilled seamstress...who needs [no loom to be set up]..." (Kennedy 1997:266) is not acceptable to my mind. For the meaning of *k̲arqā'* as "a woman incompetent to do her work (either because she is inept, or because as a woman of rank she is not used to do house works)" see Ibn Qutayba 1904:336; al-ʿAskarī 1988:1, 424: al-Marzubānī 1965:162; al-Ǧāḥiẓ 1932:2, 225-226. For the spider's web (*nasīǧ al-ʿankabūt*, "that which the spider weaves") as a standard reality-item of the drinking scene (whether real or poetic) see al-Ǧāḥiẓ 1943:2, 337-339.

(25) As though they are pearls strewn by maidens excited by the game of love[8]

2. *Dā' 'Anka Lawmī* (Arabic text: Abū Nuwās, *ibid.*:2-4)[9]

(1) Censure me not, for censure but urges one on![10]; cure me rather with the cause of my ill—
(2) A pale [wine], whose house is not visited by sorrows, imparting joy even to the rock that touches it
(3) Received from the palm of a woman clad as a man, whose lovers are two: the fornicator and the sodomite[11]
(4) As she brought the wine-jug on a dark night her face emitted a bright light
(5) She cast from the lip of the grail pure [wine]—looking at it is like falling asleep![12]
(6) More gentle than water, which ills suits her delicate [nature]. Water is too coarse to mix with it
(7) But if you were to mix light into [the wine]—it would mix well, and generate a multitude of lights
(8) It was passed around men by whom Fate is humbled, bringing upon them only what pleases them
(9) For it (i.e., the wine) do I cry, not for the spot at which Asmā' and Hind once alighted
(10) No tent is to be set up for Durra[13], no camels and sheep are to roam around her—far from it!

---

[8] For the impact of Abū Nuwās's image of bubbles as scattered pearls see al-Ma'mūn's reaction towards the sight of scattered pearls in the famous Būrān's wedding (e.g., al-Ṯa'ālibī 1965:166).

[9] The translation of this poem is based on that of Philip Kennedy (1997:267-268), with changes. Cf. also Wagner's German translation and notes (1965:297-298).

[10] I prefer Hamori's rendering of *iġrā'u* (1969:25).

[11] Literally: "one with a vagina, clad as one with a phallus." Abū Nuwās refers here to the fashion of *ġulāmiyyāt*, maids dressed and shaped to look like young men. For a description of the *ġulāmiyyāt* in connection with the Caliph al-Amīn, patron of Abū Nuwās, see Ibn Qutayba 1963:4, 318. As explained there, the style was invented by Zubayda, wife of the Caliph Harūn al-Rashīd and mother of al-Amīn, in order to distract her son's mind from favoring male servants. It later became fashionable inside and outside the court. Cf. Ibn Manẓūr 1992:122; Abū Nuwās 1980:116, 283.

[12] The idea is that one should not waste time looking at the wine and admiring it, but hurry up and drink it. Cf. Abu Nuwās, *ibid.*:86.

[13] A jāriya of Abū Nuwās. Cf. Abū Nuwās 1988:1, 91.

(11) Tell him who would claim philosophy as part of his knowledge: "You have learned some things, but much more escapes you;
(12) Do not deprive [me] of God's forgiveness, if you yourself are a man abstaining from sin; to deprive me of this is a blasphemy."

3. *Wafityāni Ṣidqin* (Arabic text: Abū Nuwās, *ibid.*:130-132)

(1) Alas to true friends,[14] whose mount I have diverted to the wine sellers' house upon which we alighted at noon-time
(2) And when the sash revealed that he was not Muslim we thought well of him and he thought ill of us
(3) We asked: "Do you belong to the religion of Christ, Son of Mary?" and he turned away and said: "'Tis a heresy!"
(4) But a Jew will appear to like you, while in secret he will harbour betrayal
(5) I asked him: "What is your name?" and he said: "Samaw'al; but my nickname is Abū ʿAmr, though there is no ʿAmr"[15]
(6) This Arabic nickname has not honoured me, nor has it brought me fame or glory;
(7) It was merely light on the tongue, with few letters; unlike another whose sound is dull"
(8) admiring the elegance of his words we said: "well said, Abū ʿAmr, and now give us good wine!"
(9) He turned away sullenly, dividing his glance, looking now at our feet now at our faces
(10) He said: "By my life, had you alighted upon someone other than me, I would have rebuked you, but [this time] I will generously excuse you!"
(11) He brought the wine all bright and golden and we could not but bow to it
(12) We set off planning to stay but three days, but they were so pleasant that we stayed there a month

[14] For a discussion of Abū Nuwās's use of *wāw al-rubba* see Hamori 1969:11-15.

[15] This is an allusion to a line by the famous poet Mağnūn Laylā, who said about his beloved Laylā: "My heart refuses to love anybody but an *ʿāmiriyya* (a woman of the ʿĀmirī tribe); her nickname is [Umm] ʿAmr, though she has no [son by the name of] ʿAmr" (al-Iṣbahānī 1992:2, 51). Cf. also al-Saraqustī 1972:124.

(13) A mischievous band, the like of whom time has never seen, though I am one of them; I am neither clean nor free of [their mischief]

(14) And when the time of prayer is close, they urge for yet more wine, so that they miss their prayer while being drunk

4. *Wakammāratim Lillahwi* (Arabic text: Abū Nuwās, *ibid.*, 317-318)

(1) Three nights we travelled towards a wine-seller, a woman with a gift for entertainment

(2) And the night covered and surrounded us like a rope; so dark you could see neither man nor jinn

(3) Accompanying us, only the sky with its stars hanging everywhere we turned

(4) Until we knocked on her door in the midst of the night and she asked: "who is knocking?" and we replied: "we are

(5) Youths who became acquainted at your door. We were not due here, but night has overtaken us

(6) If you do not let us in, we shall disperse; but if you gather us through wine—we shall stay together!"

(7) She said to us: "Welcome to true men, amongst who I see no weakness of mind"

(8) We came to her trusting her generosity and when she saw us she bowed and greeted us

(9) We said to her: "weigh the exact measure, full jars of wine, no more no less!"

(10) And she brought us wine, shining in its glass like a sun whose rays imitate in their beauty the rays of a [glass] lamp

(11) I said to her: "what is your name, and the price—tell us clearly its price, so that we may visit you as long as we live!"

(12) She answered: "Ḥanūn is my name, and the price: three [cups] for nine [dirhams]—this is how we sell to everybody else"

(13) When the night turned away, or nearly so, she came to us with a scale, to weigh our money

(14) And I said to her: "we have come with little money—would you accept one of us as pledge?"

(15) She answered: "I'll make you my pledge, so if I will not be paid rightly—I will have you kept in prison for ever!"

2.1. *Reality-items and imagery*

A cursory look at these four poems immediately reveals a gap between the first two poems on one hand, and the next two poems on the other, in their representations of reality. For example, the descriptive parts of poems 1 + 2 (lines 16-25; lines 2-8 respectively) are written in very rich figurative language, composed mainly of metaphors. In poem 1 the wine is referred to as a young female figure—*bintu daskaratin*, the daughter of a monastery, or tavern (Rice 1958:29: a wine-hall)—who is simultaneously old. In order to reach out to her the poet tears away her "veil," which is woven loosely with no hem to it, a product of such an unskilled weaver that there is no point in building a loom for her; then he stabs the hips of this female figure with the point of a sharp tool and here she comes, looking like fire. Gold and silver passed the wine over to all the drinking-mates. The wine looked so much like gold, that you could not tell which was the real gold—the cups, or the wine—and the only difference was that one was solid gold, while the other was liquid. Some of the cups were smooth and blank, some held reliefs of priests with crosses, reading from the Evangel, above them a sky of wine, whose stars were bubbles. The sparkling bubbles looked like pearls in the hands of young ladies, moved by the excitement of courting games.

In poem 2 (line 2-8) the wine is also referred to as a female figure; she is fair (yellow, or rather pale—a sign of lovesickness), yet agony never enters her home, and she could even make a stone move with joy. The wine is served by a *ġulāmiyya* (described in two harsh metonymies), a girl dressed like a boy of a homosexual nature (*ġulām*). At night, when she brings the *ibrīq* with the wine, her shining face lights up the whole room. From the mouth of the *ibrīq* she pours a wine so pure and delicate, that even water cannot suit to be blended with it, being too coarse. Light is the only match for such wine, and the result of such intermingling would be the birth of gleams and glares. This wine was passed around.

The language of these poems is figurative, and rich in metaphors and similes. It is obviously not meant to represent reality "as it is." And yet, these metaphors and similes have no sense, no meaning whatsoever, without the context of "reality." Who is this weaver, for instance, and why is she regarded as so incompetent? The answer is, of course, the spider (feminine gender in Arabic), which is a bad weaver because the web it creates is "loose and has no fine hem."

This metaphor fits in perfectly with the logical order of the acts involved in the preparation for drinking: going to where the wine jars were kept and choosing the appropriate one, cleaning off the webs that have accumulated during the long period while the wine matured, wielding a special tool on the upper narrow part of the wine jar (where it was sealed with clay: *k̲aṣrahā*, "her hips"), pouring the wine into the golden and silver cups, ornamented with reliefs of Christian themes, because the drinking took place in a monastery. The second poem, also recalls preparation: the mixing of the wine with water, and finally the bubbles that rise to the surface of the wine as a cause of the pouring and the mixing. The imagery, elaborated as it is, is based here on reality-items and is organized according to a mimetic order. Reality-items are present; nevertheless, their function is not necessarily a descriptive one.

2.2. *Dialogue and authenticity*

Let us now turn to the latter two poems. It is striking how few lines here are purely figurative. In both poems only one line is dedicated to a metaphoric description of the wine. Instead, a dialogue takes up a great part of the poem: seven out of 14 lines in poem no. 3; nine out of 14 lines in no. 4. In both poems the dialogue is taking place between the poet, who arrives at a tavern with his friends late at night in order to drink wine, and the vintner.

On one hand, then, are wine poems founded on a metaphoric description of the wine, and, on the other hand, wine poems which are founded on dialogue. The first type is abundant in details about what things looked like in these drinking parties; the second type is nearly devoid of such details. We are told nothing of what the wine hall in the tavern looked like, the shape of the cups and the other vessels, whether it was mixed with water, etc. Almost all we have is a conversation between two figures, not all of it even specifically about wine. And yet, if we ask ourselves which type of poem is more "authentic,"—that is, more successful in creating a sense of "reality as it is"—we would no doubt vote for the second type. Although these poems offer no visual descriptions of the drinking sessions that took place in the tavern, we can surely have an idea of what they were like, of the light, bohemian and humorous atmosphere of those sessions.

This seems paradoxical, if we identify literary items (materials, devices) with their function. If we expect to find a "realistic" description every time we have a literary model that uses reality-items (and uses them heavily), than it would seem to be a paradox. But literary items have different functions, and act differently, within different literary models. This is what creates dynamics and evolution in literature—when certain literary items are borrowed from one model by another, used in a different way, have new functions, and thus alter the whole model. In our case, the function of the reality-items is not to "convey reality," or create a "realistic impression"—realism is not at all a poetic aim for these genres of Abbasid poetry (nor is it likely the aim of any classical Arabic poetry). Reality-items are merely a basis, a point of departure, for the elaboration of highly sophisticated imagery that strives so hard to surprise the reader, that it is developed like a series of riddles. The reality-items that appear in the text are "solutions" to these metaphoric "riddles"; nevertheless, it is the riddle which is important, not its solution.

But what happens if a poet who is fond of poetic innovations, like Abū Nuwās, wants to refresh a conventional poetic genre—wine poetry—by introducing a new theme such as the Bacchic tavern experience? He is confronted with a need for "fresh" literary techniques, that would serve to introduce the new theme into the established genre. Abū Nuwās sought to convey the realistic atmosphere of a Bacchic tavern, as opposed to a metaphoric representation. What literary techniques in the conventional poetic repertoire were open to him for this purpose? Imposing the realistic function on reality-items, as might seem natural in other cases, is a not a viable option for the poet at this stage, for reality-items are already engaged in figurative functions. Dialogue, however, does seem to offer a ready option. Although not unfamiliar to poetic practice, dialogue was rarely used in poetry (and then only in very small segments), and never in a way that would contradict the realistic function. Thus, Abū Nuwās chose dialogue for creating an impression of "authentic" atmosphere.

3. *The function of dialogue in classical Arabic literature*

In fact, the choice was not accidental, nor even entirely new. In the literary repertoire of classical Arabic literature the association of dialogue with authenticity has already been well established—in the genre of *ḥadīṯ*, and actually in every prose genre that emerged out of oral transmission, or even those that only used its literary model. In the tradition of oral transmission dialogue was *the* literary means to create credibility, to persuade an audience that a certain text was true, that it related events as they really happened, or as they were said to have happened. The central place of dialogue in the *ḥadīṯ* has to do with the basic ontological status of text in the oral tradition.

In principal, while in written literature a text is divorced from its creator, and its ontological status is gained merely by the fact that it is written, in oral tradition the situation is different. A text separated from its creator could not be considered as "text." It would never have gained ontological status, had it not been introduced as speech (*qawl*), a saying from the mouth of speaker. Thus the only item reported in oral tradition is what people have said, or related. This is where transmission chains become so important. In this situation, it becomes clear why dialogue rather than narration became so central in classical prose.

Being central in prose, dialogue could by no means be regarded as the characteristic feature of the prosaic "authentic" text. So when borrowed by poetry, dialogue would in no way have to imitate actual speech in order to achieve an authentic impression—not a vernacular dialogue, not even "third language" (cf. Somek̲ 1981). It would simply be a dialogue, no more, with all the constrains of metrics and line length imposed upon a poetic dialogue. The mere use of a dialogue was enough here to create the realistic impression.

Actually, the realistic function entered poetry through the back door, so to speak, in the context of a humorous, rather than serious, frame of reference (cf. Sadan 1983). As mentioned earlier, serious poetry had no interest in being realistic. Humorous poetry could behave differently, because it did not have this official obligatory status of "poetry." Thus almost every time we find a dialogue in poetry, be it in *ġazal*, *k̲amriyyāt* or even *hiǧā'*—it is associated in one way or another with humor, and a frivolous atmosphere. It is worth mentioning that the first signs of fiction in classical Arabic prose—a great innovation at the time—also appeared in a light, humorous framework. This was the *maqāma*,[16] which was first regarded as *hazl* rather than *ǧidd*, and had to do with parodyzing serious texts, and

[16] See ch. 1; Drory 1998:508.

drawing comical pictures of everyday life. Again it was the unofficial, and therefore non-obligatory, status of *hazl* that made it possible for a new attitude towards reality to be introduced into Arabic literature.

As a qualification, I am quite aware of the fact that the picture here of dialogue in Abū Nuwās's poetry is certainly somewhat too clear cut. Firstly, Abū Nuwās did not invent the use of dialogue in poetry, it was already there in Ǧāhili and Ummayad poetry—although on restricted scale—serving mainly love themes; and we can even find a dialogue with a wine merchant as early as al-Aʿšā's Bacchic poetry (al-Aʿšā 1983:69-70 [ll. 13-15]). Secondly, dialogue did not always play such a salient and formative role as it played for the two poems discussed here, and seldom did it play this role all alone. There were usually other factors that had to be considered, like narration, relation between metric and semantic units, and so on. These and other important factors are not treated here in order to make the point. Accounting for a more subtle and complex picture of the function of dialogue in poetry—and in prose—is work yet to be done.

CHAPTER FOUR

THE POETICS OF RHYME IN CLASSICAL ARABIC LITERATURE

Introduction

Classical Arabic literature is abundant in rhymed poetry and prose. The earliest known examples of poetry and *sağʿ* are rhymed, rhyme being a necessary condition for their very composition[1]. Rhymed texts were part of practically every genre of Arabic literature: in addition to the Koran and poetry, we find rhymed prose in royal and administrative writings, in secular speeches, religious sermons, prayers, essays, epistles, prefaces to treatises and books, chronicles, and of course letters—*adab* and *maqāmāt*. Rhyme was, in fact, the most common means used to elevate a text: to mark it as official and festive, or grant it a certain formal status.[2] Yet, despite the common use of rhyme and its wide distribution throughout classical Arabic literature, it failed to attract scholarly attention, and very little research has been done on the subject. The only exceptions are several résumés dealing with the Arabic theory of rhyming as formulated in Abbasid treatises on rhyme, which relate exclusively to poetry.[3] The situation is remarkably different with regard to metre. This seems to be a constant focus of interest and a source of inspiration for new hypotheses materializing, every now and then, in an attempt to explain the nature and behavior of metre, but more so to discuss the medieval Arabic theory of metrics.[4]

The present study aims at describing the basic rules and norms which regulate the rhyming system in classical Arabic texts. I choose to address these rules and norms with the term "poetics," making use of two connotations for this term:

---

[1] See Lord 1974:13-29; Monroe 1972; McDonald 1978; Zwettler 1978.

[2] For a similar function in Hebrew, which also involved rhyme, see ch. 7, especially section 3.3.

[3] See, for instance, Freytag 1830:296-333; De Sacy 1831:2, 651-661; Wright (1967) 1862:2, 350-258; Bonebakker; For a modern suveys see Naṣār 1980; Mannāʿ 1989;.

[4] See Weil 1958; 1960; Bohas 1974; Stoetzer 1989.

(a) "Descriptive poetics," in the sense of reference to the conceptual framework of the research and implying a systematic description of the Arabic rhyming system, based on an analysis of the structure and behaviour of rhyme in rhymed texts of both poetry and prose. The description should address questions such as: is the rhyming effect created mainly by a repetition of vowels, or of consonants; does a root or a morphological consonant bear any relevance to the participation of consonants in the rhymeme; is the structure of the rhyme regulated by rules which determine the permitted and the prohibited, or rather is it regulated by norms, which only determine the accepted and the non-accepted, leaving room for the individual or common aesthetic taste; do changes in literary fashions create new demands for rhyme, or is rhyme a conservative institution in comparison to other institutions of literary text (such as thematics, metaphorics, syntactic and semantic organization of the poetic line, metrics)? The answers to these and other questions would in fact bear upon both issues: the rhyming system as a matter in itself, and the aesthetic demands imposed on rhyme in classical Arabic literature by changing literary taste.

(b) "Poetics" in the sense of reference to the object of the research, indicating the variety of declared claims within a literate community concerning its literature: how is it regarded by the members of that community, what are their aesthetic (and other) demands of it. In our case this is a description of the poetics of rhyme as perceived by the scholars of prosody and literary critics, based on an analysis of the Arabic theory of rhyme as presented in the Abbasid treatises on rhyme.

This study can thus be defined as research in descriptive poetics, dealing with two essential topics: the phenomenon of rhyme in classical Arabic literature, and the medieval Arabic poetics of rhyme.

For the purpose of presenting a systematic description of the institution of rhyme in classical Arabic literature a very wide corpus of texts had to be considered. In fact, all rhymed texts of the "classical Arabic literature" (approximately 500 CE till 1258, the accepted date for the end of the Abbasid period) should have been taken into consideration. However, strophic poems which already began to appear during this period—*Musammaṭāt* in the East and the *Muwaššaḥāt* in the West—are not discussed here. Quantitatively, no restrictive framework was set for the corpus. It was intended to be based on a sample, and yet to examine as many texts as required. In poetry, several dozen *dīwāns* belonging to different periods of classical literature (Ǧāhili, Ummayad, Abbasid) were examined, as well as poems quoted in historical chronicles and several *adab* anthologies—a total of several thousand texts of poetry. In rhymed prose, the following texts were examined: the Koran; anthologies of epistles and speeches, mainly from the Ummayad and Abbasid periods (the authenticity of such compositions attributed to previous periods is still questionable); abstract essays; prefaces to books; the *maqāmāt* of al-Hamaḏānī and al-Ḥarīrī—in all, several hundred texts of rhymed prose.

It should be emphasized, that this large corpus of rhymed texts is not considered historically, but rather as a means of analyzing the structure and behavior of a single aspect of the texts. In the course of the analysis the historical perspective is only referred to occasionally in order to point out diachronic changes in the rhyme; this is mainly done in the case of rhymed prose, since in classical Arabic poetry the rhyming system tends to be rather monolithic and show but little change from Ǧāhiliyya times up to the end of the Abbasid period.

In the course of the presentation, the rhyming system of poetry is discussed before that of prose, and the reference to the latter is always against the background of the former. The reason for this is that, due to the privileged status of poetry in classical Arabic literature, the rhyming system of poetry is perceived as a master system of the classical Arabic text in general, to which poetry appears to be better committed than does rhymed prose.

It should be emphasized that this study confines itself to questions regarding the structure and behavior of rhyme. Relationships between rhyme and other aspects of the Arabic language are outside the scope of the discussion. Important issues—such as morphological changes in the rhyming words, or the distribution of consonants in a rhymeme as compared to their general distribution in the language—are hardly touched upon. Another important issue, the correlation between rhyme and syntax, is only briefly referred to in the last chapter, "Conclusions and Perspectives." In fact, the research in classical Arabic rhyme is only beginning.

The examples of rhyming words are presented here using the following conventions: the point to be illustrated is highlighted by the use of bold capital letters, while the remaining sounds of the word are presented in small letters. Thus capital letters can represent different phenomena, depending on the issue discussed, but generally they indicate the regularly repeating sounds which make up the rhymeme.

PART ONE

THE BASIC RHYMING MODEL OF CLASSICAL ARABIC POETRY

1. *Definition*

The rhyme of classical Arabic poetry can be defined as "an exact terminal rhyme," meaning a pattern of sounds recurring at the end of each line (*bayt al-šiʿr*) of a poem, at least in the last syllable, but usually in more than one syllable of every line.

1.1. *Rhymeme*

The rhymeme[5] is the particular group of sounds which repeats at the end of every line throughout the entire poem. This group of sounds includes an obligatory "determining sound," called *rawiyy* in medieval Arabic treatises on rhyme, as well as sounds occuring both before and after the *rawiyy*. The rhymeme includes the *rawiyy* and all successive sounds if any exist; under certain conditions, preceding sounds are also included, even if they do not form a continuous sequence with the *rawiyy*.

Examples:[6]

(1) fariğ**ĀMUHĀ**—sil**ĀMUHĀ**—waḥar**ĀMUHĀ**—farih**ĀMUHĀ**—irz**ĀMUHĀ**

(Labīd, Tibrīzī 1894:27)

(2) hab**ŪBŪ**—surḥ**ŪBŪ**—'s-sab**ĪBŪ**—raṭ**ĪBŪ**—'l-qul**ŪBŪ**

(ʿAbīd b. al-Abraṣ, *ibid.*:162)

(3) taki**FŪ**—mukٍtali**FŪ**—'l-ʾunu**FŪ**—waka**FŪ**—ġura**FŪ**

(ʿAmr b. Imriʾ al-Qays, Qurašī 1963:237)

(4) wayaht**ADĪ**—bi'l-y**ADĪ**—wazabarġ**ADĪ**—watart**ADĪ**—lahu n**ADĪ**

(Ṭarafa, Tibrīzī 1894:30)

(5) 'l-munaʿʿ**ATĪ**—waʿall**ATĪ**—'l-muṣaww**ATĪ**—waʾazall**ATĪ**—bimuny**ATĪ**

(al-Šanfarā al-Azdī, Mufaḍḍal 1964:111-112)

---

[5] This term was first formulated and employed by Benjamin Harshaw (Hrushovski) in his works on Hebrew rhyme. See Hrushovski 1971a, 1971b.

[6] The rhymeme is marked by the bold capital letters.

(6) 'l-ḥaw**ĀfIRĀ**—š**ĀdIRĀ**—'l-'ay**ĀṣIRĀ**—q**ĀdIRĀ**—waq**ĀṭIRĀ**
(Maqqās al-ʿĀ'iḏī, *ibid.*:306)
(7) bi'adn**ĀHŪ**—'aġl**ĀHŪ**—'anf**ĀHŪ**—tamann**ĀHŪ**—bišir**ĀHŪ**—wa'l-l**ĀHŪ**
(Ṯaʿālibī 1956:3, 76)
(8) yuṭa**LLŪ**—mustaqi**LLŪ**—tuḥa**LLŪ**—ṣi**LLŪ**—'l-'aǧa**LLŪ**
(Ta'abbaṭa Šarran, Abū Tammām 1972:1, 343)
(9) 't-tahni'**ĀTĪ**—ʿaraf**ĀTĪ**—'l-mīq**ĀTĪ**—'l-'aṣw**ĀTĪ**—b'ṣ-ṣal**ĀTĪ**—šahw**ĀTĪ**
(Ṯaʿālibī 1956:2, 183)
(10) 'l-mak**ĀNĪ**—'l-'alw**ĀNĪ**—'l-'urǧuw**ĀNĪ**—'anū širw**ĀNĪ**—'n-nuʿm**ĀNĪ**
(*ibid.*:2, 241)
11) ka'l-huǧ**RĪ**—wa'l-qah**RĪ**—yas**RĪ**—tam**RĪ**—'l-ḥum**RĪ**
(Ḵidāš b. Zuhayr, Qurašī 1963:189)

1.1.1. *The* rawiyy

If the last consonant in the line is a root-consonant at least in some of the rhyme members, this consonant is recognized as the *rawiyy*, or the "determining sound" of the rhymeme. If the last consonant is not a root-consonant in any of the rhyme members, then the *rawiyy* would be the consonant preceding the last. The *rawiyy* is a "determining sound" in the sense that it is the only consonant in the rhymeme which is both necessary and sufficient for the existence of the rhymeme. A minimal rhymeme is one consisting of a *rawiyy* alone.

The *rawiyy* is usually a root-consonant, the last in the line throughout the entire poem. As classical Arabic poetry generally rhymes in open syllables, the rhymeme also includes the vowel of the *rawiyy* (one of three: **i**, **a**, **u**). This vowel is always pronounced as a long vowel.

(12) 'n-nahā**RŪ**—tiʿā**RŪ**—'l-maġā**RŪ**—qiṭā**RŪ**—fasā**RŪ**
(Bišr b. Abī Ḵāzim, Mufaḍḍal 1964:339)
(13) maḍrū**BĪ**—maḥrū**BĪ**—makrū**BĪ**—taḏbī**BĪ**—'l-'anābī**BĪ**
(Salāma b. Ǧandal, *ibid.*:122)
(14) tarī**MĀ**—'l-wušū**MĀ**—'r-rusū**MĀ**—saqī**MĀ**—suǧū**MĀ**—'r-rasī**MĀ**
(Rabīʿa b. Maqrūm, *ibid.*:181)

In practice, a minimal rhymeme consisting of only a consonant is infrequent; it occurs only when the last vowel is shortened due to a metrical constraint:

(15) waʿāmi**R**—'l-muʿāši**R**—yufāḵi**R**—mayāsi**R**—'l-'awāṣi**R**
(Ḥuṭay'a 1957:174)

(16) 'r-raqa**M**—yastaqi**M**—bi'l-qala**M**—'l-'uṭu**M**
(Ibn Muqbil, Buḥturī 1910:167)

The *rawiyy* may also be a silent consonant, that is, a letter which functions morphologically as a consonant and phonetically as a vowel:

(17) haw**Ā**—'t̲-t̲ar**Ā**—'d-duǧ**Ā**—'at**Ā**—ǧan**Ā**
(Suwayd al-Marāt̲ī al-Ḥārit̲ī, Abū Tammām 1972:1, 347)
(18) fa'r-raḫ**Ā**—yuštaw**Ā**—bak**Ā**—'l-ḥaš**Ā**—'l-qir**Ā**—'ṣ-ṣuw**Ā**
(al-Rāʿī al-Numayrī, *ibid.*:2, 219)

From the perspective of sound, the rhymeme in examples 17 and 18 consists of only a vowel. In traditional script, this vowel is expressed by one character which represents one of the two root-consonants: *wāw* or *yā'*. The Arabic theory of rhyme, which describes the *rawiyy* in terms of letters (see 2.2), considers this vowel-sound a proper *rawiyy*. This type of sound-poor rhymeme is more common with the addition of a morphological suffix, though the suffix alone is not generally considered sufficient to form a rhymeme:[7]

(19) 'at̲āf**ĪHĀ**—'āf**ĪHĀ**—'uk̲z**ĪHĀ**—unād**ĪHĀ**
(Ḥuǧr b. Ḥayya al-ʿAbsī, *ibid.*:2, 307)
(20) yuwār**IHĪ**—k̲awāf**ĪHĪ**—mā f**ĪHĪ**—qās**ĪHĪ**
(T̲aʿālibī 1956:4, 67)
(21) wābi'ab**ĀHUMĀ**—fadaʿ**ĀHUMĀ**—kil**ĀHUMĀ**—san**ĀHUMĀ**—munṣal**ĀHUMĀ**
(ʿAmra al-K̲at̲ʿamiyya, Abū Tammām 1972:1, 449)

1.1.2. *The morphology of the rhymeme*

From the definition of the *rawiyy*, the following condition for its morphological nature is inferred: the *rawiyy* has to be a root-consonant. Morphological suffixes cannot form a rhymeme, except in very rare cases. This restriction should be understood in light of the fact that in ancient Arabic poetry a single rhymeme is retained throughout

[7] At the same time, words in which the third root letter is *wāw* or *yā'* sometimes rhyme with words in which the third root letter is a consonant; in such a case, their second root letter is the *rawiyy*:

'l-ʿuq**LŪ**—yaʿ**LŪ**—wa'l-maḥ**LŪ** (al-Ḥārit̲ b. K̲ālid, Abū Tammām 1972:2, 92)
wanaǧta**DĪ**—yuḥma**DĪ**—muk̲alla**DĪ** (Ḥuṭay'a 1957:161)
's-sum**RĪ**—tas**RĪ**—taq**RĪ**—ṣak̲**RĪ** (al-K̲ansā', Buḥturī 1910:271)

the entire poem. A rhyming pattern of morphological suffixes alone would seem dull and barren in this case, even more so for long *qaṣīdas*. A morphological suffix can be added to the root-consonant, but cannot substitute for it; when appearing as an additional element, the suffix must repeat in all the rhyme members throughout a poem:

(22) maqā**MUHĀ**—wašā**MUHĀ**—saqā**MUHĀ**—huyā**MUHĀ**—ḥimā**MUHĀ**
(D̲ū al-Rumma 1919:636)

(23) ǧawā**BAKĀ**—'asā**BAKĀ**—'aṣā**BAKĀ**—'arā**BAKĀ**—t̲iyā**BAKĀ**
(Du'alī 1954:194-195)

However, when a root-consonant is present in at least some of the rhyme members, a morphological consonant may alternately rhyme with it:

(24) taʿrifū**NĪ**—'l-ǧabī**NĪ**—liḥī**NĪ**—'l-'arbaʿī**NĪ**—'š-šu'ū**NĪ**
(Suḥaym b. Wut̲ayl, Buḥturī 1910:13)

(25) ġud̲ī**TŪ**—'l-buyū**TŪ**—'urī**TŪ**—'l-mustamī**TŪ** (Aṣmaʿī:83)

(26) 'l-mutalāḥi**KĪ**—riḥāli**KĪ**—'l-hawāli**KĪ**—waḥāri**KĪ**—dāri**KĪ**
(D̲ū al-Rumma 1919:412)

(27) faha**LAK**—qata**LAK**—k̲ata**LAK**—'s-su**LAK**—yaku **LAK**—'aǧa**LAK**
(Ta'abbaṭa Šarran's sister, Abū Tammām 1972:1, 379)

Example 27 demonstrates a case where, although the morphological consonant **k** rhymes with a root-consonant, the preceding consonant **l** (along with its vowel) also takes part in the rhymeme (otherwise of a single consonant and no vowel) in order to strengthen it. However, this is an exceptional example and not the rule.

Only when two consecutive morphological consonants repeat in all the rhyme members a rhymeme is constituted, in which the first of the two morphological consonants becomes the *rawiyy*, while the root-consonant is left out:

(28) maʿlūfā**TIHĀ**—ḥāǧā**TIHĀ**—waʿafraniyyā**TIHĀ**—ʿilā**TIHĀ**—ḥudā**TIHĀ**
(anonymous, *ibid.*:2, 388)

(29) siwā**HUMĀ**—qad̲ā**HUMĀ**—kilā**HUMĀ**—laǧazā**HUMĀ**
(Kut̲ayr, *ibid.*:2, 96)

In other words, three consonants appear to be considered already overabundant for a rhymeme.

1.1.3. *The maximal condition for consonants in a rhymeme*
We can now establish the following maximal condition for a rhymeme: it must not include more than two consonants. As mentioned above (1.1.1), the first of these consonants must be a root-consonant in at least some of the rhyme members. The second consonant, if present, would inevitably be morphological. At times both consonants are morphological, in which case the root-consonant is excluded. According to the basic norm of classical poetry, the root-consonant which precedes the *rawiyy* in all of the rhyme members is never included in the rhymeme (for deviations, see 1.4).

1.1.4. *The function of vowels in the rhymeme*
Our discussion has thus far referred to the organization of consonants in the rhymeme; yet vowels, too, have a function in the organization of rhymeme sounds. As previously stated, the vowel of the *rawiyy* is also part of the rhymeme. In fact, the rhymeme includes vowels both before and after the *rawiyy*—up to two syllables before the *rawiyy* and one after, if such a syllable occurs. The sound pattern is continuous and parallel from the *rawiyy* until the end of the line, i.e., all the consonants and vowels repeat in the same order. This, however, is not the case with the vowels before the *rawiyy*. Let us examine the following examples:

1.1.4.1. Long open syllable before the *rawiyy*

1.1.4.1.1. The vowel of the syllable *is* **a**

(30) 'l-ʿaz**Ā'Ū**—'l-buk**Ā'Ū**—'l-baq**Ā'Ū**—fan**Ā'Ū**—liq**Ā'Ū**
(Ḥuṭay'a 1957:109)
(31) 'l-qiṭ**ĀRĀ**—'l-'iṣ**ĀRĀ**—'l-nim**ĀRĀ**—'l-k̲im**ĀRĀ**—f'staṭ**ĀRĀ**
(D̲ū al-Rumma 1919:193)
(32) 'l-b**ĀQĪ**—išf**ĀQĪ**—mušt**ĀQĪ**—s**ĀQĪ**
(Abū Nuwās 1962:436)

In examples 30-32 *a long open syllable, whose vowel is* **a**, precedes the *rawiyy* in all the rhyme members. Similar to the *rawiyy*, it is a regularly-repeating element and therefore forms a part of the rhymeme.

1.1.4.1.2. The vowel of the syllable is **u** or **i**

(33) masǧ**ŪMŪ**—tash**ĪMŪ**—mahǧ**ŪMŪ**—'r-rawās**ĪMŪ**—ma<u>d</u>m**ŪMŪ**
(<u>D</u>ū al-Rumma 1919:568)

(34) mard**Ū'Ā**—r**Ī'Ā**—ṭul**Ū'Ā**—naq**Ī'Ā**—muṭ**Ī'Ā**
('Umar b. Abī Rabī'a 1901:54-55)

(35) 'r-rab**ĪḤĪ**—wa't-talw**ĪḤĪ**—'l-m**ŪḤĪ**—'l-l**ŪḤĪ**—'r-r*ĪḤĪ*
(Abū Nuwās 1962:178)

Here a long open syllable, whose vowel is alternately **i** or **u**, precedes the *rawiyy* in all the rhyme members, and thus forms a part of the rhymeme.

The following rule may now be formulated: if the open syllable preceding the *rawiyy* is long, it is part of the rhymeme. Its vowel may be **a**, **i** or **u**. Vowels **i** and **u** rhyme with one another, but not with the vowel **a**.[8]

1.1.4.2. Long closed syllable before the *rawiyy*

(36) nağ**DŪ**—wa'l-bū**DŪ**—ṣad**DŪ**—wad**DŪ**—wa'l-ğid**DŪ**
(Ḥuṭay'a 1957:140)

(37) naṣ**RĀ**—'l-qaf**RĀ**—<u>k</u>ub**RĀ**
_(anonymous, Abū Tammām 1972:2, 232)

(38) 'n-naḥ**SĪ**—'l-'in**SĪ**—ka'ṭ-ṭar**SĪ**—naf**SĪ**—'š-šam**SĪ**
(Abū Nuwās 1962:369)

In examples 36-38, a *long closed syllable*, whose vowel varies randomly, precedes the *rawiyy* in all the rhyme members. The rhymeme in these examples is therefore strengthened not by a repeating sound, but by the very regularity of the syllable pattern.

1.1.4.3. Long open syllable + short syllable before the *rawiyy*

(39) raw**Ā**ǧi'—'l-bal**Ā**qi'—'l-<u>k</u>aw**Ā**ḍi'—'l-bar**Ā**qi'—'n-naw**Ā**ṣi'—
(<u>D</u>ū al-Rumma 1919:332)

(40) 'l-'an**Ā**fi**Š**—faw**Ā**ri**Š**—'l-qal**Ā**ni**Š**—'aw**Ā**bi**Š**
(al-'Abbās b. Mirdās, Buḥturī 1910:48)

(41) biġ**Ā**fi**LĪ**—'<u>t</u>-<u>t</u>**Ā**ki**LĪ**—wafaw**Ā**ḍi**LĪ**—ġay**Ā**ṭi**LĪ**—bi'aṣ**Ā**'i**LĪ**
(*ibid.*:191)

[8] See Wright 1967:2, 353. The medieval Arab grammarians were also aware of this rule; see 2.2.1.3.

(42) ṭul**ŪLUHĀ**—ḏuy**ŪLUHĀ**—yaġ**ŪLUHĀ**—wuṣ**ŪLUHĀ**—ġal**ĪLUHĀ**

(Ḏū al-Rumma 1919:545)

In examples 39-42, the *second* syllable before the *rawiyy* is a *long open syllable*, followed by a short syllable. The previously formulated rule referring to the rhyming pattern of long syllables (1.1.4.1) can be applied in this case as well. The vocalization of the short syllable is not fixed.[9] It should be noted that due to the morphological structure of the Arabic language, a rhyming scheme of **i/u** in the second syllable before the *rawiyy* is indeed very rare: it can only occur in words belonging to the third or sixth conjugation, past tense, passive voice: *fūʿila, tufūʿila.* On the few occasions in which such a rhyming pattern does occur (as in example 42), it is formed with an addition of a morphological suffix to the word. This pattern is essentially a rhymeme of type 1.1.4.1.2, with the addition of a morphological suffix (see 1.1.7)

1.1.4.4. Long closed syllable + short syllable before the *rawiyy*

(43) **maġ**ḍa**BŪ**—**ağ**da**BŪ**—'l-'**ar**na**BŪ**—'l-'**ar**ka**BŪ**—**fa'ġ**ḍa**BŪ**

(al-Musayyab b. ʿAlas, Buḥturī 1910:21)

(44) **aw**wa**LĀ**—**aq**ba**LĀ**—**miġ**za**LĀ**—**mik**ḥa**LĀ**—bi'**an**na **LĀ**

(al-Aʿrağ b. Mālik, *ibid.*:38)

(45) **yaḥ**ḏa**RĪ**—**mus**fi**RĪ**—'l-'**aq**fa**RĪ**—**mi'**za**RĪ**—**am**ta**RĪ**

(Muqāʿis al-Kilābī, *ibid.*:18)

In this group, the second syllable which occurs before the *rawiyy* is a *long closed syllable*, followed by a short syllable. This particular regularity of syllable pattern is the element which repeats in all the rhyme members, and thus constitutes part of the rhymeme.

1.1.4.5. Two short syllables before the *rawiyy*

(46) 'l-'uğu**DŪ**—wa'l-wati**DŪ**—aḥa**DŪ**—wamuʿtama**DŪ**—muntafa**DŪ**

(al-Mutalammis al-Ḍubaʿī, *ibid.*:20)

(47) nağa**MĀ**—fahi**MĀ**—raġa**MĀ**—sala**MĀ**—ğaši**MĀ**

(ʿUmar b. Abī Rabīʿa 1901:75)

[9] In the above examples it does appear to be fixed; this is not, however, necessarily a result of the rhymeme, but is due to the repetition of the same grammatical forms.

(48) 'l-ḥiqa**BĪ**—ʿağa**BĪ**—wa'l-ḥasa**BĪ**—'l-kuṯu**BĪ**—'l-k̲ari**BĪ**
(*ibid.*:179-180)

In these examples, *two short syllables* precede the *rawiyy*, without a definite order of their vowels. Thus, these syllables are not part of the rhymeme.

1.1.5. *Significance of the long syllable in the rhymeme*
It becomes evident now, that the sequence and quality of the last two syllables before the *rawiyy* play an important role in the structure of the rhymeme. A study of examples 30-48 will reveal that there are actually five distinct patterns of short and long syllable arrangements which precede the *rawiyy*. Four of these five patterns include a single long syllable, which either directly precedes the *rawiyy*, or comes two positions before it. Within each pattern, however, the long syllable repeats at a fixed position in all the rhyme members, thus helping to strengthen the effect of the rhymeme. Only one particular pattern (1.1.4.5), having short syllables only, leads to the formation of a rhymeme consisting of a *rawiyy* alone. In all the other patterns, the long syllable is part of the rhymeme; if a short syllable separates this long syllable from the *rawiyy*, the vowel of the short syllable may sometimes also participate in the rhymeme (depending upon the choice of grammatical form).

The four patterns in which there is a long syllable may actually be presented in two basic patterns of syllable arrangement:

Pattern sequence	Syllable
1.1.4.1 1.1.4.2	— —
1.1.4.3 1.1.4.4	— V —

1.1.6. *Long open syllable as opposed to long closed syllable*
Although reduced to two basic patterns, there is still a difference between rhymemes 1.1.4.1 and 1.1.4.2, as there is between 1.1.4.3 and 1.1.4.4. This difference derives from the nature of the long syllable joining the *rawiyy* to form the rhymeme. Words of a long open syllable will rhyme with each other, as will words having a long closed syllable; but a word having a long open syllable will never

rhyme with a word having a long closed syllable, even when they have the same syllable pattern and *rawiyy*. There is also another restriction with regard to long open syllables: vowels **ī** and **ū** rhyme with each other but not with the vowel **ā** (1.1.4.1.1 as opposed to 1.1.4.1.2; examples 39-41, as opposed to example 42).

1.1.7. *Relation to grammatical forms*
The two restrictions—the distinction between open and closed syllables, and between the vowels **i/u** and the vowel **a**—function as "grouping rules" which classify the grammatical forms of the Arabic language into rhyme groups. Certain grammatical forms rhyme with one another, but not with other grammatical forms, even if the syllable arrangements and *rawiyy* permit such rhyming. Such is the case, for instance, in the selected following examples in which the grammatical forms *mufʿal, mafʿal, yufʿal* (as well as *yafʿal, yufʿil, faʿlal*) rhyme with each other, but not with the grammatical forms *fawāʿil, mafāʿil, faʿālil, yufāʿil, afāʿil*, etc., even though these have the same syllabic arrangement and may also have the same *rawiyy*. Thus, too, the forms *fuʿūl, faʿīl, tafʿīl, mafʿūl*, etc., form a group, as opposed to the various forms of *f(a, u, i)ʿl*. A parallel, but nevertheless separate group, is *f(a, u, i)ʿāl, afʿāl, mifʿāl*, etc,; another group is *fuʿul, faʿil, fuʿal, yaftaʿil, muftaʿil*, etc. These grammatical forms include both nouns and verbs, as well as various combinations of these (and of prepositions) with pronouns. The use of pronouns allows for a more flexible manipulation of the language; a word used for one pattern can also serve, with the addition of a pronoun, for another pattern: *ġalīlū* forms pattern 1.1.4.2, where as *ġalīluhā* forms pattern 1.1.4.3.

1.2. *The basic rhyming norm of classical poetry*

Each of the five patterns of syllable arrangements constitutes a rhymeme in itself, since each has its own regularity of repeating sound elements in addition to the *rawiyy*, which is present in all five. Classical Arabic poetry can thus be described as employing five types of rhymemes, which together form the basic rhyming norm. Any type of rhymeme may be selected for a particular poem, but the selected rhymeme must be sustained throughout the poem and not be replaced by another. At its maximal possibility, the rhymeme encompasses the last three syllables of the rhyme member. The *rawiyy* is positioned in the last syllable of the rhyme member, unless a mono-syllabic morphological suffix is present; in that case, the *rawiyy*'s position would move to the syllable before the last. In the case of a bi-syllabic morphological suffix, the *rawiyy* would be excluded from the rhymeme (cf. 1.1.3).

The rhyming norm formed by the five types of rhymemes (which are mutually exclusive in classical Arabic poetry) is both minimal and maximal, in the sense that each rhymeme determines exactly which sound elements repeat throughout an entire poem, and, that there is no addition or deletion of sounds. The five sound patterns are fixed; there is, however, a certain measure of choice with regard to the consonants of the rhymeme: the minimum is one consonant, the maximum, two.

The five types of rhymemes may be formulated as follows:

1.1.4.1 **V** C**V**
1.1.4.2 **vc** C**V**
1.1.4.3 **V** cv C**V**
1.1.4.4 **vc** cv C**V**
1.1.4.5 cv cv C**V**

(**c** indicates consonant; v indicates vowel; a capital letter indicates those elements which are part of the rhymeme; **bold** indicates a long open syllable; **bold underline** indicates a long closed syllable which is part of the rhymeme;)

In most instances, the rhymemes end in **V**, and less frequently, in C.

All five types of rhymemes can be described as deriving from one phonological scheme of a maximum of three syllables (the last in each rhyme member), whose variables are as follows:

1. **V** (cv) C**V**
2. **vc** (cv) C**V**
3. cv cv C**V**

1.3. *The aesthetic norm*

The *rawiyy* is the only part of the rhymeme whose consonants and vowels retain a uniform sound throughout all five types of the rhymeme. Apart from the *rawiyy*, each rhymeme retains its own particular sound pattern, which is constructed upon a fixed syllable arrangement, rather than on the repetition of consonants. This norm can be regarded as imposing quite severe constraints on the poet, but, on the other hand, as compensating for a sound-poor rhymeme in which only one consonant is obligatory. It seems that the effect produced by repeated morphological patterns in the rhymeme was not considered a flaw, but rather the opposite: the repetition of a fixed vowel (and syllable) arrangement at the ends of lines resulted from repeating the same grammatical forms apparently served to strengthen and enrich the aesthetic effect of a rhymeme, otherwise based exclusively on the *rawiyy*. The way to compensate for a sound-poor rhymeme based solely on a *rawiyy* was thereby not found in the addition of rhyming *consonsants*, but rather in the syllabic *patterns* of rhyming.

1.4. *Some Deviations from the basic classical rhyming norm*

1.4.1. *Abū al-ʿAlāʾ al-Maʿarrī*

The only poet who consciously attempted to enrich the sound of the rhymeme by the addition of consonants was Abū al-ʿAlāʾ al-Maʿarrī of northern Syria (d. 1057). Al-Maʿarrī composed a *Dīwān* of over 1500 poems (entitled *Luzūmu mā lā yalzamu*—"self-obligation where one is not obliged"), in which every poem has a rhymeme of at least two consonants. The poet thus demanded more of himself, above and beyond the requirements of the basic classical rhyming norm. In most of his poems, he adds a root-consonant before the *rawiyy*, so that both consonants of the rhymeme are root-consonants:

(49) ʾt-**TĀǦĪ**—bifir**TĀǦĪ**—muh**TĀǦĪ**—muḥ**TĀǦĪ**—biʾir**TĀǦĪ**
(Maʿarrī 1971:1, 270)

(50) ʾl-qa**D**a**RŪ**—waʾl-ha**D**a**RŪ**—ʾl-ḵa**D**a**RŪ**—ġu**D**a**RŪ**—ma**D**a**RŪ**
(*ibid.*:1, 478-479)

(51) qur**Z**u**LŪ**—tan**Z**i**LŪ**—yah**Z**i**LŪ**—taġ**Z**i**LŪ**—yub**Z**a**LŪ**
(*ibid.*:2, 287)

In about ten percent of these poems, the rhymeme is composed of both morphological and root-consonants. The various combinations of these two elements result in the following phenomena:

(A) In the case of two morphological consonants, the root-consonant preceding the *rawiyy* is not included in the rhymeme, and thus al-Maʿarrī's maximum norm of three consonants per rhymeme is still preserved:

(52) suʿ**ĀTUHĀ**—sāʿ**ĀTUHĀ**—duʿ**ĀTUHĀ**—wuʿ**ĀTUHĀ**—tabiʿ**ĀTUHĀ**
(*ibid.*:1, 208)

(53) ā**TĀKUMŪ**—maw**TĀKUMŪ**—aʿ**TĀKUMŪ**—muš**TĀKUMŪ**—wafa**TĀKUMŪ**

(*ibid.*:2, 412)

(B) In most poems in which the rhymeme includes a morphological consonant after the *rawiyy*, al-Maʿarrī does not add a root-consonant before the *rawiyy*, despite the fact that a morphological consonant is not considered the determinant of the rhymeme (cf. 1.1.2). In such cases, the rhymeme stands on two consonants alone: a root-consonant and a morphological consonant (the maximum number of consonants permitted by the classical norm):

(54) a*d***ĀʿŪHŪ**—muṭ**ĀʿŪHŪ**—b**ĀʿŪHŪ**—aḍ**ĀʿŪHŪ**—d**ĀʿŪHŪ**

(*ibid.*:2, 595-596)

(55) 'š-šaha**WĀTĪ**—'l-k̲uṭu**WĀTĪ**—'l-laha**WĀTĪ**—'l-haba**WĀTĪ**—wa'l-k̲ama**WĀTĪ**

(*ibid.*:1, 223)

(C) In a few cases, al-Maʿarrī upholds the rule which states that a morphological consonant can not be considered the determinant of the rhymeme, and adds the root-consonant before the *rawiyy*. A rhymeme of three consonants is thereby formed:

(56) k̲a**B**a**BNĀ**—ra**B**a**BNĀ**—da**B**a**BNĀ**—ta**B**a**BNĀ**—ha**B**a**BNĀ**

(*ibid.*:2, 585)

(57) k̲**ĀM**i**LĪNĀ**—**ĀM**i**LĪNĀ**—muʿ**ĀM**i**LĪNĀ**—k**ĀM**i**LĪNĀ**—ḥ**ĀM**i**LĪNĀ**

(*ibid.*:2, 528)

(D) If the morphological consonant is not followed by a vowel, in other words, if the last syllable of the rhymeme is a closed one, then two root-consonants almost always participate in the rhymeme, in an apparent attempt to embellish the rhymeme:

(58) ham**MĀMĀH**—šam**MĀMĀH**—aw **MĀMĀH**—zam**MĀMĀH**—ram**MĀMĀH**

(*ibid.*:2, 435)

(59) tak̲**B**i**ṬŪN**—tastan**B**i**ṬŪN**—taʿ**B**i**ṬŪN**—tar**B**i**ṬŪN**—taġ**B**i**ṬŪN**[10]

(*ibid.*:2, 585)

[10] A closed syllable having a long vowel, as in this example, is not familiar in

(E) Rhymemes of which the last consonant is morphological are sometimes strengthened by the inclusion of the root-consonant before the *rawiyy*; this root-consonant does not appear regularly throughout the poem, but rather in certain clusters of rhyme members. These clusters (whose additional root consonant may vary from one to another) are generally not successive; they occur sporadically throughout the poem:

(60) wa'ar**HaQATHŪ**—az**HaQATHŪ**—ad**HaQATHŪ**—raw**WaQATHŪ**—ṭuw**WiQATHŪ**—aw**HaQATHŪ**—ʿaw**WaQATHŪ**—ʿul**LiQATHŪ**—wa'ak̲**LaQATHŪ**—ṭal**LaQATHŪ**—an**TaQATHŪ**—aʿ**TaQATHŪ**
(*ibid.*:2, 597)

(61) tah**Ğu WĀNĪ**—yas**ĞuWĀNĪ**—yad̲u**WĀNĪ**—yan**ĞuWĀNĪ**/ tağ**FuWĀNĪ**—taq**FuWĀNĪ**—taʿ**FuWĀNĪ**/[...] yak̲**LuWĀNĪ**—yaq**LuWĀNĪ**—yağ**LuWĀNĪ**—yaġ**LuWĀNĪ**
(*ibid.*:2, 580)

(F) Despite the maximum norm of three consonants per rhymeme, we find that some short poems deviate from this norm by adding more consonants to the rhymeme:

(62) sa**RĀ'iRIKUM**—ḥa**RĀ'iRIKUM**—ğa**RĀ'iRIKUM**—ḍa**RĀ'iRIKUM**—d̲a**RĀ'iRIKUM**—ma**RĀ'iRIKUM**
(*ibid.*:2, 487)

(63) **DĀRIHIM**—iṣ**DĀRIHIM**—aq**DĀRIHIM**—muz**DĀRIHIM**
(*ibid.*:2, 492)

A similar phenomenon can also be found in the short *waṣf* poems (see 1.4.2).

Al-Maʿarrī strengthens the uniformity of sound in the rhymeme in an additional way—by not adhering to the rule allowing the long vowels **ū** and **ī** to rhyme with each other. Rather, he limits himself to rhyming **ū** separately and **ī** separately in deviation from the classical norm.

All the other elements of the rhymeme in the *Luzūmiyyāt* poems conform to the classical norm, and al-Maʿarrī employs all five types of rhymemes.

---

the rhyming system of ancient poetry. It appears in written poems from approximately the tenth century onward. This has to do with a change in intonation; Cf. A discussion of the subject in an Arabic book on poetics from the fourteenth century: Hoenerbach 1956:58-59 (Arabic text).

We can summarize al-Maʿarrī's rhyming scheme as follows: he follows the classical norm:

(A) in limiting the rhymeme to the last three syllables of the line (there are few exceptions);

(B) in using all five rhymeme types, that is, in keeping to the same location of the vowels and syllables (with a difference in **ī** and **ū**, as mentioned).

He deviates from the norm in his use of *consonants*:

(A) by setting a minimum of two consonants, usually root-consonants, to a rhyme;[11]

(B) by setting a maximum which is the maximum of sound repetition possible in a rhyming system: all consonants, except one, repeat.

In the rhyming of morphological and root-consonants together (as stated, in about ten-percent of the poems), al-Maʿarrī exploits all the possible combinations of these two types of consonants, within a three-syllable framework:

syllables (ordered from the end of the line)

	3	2	1
		r	r
range	r	m	m
of consonant		r	m
consideration	r	r	m
	r	r	m

(r = root-consonant; m = morphological consonant)

As far as the rhyming effect is concerned, al-Maʿarrī's rhymes sound much richer than those of classical rhyme. In addition to his use of the extra consonant, al-Maʿarrī often remains consistent with the same grammatical forms throughout each poem; thus additional sounds inevitably repeat—the sounds of short vowels and of morphological consonants in the beginning or in the middle of the rhyming word. This is due, in my opinion, to a conscious effort to intensify the rhyming effect—not simply by adding consonants to the rhymeme—but by repeating the same morphological pattern, thereby emphasizing the scheme of syllabic arrangements which determines the

[11] The term *luzūmu mā lā yalzamu*, meaning the addition of rhyming consonant before the *rawiyy*, became an accepted term in the later books on rhetoric, among the "embellishments of form." See, for example, al-Sakākī 1938:3, 105. Cf. also note 11.

rhyming effect to an Arab ear. We see, therefore, that from the perspective of the aesthetic rhyming effect, al-Maʿarrī still follows the classical norm of rhyme.

Al-Maʿarrī's *Dīwān* is unique also in the utilization of all the letters of the Arabic alphabet as *rawiyy* (the Arab poets mainly rhymed those consonants which were common at the end of words, not all the consonants of the language), and in the rhyming of every letter as *rawiyy*, in all four possible vowel combinations: when the vowels of the letter are **u**, **i**, or **a**, and when it has no vowel. Al-Maʿarrī was highly sensitive to rhyme, and completely familiar with the Arabic theory of rhyme, as is evident from the exhaustive, relatively original summary of it in his introduction to *Luzūmu mā lā yalzamu* (Maʿarrī 1971:1, 5-39). In this introduction he enumerates the three constraints he imposes upon himself in the *Dīwān* (the addition of a consonant, plus the two restrictions mentioned above); yet he is not explicit as to the reason for these constraints "where one is not obliged." One can only assume, from the tenor of his words in the introduction, from the nature of his poems, and from his character as a poet, that he wished to prove his genius as a dexterous composer of poetry, and one greater than any other Arabic poet.

Al-Maʿarrī's characteristic rhyming scheme affected the length of his poems: most of them are about four-five lines each, and particularly difficult to understand. He uses this scheme only in this one *Dīwān*, and not in his other compositions. It thus remains an exceptional phenomenon in Arabic poetry, without many followers.[12]

1.4.2. *The* waṣf *poems*

Waṣf poems, whose emergence in the Arabic poetic tradition is generally connected with the development of each section of the long *qaṣīda* into independent pieces (*qiṭaʿ*), became a full-fledged poetic genre in the tenth century. Ibn al-Muʿtazz (d. 908) is generally accepted to be the first who developed these poems into an independent genre. The *waṣf* poems are short, containing only several lines

---

[12] Approximately one hundred years later, the Andalusi al-Saraqustī (d. 1143) borrowed the idea of *luzūm mā lā yalzam* and applied it to rhymed prose in order to compete with al-Ḥarīrī's *maqāmāt*. He wrote fifty *maqāmāt* which he entitled *al-Maqāmāt al-luzūmiyya*, in which he, too, "obliged himself where one is not obliged:" he rhymed as a rule with two root-consonants, and very often with three and sometimes more, even if not in fixed positions, in a method similar to that of the *waṣf* poems (al-Saraqustī 1982; 1995).

(an average of two to seven); they describe a single object, such as a candle, a blooming garden, an apple, a cloud, or a beloved's face, in an enriched metaphorical language. The *waṣf* poets demonstrate great awareness of the poetic language, including its non-semantic aspects, of which the rhyme is a part. The sounds of their rhymemes are usually corresponding to the sound-pattern of the complete line, or of the entire poem. For example:

A three-line poem:

 (64) –bim**IṢBĀḤIHĀ**—**IṢBĀḤIHĀ**—**IṢLĀḤIHĀ**

(al-Sarī al-Raffāʾ 1936:75)

A four-line poem:

 (65) –ʾš-**ŠaFaQĪ**—a**RiQĪ**—yaʿ**ŠaQĪ**—ʾl-Ma**FRIQĪ**—Ma**ŠRIQĪ**

(Mīkālī 1908:37)

A two-line poem:

 (66) –ʾl-ḥi**KMATĪ**—Kaʾl-**MA**yyi**TĪ**

(Ibn Ḥamdīs 1879:63)

A three-line poem:

 (67) ʾl-ba**DĪʿĪ**—ʾr-Ru**ǧŪʿĪ** —ʾd-Du**RŪʿĪ**

(Ṯaʿālibī 1956:1, 39)

The trend here is toward a minimal difference, often of only one consonant, between one rhyme member and the next. The additional rhyming consonants have no set location within the rhymeme. The ancient *qaṣīdas* may also organize sporadic additional root-consonants with no fixed location to rhyme within small groups of rhyme members, such as in the *Muʿallaqa* of Labīd. The difference, however, is that the *waṣf* poems show a conscious striving toward as many rhyming consonants as possible, as part of the sound-rich norm of the genre, whereas the organization of rhyming groups in the *qaṣīdas* appears coincidentally and seems unintentional.

 This striving toward a sound-rich rhyme is typical not only of the *waṣf* poems, but also of late classical Arabic poetry in general. One may therefore describe diachronically the difference between the early (seventh, eighth and ninth centuries) and the late classical Arabic poetry (ninth and tenth centuries and onward) from the perspective of the rhyming norm as follows: early classical poetry strives towards a minimum of consonants in the rhymeme, and creates a rhyming effect by repetition of syllabic arrangements, whereas late classical poetry attempts, as a general trend, to intensify the rhyming effects by the addition of consonants to the rhymeme, perhaps because the effect of the morphological pattern has already become trite and automatic.

PART TWO

THE MEDIEVAL ARABIC THEORY OF RHYME

The first part of the chapter on rhyme presented an attempt at a systematic description of the classical Arabic rhyming system as reflected in the actual rhymed texts. The present part discusses the medieval Arabic theory of rhyme, focusing on two aspects. First, the manner in which Arab theorists understood and analyzed the phenomenon of rhyme. Second, their poetics of rhyming, namely, their aesthetic perceptions of it: what they permitted or forbade in the practice of rhyming, what they liked or disliked regarding it, what they considered favourable or poor.

The Arabic theory on rhyme was established by grammarians in the ninth century and developed in the tenth and eleventh centuries due to a scholarly interest in the subject of both grammarians and poeticians. Special treatises, sometimes chapters in more general compilations, were dedicated to the two "sciences" of Arabic prosody: metrics (*ʿilm al-ʿarūḍ*) and rhyming (*ʿilm al-qawāfī*). The treatises were usually somewhere between theoretical descriptions of rhyme and didactic handbooks for the practice of rhyming.

2.1. *The* qāfiya

Similar to the Hebrew word *ḥarūz*, the Arabic word for rhyme, *qāfiya*, was originally used to signify several concepts related to poetry (for its origin see Bonebakker). Only with the development of linguistic and poetic theory did the *qāfiya* receive its later, narrower, technical denotation. The beginnings of medieval Arabic theoretical thought on the subject of rhyme are manifested in the first attempts to employ the word *qāfiya* as a theoretical term; that is, to define the unit of sounds repeating at the line endings of a poem.

Al-Akfaš, (Abū al-Ḥasan Saʿīd b. Maṣada, of Basra and Baghdad, d. ca. 830), the author of the earliest known treatise on rhyme, begins his book with a discussion on the question of what is *qāfiya* [Akfaš 1970:1-7; see also Tanūkī 1970:58-59; Ibn Rašīq 1972:1, 151-154]. It is evident from the discourse that the word (as well as other prosodic terms) did not have one specific meaning in his day. The term was used to indicate an entire *qaṣīda*; a single line; the second hemistitch only; "the end of a line" (*āḵir al-kalām*), apparently referring to the last syntactical or metrical unit of the line; the last word of a line; or even the *rawiyy* alone.

Al-Aḵfaš focuses his discussion primarily on those definitions which position the *qāfiya* at the ends of lines. This may be indicative of the fact that he is not interested in a semantic debate for its own sake, but prefers to define the particular structural unit of the *qaṣīda* which creates the rhyme. Al-Aḵfaš quotes al-Ḵalīl's definition of the term *qāfiya*, as well as introducing his own definition. There are four definitions of the term *qāfiya*, which are listed below in chronological order:

2.2. *Al-Ḵalīl's two definitions as distinguished from other definitions of the* qāfiya

1. Two definitions of the *qāfiya* are attributed to al-Ḵalīl b. Aḥmad (Basrian, d. 786):

(A) that which is between the last letter of the line and the first quiescent letter before it, including the movent letter [or: the vowel of the letter[13]] before this quiescent letter.

(B) that which is between the last two quiescent letters of the line, including the last quiescent letter only.[14]

According to definition (A), the *qāfiya* in the rhyming words: *ǧānibū—taqārubū—'lmarāḥibū* would then be:

(68) ǧ**ĀNIBŪ**—taq**ĀRUBŪ**—'lmar**ĀḤIBŪ**

and according to definition (B):

(69) ǧā**NIBŪ**—taqā**RUBŪ**—'lmarā**ḤIBŪ**

---

[13] There are two versions of this definition:

a) *mā bayna āḵiri ḥarfin mina 'l-bayti ilā awwali sākin yalīhi maʿa 'l-mutaḥarriki 'l-ladī qabla 's-sākini.* (Aḵfaš 1970:6; Anbārī 1956:51; Tibrīzī 1966:342).

b) *as-sākināni 'l-āḵirāni mina 'l-bayti wamā baynahumā maʿa ḥarakati mā qabla 's-sākini 'l-awwali minhumā.* (Tanūḵī 1970:59; Ibn Rašīq 1972:1, 151; *Lisān*: s.v. *qāfiya*).

[14] *mā bayna 's-sākinayni 'l-āḵirayni mina 'l-bayti maʿa 's-sākini 'l-āḵiri faqaṭ* (Tanūḵī 1970:59).

In the rhyming words: *walā yadī—midwadī—yaǧmudī*, the *qāfiya* would be according to definition (A):

(70) wal**Ā YADĪ**—m**IDWADĪ**—y**AǦMUDĪ**

and according to definition (B):

(71) walā **YADĪ**—mid**WADĪ**—yaǧ**MUDĪ**

2. The following definition of the *qāfiya* is attributed to Quṭrub, Abū ʿAlī Muḥammad b. Aḥmad (Basrian, d. 821):
   The letter on which the *qaṣīda* is constructed, and it is the letter called *rawiyy*.[15]

Consistent with this definition, the *qāfiya* in examples 68 and 69 would be **BŪ**, and in examples 70 and 71, **DĪ**.

3. Al-Akfaš defines the *qāfiya* as the last word in the line.[16]
4. Ibn Kaysān (Abū al-Ḥasan Muḥammad b. Aḥmad, Baghdadian, d. 911 [or 932]) defines the *qāfiya* as: Anything that repeats regularly at the end of the line.[17]

Abū Mūsā al-Ḥāmiḍ (Sulaymān b. Muḥammad, Baghdadian, d. 917) ventures further in the definition he proposes, which is: The letters and vowels which the poet must repeat at the end of each line.[18]

All four definitions attempt to determine exactly what the elements are which repeat at the line endings, and to define them as a single unit. Al-Kalīl, al-Akfaš, Ibn Kaysān, and subsequently Abū Mūsā al-Ḥāmiḍ, all recognized the regularity of some additional elements to the *rawiyy*, and sought a way to include them into the definition of the *qāfiya*. Interestingly so, it is al-Kalīl, the earliest of the four

[15] *al-ḥarfu ʾl-ladī tubnā ʾl-qaṣīdatu ʿalayhi wahuwa ʾl-musammā rawiyyan.* (*Lisān*: s.v.; Tanūkī 1970:59; Akfaš 1970:1). Al-Anbārī attributes this definition to Taʿlab (Anbārī 1956:51); Ibn Rašīq attributes it to al-Farrāʾ (Ibn Rašīq 1972:1, 153); Ibn ʿAbd Rabbihi quotes this definition only (Ibn ʿAbd Rabbihi 1965:5, 496).

[16] *Ākiru kalimatin fī ʾl-bayti* (Akfaš 1970:1; Tanūkī 1970:59).

[17] *kullu šayin lazimat iʿādatuhu fī ākiri ʾl-bayti* (*Lisān*: s.v.). Ibn Kaysān himself attributes this definition to al-Kalīl (Ibn Kaysān 1859:48), but consistently calls the *rawiyy* by the name *qāfiya*.

[18] *mā yalzamu ʾš-šāʿiru takrīrahu fī kulli baytin mina ʾl-ḥurūfi waʾl-ḥarakāti* (Tanūkī 1970:59; Ibn Rašīq 1972:1, 153)

theorists, who attempted to designate boundaries for the *qāfiya* most precisely, by referring only to the phonetic elements of the language. While quoting al-Ḵalīl's definition, his disciple al-Aḵfaš offers a definition of his own, which is quite misrepresentative, as a *qāfiya* is rarely identical with a word: it is generally located within part of a word, and sometimes in more than just a word. This peculiar definition of the *qāfiya* should be considered in light of the nature of al-Aḵfaš's scholarly activity. While al-Ḵalīl was a man of theoretical thinking, and one who created new paradigms in several linguistic fields of which metrics is only one example, al-Aḵfaš's approach was more empirical. His treatise on rhyming is particularly replete with linguistic material collected from the speech of the Bedouins, whose Arabic was highly regarded at the time as "pure" and correct. His definition is based not on a theoretical speculation, but rather on the way in which people used the word *qāfiya*.[19] Al-Aḵfaš justifies his definition in this manner: "Would a poet ask you: rhyme me rhymes, you will not rhyme him half-lines, but words, like *ǧulām* and *salām*" (Aḵfaš 1970:5).

Ibn Kaysān, in his turn, offers a rather tautological definition; its formulation is obviously correct, but it does not define the boundaries of that particular unit which repeats at the ends of lines. Quṭrub's narrower definition, which bases the *qāfiya* on the *rawiyy* alone and ignores the additional repeating elements, is also not without a certain logic, since the *rawiyy* is indeed the most prominent component of the *qāfiya*. It is the only one which always repeats in all the *qāfiya*-types—to the extent that the *qaṣīdas* were named according to their *rawiyy*—whereas the other repeating elements do not all occur in the same *qāfiya* (see also Tanūḵī 1970:75; Ibn Rašīq 1972:1, 153).

Of the four definitions just mentioned, only al-Ḵalīl's two definitions, particularly his first, continued to dominate the Arabic theory of rhyme. The definitions of al-Aḵfaš and Quṭrub were occasionally quoted in compositions on rhyme (for example, Anbārī 1956:51; Tanūḵī 1970:59), but they have not been further discussed. Al-Ḵalīl's definitions were continually referred to in medieval treatises on

---

[19] A recurring sentence in this treatise is: *walaysat tu'ḵadu 'l-asmā'u bi'l-qiyāsi ... innamā nanẓuru mā sammathu 'l-'arabu fanattabi'uhu* ("One should not treat these terms as if they were derived from a [certain] rule. We simply observe which terms were given by the Arab [Bedouins], and to these we adhere").

rhyme, most notably because the entire Arabic concept of rhyme was derived from these definitions.

Al-K̲alīl's definitions position the *qāfiya* between the two quiescent letters at the end of the line. The first quiescent letter is usually, but not necessarily, situated in the last word of the line, whereas the second quiescent letter is the final letter in the line when the line ends in a closed syllable (in Arabic, *qāfiya muqayyada*); or it is the letter which indicates a long vowel when the line concludes in an open syllable (*qāfiya muṭlaqa*). In such a case, it can be an *alif*, a *wāw* or a *yā'*. In the case of an *alif*, the letter *alif* is written; in the other two cases, the letters *wāw* or *yā'*, respectively, are not written: *'udrā; wağudūdū; 'l-manākibī, ḥarīq.*

Both the first, broader definition and the second, narrower one actually include two separate statements: the explicit formulation of the definitions simply sets the boundaries of the repeating unit—the *qāfiya*. But in positioning the *qāfiya* between the two quiescent letters at the end of the line the definitions also imply the existence of not one but actually *several* types of *qāfiya*, depending on the varying location of the first quiescent (the location of the second quiescent is fixed—the last letter in the line):

(72) 'n-naw**ĀĞIYĀ**—lay**ĀLIYĀ**—d**ĀNIYĀ**
(73) 'l-'**ĪSŪ**—maġm**ŪSŪ**—ma'k**ŪSŪ**
(74) **'Ṣ-ṢADA'**—m**Ā ṢANA'**—yu**TTABA'**
(75) fa'lḥa**TRĪ**—wabi'ssi**DRĪ**—wa'abā' ba**KRĪ**
(76) farig̃**ĀMUHĀ**—sil**ĀMUHĀ**—waḥar**ĀMUHĀ**

Both definitions of the *qāfiya* imply, then, that the rhymeme contains more than just the *rawiyy*, and that the addition of extra elements to the *rawiyy* creates several possibilities of *qāfiya*, each of which is employed exclusively throughout a poem. The difference between the two definitions seems to be that, whereas definition (A) includes in the *qāfiya* the movent letter which precedes the first quiescent letter (or, according to the version of that definition, only the vowel of the movent letter), definition (B) sets the boundary of the *qāfiya* on the first quiescent letter itself. In effect, this difference reveals two distinct principles of classifying the *qāfiya* into its various types. As will be further discussed in the following sections, the basic conception of which there is not one, but rather several types of *qāfiya*, is the foundation upon which the entire Arabic theory of rhyme lies. Although this conception is not expressed explicitly in the Arabic dis-

cussions on rhyme, the attempt to formulate it theoretically, nevertheless, led to the formulation of two different principles of classification of the *qāfiya*-types. In most of the Arabic works on rhyme both
principles are discussed successively, with no attempt to elucidate the
relationships between them, or, to offer a historical or doctrinal
explanation for their dual existence. Moreover, both principles are
ascribed to the same scholar, al-Ḵalīl,[20] who is considered to be the
founder of the Arabic theory of rhyme.

2.2.2. *The first method of classifying the* qāfiya

The primary principle of classification of the *qāfiya* is based upon a
distinction between the essential components of the *qāfiya*: those which
appear in it consistently (that is, successively in a fixed location,
lawāzim), and those components which may be variable. Thus, the
qāfiya is defined as including six letters and five vowels—counting
from the end of the line backwards. This is a maximal range which
theoretically includes all the types of *qāfiya* together. Each of the letters
and vowels was assigned a special name, which, in itself, proves that
each 'letter' was perceived as a distinct element of the *qāfiya* (cf. for
example Ibn Rasīq 1972:1, 161).

2.2.1.1. The 'letters' of the *qāfiya*

The most noticeable of these 'letters' is the *rawiyy*, which is generally defined as "the letter on which the *qaṣīda* is constructed." Its
position within the *qāfiya* is always determined: when appearing in
a closed syllable, it is the last letter in the line, and in an open syllable, the letter before the last (or the second before the last). All
consonants can function as *rawiyy* (see Aḵfaš 1970:10; Tanūḵī 1970:74-
75; Maʿarrī 1971:1, 6; Ibn Kaysān 1859:68; Anbārī 1956:52; Mubarrad 1973:3; Ḥimyarī 1948:87; Damanhūrī:80; Tibrīzī 1966:149-150).

The 'letters' after the *rawiyy* are:

waṣl (or *ṣila*)—one of the letters *alif*, *wāw*, *yāʾ*, *hāʾ*, following the
rawiyy and indicating a long vowel:

---

[20] See Aḵfaš 1970:7-9; Tanūḵī 1970:59-62; But Ibn Kaysān, who considers al-
Ḵalīl as the first to assign names to the vowels and consonants (Ibn Kaysān 1859:48,
54), does not attribute to him the assignment of the five names of the *qāfiyas* (*ibid.*:

(77) f'nfara**QĀ**—mā ʿali**QĀ**
(78) tara**KŪ**—sala**KŪ**
(79) takalla**MĪ**—wa'sla**MĪ**
(80) 'l-ʾarbaʿ**AH**—'l-ḵayḍʿ**AH**
(81) sulla**MUH**—yaʿla**MUH**
(82) fiqra**TIH**—širra**TIH**

alif lengthens the vowel **a**, *wāw* the vowel **u**, *yāʾ* the vowel **i**, and *hāʾ* lengthens all three vowels.

ḵurūǧ—one of the letters *alif*, *wāw*, *yāʾ*, succeeding a movent *hāʾ* (in the morphological function of a third-person pronoun for both masculine and feminine) and indicating its vowel:

(83) mawki**BUHĀ**
(84) nuʿalli**LUHŪ**
(85) naʿ**ṢIHĪ**

The movent *hāʾ* is considered a *waṣl*.
The letters before the *rawiyy* are:

ridf—one of the letters *alif*, *wāw*, *yāʾ*, preceding the *rawiyy* and indicating that the vowel in the syllable before the *rawiyy* is a long one:

(86) ṭar**ĪQ**—bi'l-maḍ**ĪQ**
(87) 'l-fut**ŪQ**—'l-ḥuq**ŪQ**
(88) qaṭ**ĀMĪ**—w'ssal**ĀMĪ**
(89) ṭar**ŪBŪ**—maš**ĪBŪ**

The long vowels **ī**, **ū** can rhyme with one another, but not with the long vowel **ā** (cf. 1.1.4.1.2).

ta'sīs—the letter *alif*, indicating the long vowel **ā** in the second syllable before the *rawiyy*:

(90) t**Ā**mi**R**—'d-daw**Ā**'i**R**
(91) 'n-naw**Ā**ši**ZŪ**—ḥ**Ā**ǧi**ZŪ**

daḵīl—the letter between the *ta'sīs* and the *rawiyy*. Any consonant can be the *daḵīl*. Its vowel, which varies, yet is usually a *kasra* (**i**), is always short:

(92) t**Ā**m**IR**—'d-daw**Ā**'**IR**
(93) 'n-naw**Ā**š**IZŪ**—ḥ**Ā**ǧ**IZŪ**

The *da<u>k</u>īl* is the only element in the *qāfiya* whose sound varies, and only its location is fixed; thus some treatises on rhyme do not mention it (such as those of al-A<u>k</u>faš, al-Maʿarrī and his disciple, al-Tanū<u>k</u>ī).

2.2.1.2. The vowels of the *qāfiya*
The *qāfiya*'s vowels are:

mağrā—the vowel of the *rawiyy* (obviously in an open syllable; in a closed syllable the *rawiyy* has no vowel).

nafā<u>d</u>—the vowel of the *hā'*, when there is a *<u>k</u>urūğ* following it.

ḥa<u>d</u>w—the vowel of the letter preceding the *ridf*. This is, in fact, the vowel which is indicated by the *ridf* to be long, and upon which the *ridf* is dependent: when the vowel is **i**, the *ridf* is *yā'*; when the vowel is **u**, the *ridf* is *wāw*; and when the vowel is **a**, the *ridf* is *alif*.

tawğīh—the vowel of the short syllable before the *rawiyy*. When the *qāfiya* includes a *ta'sīs*, this is the vowel of the *da<u>k</u>īl*.[21]

rass—the vowel of the letter before the *ta'sīs*. It is always **a**, just as the *ta'sīs* is always *alif*.

The six letters which, in their various combinations, form the *qāfiya* signify long vowels, with the exception of the *da<u>k</u>īl* and the *rawiyy* (and also the *waṣl*, when it is succeeded by a *<u>k</u>urūğ*). Their location is fixed and repeats in every *qāfiya*-type in which they appear throughout the poem. The only variations permitted are the rhyming of the *ridf wāw* with *yā'* (which also implies a change in the vowel of the letter before the *ridf*), and alternations in the short vowels. However, when a short vowel, often **i**, is located between a long vowel and the *rawiyy*, it tends to repeat throughout the entire poem.

2.2.1.3. Types of *qāfiya* according to the first method of classification
As was previously mentioned, defining the components of the *qāfiya* by naming them indicates an awareness of the fact that the *qāfiya* includes other elements in addition to the *rawiyy*. Not every theorist, however, ventures much further beyond this awareness to discuss the relationships between the various elements of the *qāfiya*, that is, to actually analyze its different types. Al-A<u>k</u>faš, for instance, discusses all the *qāfiya*-components (the 'letters' and 'vowels'), as if appearing as one group simultaneously in the *qāfiya*. Yet some the-

---

[21] Some refer to the vowel of the *da<u>k</u>īl* as *išbāʿ*. See Anbārī 1956:55; Maʿarrī 1971:1, 17-20; Ḥimyarī 1948:101; Tibrīzī 1966:108.

orists[22] do use the method of classifying the *qāfiya* into its components discussed here to introduce *qāfiya*-types, and classify them according to the various possible combinations of its components.

All the treatises on rhyme, except those of al-Akfaš and of al-Anbārī, describe nine *qāfiya*-types:

1. *qāfiya muqayyada muğarrada*—a *qāfiya* ending in a *closed syllable*, having no long vowels in both syllables before the *rawiyy* (two syllables before the *rawiyy* being the maximal scope of the *qāfiya*).
2. *qāfiya muqayyada murdafa*—a *qāfiya* ending in a *closed syllable* and including a *ridf*.
3. *qāfiya muqayyada mu'assasa*—a *qāfiya* ending in a *closed syllable* and including a *ta'sīs*.
4. *qāfiya muṭlaqa muğarrada*—a *qāfiya* ending in an *open syllable* (by definition including a *waṣl*) having no long vowels.
5. *qāfiya muṭlaqa muğarrada lahā kurūğ*—a *qāfiya* ending in an *open syllable* (by definition including a *waṣl*), having no long vowels and including a *kurūğ*.
6. *qāfiya muṭlaqa murdafa*—a *qāfiya* ending in an *open syllable* and including a *ridf*.
7. *qāfiya muṭlaqa murdafa lahā kurūğ*—a *qāfiya* ending in an *open syllable* and including both a *ta'sīs* and a *kurūğ*.
8. *qāfiya muṭlaqa mu'assasa*—a *qāfiya* ending in an *open syllable* and including a *ta'sīs*.
9. *qāfiya muṭlaqa mu'assasa lahā kurūğ*—a *qāfiya* ending in an *open syllable* and including both a *ta'sīs* and a *kurūğ*.

The following table provides a graphic summary of these nine *qāfiya*-types:

	ta'sīs	*dakīl/ridf*	*rawiyy*	*waṣl*	*kurūğ*
(1)			any consonant		
(2)		*alif/wāw,yā'*	any consonant		
(3)	*alif*		any consonant		
(4)			any consonant	*alif,wāw,yā',hā'*	
(5)			any consonant	*hā'*	*alif,wāw,yā'*
(6)		*alif/wāw,yā'*	any consonant	*alif,wāw,yā',hā'*	
(7)		*alif/wāw,yā'*	any consonant	*hā'*	*alif,wāw,yā'*
(8)	*alif*		any consonant	*alif,wāw,yā',hā'*	
(9)	*alif*		any consonant	*hā'*	*alif,wāw,yā'*

[22] "It has been said: the first to divide the *qawāfī* (=*qāfiya*-types) in this way was al-Farrā', then al-Mubarrad used this division in his book called *Mukṭaṣar* (=summary, résumé)" (Tanūkī 1970:107).

What we actually have here is a description of an entire set of rhymemes. In a manner characteristic to the Arabic rhyme theory (and of medieval Arabic scientific thinking in general), this description is based on taxonomy rather than on a structural concept of identifying a minimal number of elements and accounting for their organization and their relationships. We can find detailed lists of the *qāfiya*-types (including all their possible linguistic materializations, see 2.4), but scarcely any of a formulation of the disjunctive relationships between the components of the *qāfiya* which produce the various rhymemes. Insofar as there is mention of this, it is only partial and refers primarily to the relationship between *ta'sīs* and *ridf*:

> All these letters and vowels can assemble in a *qāfiya*, except for the *ta'sīs* and the *ridf*. They do not coincide in a *qāfiya*, nor do the *rass* and the *ḥaḏw*.[23]
> The *ridf* and the *ta'sīs* do not coincide in a *qāfiya*, but rather each one appears separately in a (different) *qāfiya*.[24]
> Every poem has to be either *muṭlaq* (ending in an open syllable) or *muqayyad* (ending in a closed syllable); furthermore, the poem must have either a *ridf* or a *ta'sīs*, or neither.[25]

As a matter of fact, the classification of the *qāfiya* into nine types relates to only three possible combinations of the *qāfiya* before the *rawiyy*:

(1) a *qāfiya* in which the second syllable before the *rawiyy* is a long open syllable (*ta'sīs*).
(2) a *qāfiya* in which the syllable just before the *rawiyy* is a long open syllable (*ridf*).
(3) a *qāfiya muğarrada*, in which there is no long open syllable before the *rawiyy*.

Such a classification seemingly ignores two additional combinations, parallel to (1) and (2), in which a long *closed* syllable before the *rawiyy* exists. It seems that the medieval Arab theorists of rhyme did not notice that a disjunctive relationship existed also between closed syllables (see 1.2), presumably because these syllables had no repeating

---

[23] *wakullu hāḏihi 'l-ḥurūfi wa'l-ḥarakāti qad tağtami'u fī qāfiyatin, illā 't-ta'sīsa wa'r-ridfa, fa'innahumā lā tağtami'āni fī qāfiyatin, walā 'r-rassu wa'l-ḥadwu* (Akfaš 1970:39).

[24] *walā yağtami'u 'r-ridfu wa't-ta'sīsu ma'an fī qāfiyatin walākin yanfaridu kullu wāḥidin bi'l-qāfiyati* (Ibn Kaysān 1859:50-51).

[25] *wakullu ši'rin falā budda an yakūna muṭlaqan aw muqayyadan ṯumma lā budda an yakūna murdafan aw mu'assasan aw mu'arran minhu muğarradan* (Ibn Rašīq:1972:1, 159, 164).

sound; they may have considered these two additional combinations to be included in number (3).

2.2.2. *The second method of classifying the* qāfiya

From the fact that closed syllables were ignored by this method of classifying the *qāfiya* into separate types we learn that, although speaking in terms of 'letters' and 'vowels,' the classification was nevertheless based upon a phonetic conception of the *qāfiya*. The aim of this method was to determine which *sounds* composed the *qāfiya*, and what different rhymemes could be formed from the combinations of these sounds. The second method of classification, although employing the same terminology (more accurately, only 'vowels'), nevertheless appears to rely on the written, rather than the oral, representation of the texts.

The second method of classifying the *qāfiya* into types derives from the narrower definition of the *qāfiya* ascribed to al-K̲alīl (cf. 2.2). In accordance with this definition, and as previously stated, the last two quiescent letters at the end of the line mark the boundaries of the *qāfiya*. While the position of the second quiescent letter is fixed—it is always the last letter in the line—the position of the first quiescent letter is flexible. According to the possible positions, five types of *qāfiya* are defined (Ibn Rašīq 1972:1, 172; Anbārī 1956:55-56):

(1) *mutaqāwis*—a *qāfiya* in which there are four movent letters between the two quiescent letters.

(2) *mutarākib*—a *qāfiya* in which there are three movent letters between the two quiescent letters.

(3) *mutadārik*—a *qāfiya* in which there are two movent letters between the two quiescent letters.

(4) *mutawātir*—a *qāfiya* in which there is one movent letter between the two quiescent letters.

(5) *mutarādif*—a *qāfiya* in which the two quiescent letters are successive.

This particular method classifies the *qāfiya*-types according to length; the length being expressed by a sequence of short vowels. It is less comprehensive than the previous classification for two reasons:

(A) The vowel preceding the first quiescent letter, which takes part in some of the rhymemes, is not taken into account here. When the *rawiyy* is preceded by long open syllables, (that is, with rhymemes including a *ta'sīs* or a *ridf*), this quiescent letter is not independent, but rather signifies the length of the vowel before it: liḥ**īnī**—

bi'lyam**īnī**. The long vowel **ī** is thus a part of the rhymeme, whether it comes immediately before the *rawiyy* (as in the *ridf*), or whether a short vowel (which is not necessarily a part of the rhymeme) separates it from the *rawiyy* (as in the *ta'sīs*). The above classification applies to those cases in which closed syllables are located before the *rawiyy* in parallel positions to a *ta'sīs* and a *ridf*. The closed syllables have no fixed recurring sound, and the vowels of such syllables may be excluded from the rhymeme.

(B) Although the location of the first quiescent letter is set throughout the entire poem due to the precise syllable arrangement of the *qāfiya*—to the degree of distinguishing between a long open syllable and a long closed syllable—this does not necessarily apply to all the possible *qāfiya*-types. Thus, when several successive short syllables (at least two) precede the *rawiyy*, the location of the first quiescent letter may vary, resulting in the presence of not one, but several "*qāfiya*-types" within one poem. According to the Arabic conception of rhyme, however, these rhyming variations are fundamentally unacceptable. For example, in the following four-line poem (in the *rağaz* metre):

(94) innā a<u>k</u>āka 'ṣ-ṣidqa man kā**NA MA'AK**
waman yaḍurru nafsahu liyan**FA'AK**
waman i<u>d</u>ā raybu 'z-zamā**NI ṢADA'AK**
šattata fīhi šamlahu liyağ**MA'AK**

(Kišwān 1968:345)

The rhymeme according to our conception would be **A'AK**. Yet according to this method of classification, in the first line the rhymeme would be **NAMA'AK**, in the second line—**FA'AK**, in the third line—**NIṢADA'AK**, and in the fourth line—**MA'AK**, depending upon the number of short successive vowels between the two quiescent letters. Although this is an exceptional example, which could only occur in the *rağaz* metre, alternations between *mutadārik* (three short vowels between two quiescent letters) and *mutarākib* (two short vowels between two quiescent letters) could, nevertheless, occur quite frequently.

2.2.3. *The limitations of the second method of classification*

From the above discussion, it becomes clear that the second method of classifying the *qāfiya* retains a double weakness: on the one hand, sounds which repeat in a fixed location throughout the poem, and therefore should be considered by definition part of the rhymeme, are excluded. On the other hand, sounds which do not repeat in a fixed location throughout the entire poem, and hence should not be part of the rhymeme by definition, are included. The limitations of this method are also evident with regard to the distribution of rhymemes in classical poetry. Since the method is based on a quantitative principle—the counting of the successive short vowels—whose realization actually depends on the metre, and not on the rhyming scheme itself, a distorted picture is formed of the distribution of the *qāfiya*-types in poetry. Even a superfluous examination of classical Arabic poetry reveals that the *qāfiya*-types three and four are the most common, less common is *qāfiya*-type two, while *qāfiya*-types one and five (particularly one) are quite rare. Thus solitary instances are regarded as "types" according to this method, while heterogeneous components which should have been considered separately, are included in one single *qāfiya*-type. From the comparative perspective, the first method of classification draws a more representative picture of the actual situation in rhyming than the second one, because only essential sounds are considered in its *qāfiya*-types.

2.3. *Quantitative as opposed to qualitative arrangement*

The coexistence, in most of the compositions on rhyme, of two distinct methods of classifying the *qāfiya* (both of which are attributed to al-K̲alīl), is rather puzzling, particularly, since the first method provides a seemingly sufficient account of all the possible *qāfiya* forms, while a deficiency remains in the second method. There might be, of course, a historical explanation for this, as previously mentioned. However, it seems that each method fulfills a different function in the theory of rhyme. The second method appears to be connected rather closely to the metric system, for the discussions of it in the treatises on rhyme usually indicate in which one of the Arabic metres (and their variations) each of the method's five *qāfiya*-types can be employed. The connection is obvious, for it is the metre that determines the possible number of successive short vowels in the poem. The second method thus pertains not only to rhyme, but also to the complexity of metrics.

The difference between the two methods stems from the fact that the second method strives to organize sound-elements into a single rhyming scheme according to a quantitative principle; whereas the first method aims to organize sound-elements into a rhyming scheme according to a qualitative principle. Today we are unable to know exactly how ancient Arabic poetry was performed; however, the fact that the rhyme theorists have identified the last long vowels before and after the *rawiyy* as components of the *qāfiya* provide some evidence that the vowels were uttered in such a way as to produce sounds conspicuous enough to be included in the rhymeme. Several treatises on rhyme clarify the function of the long vowels in the rhyming scheme by relating it to the manner in which they are pronounced:

> And all this (= various grammatical deviations) is preferable to a change of *qāfiya*, as far as they [poets] are concerned, since the *qāfiya*s are what differentiate poetry from [ordinary] speech. This is because it might well happen that [ordinary] speech would have metre, which is what determines the poem [being what it is], yet it would never be called poetry unless it has rhyme as well. That is why they took great care to clarify the *rawiyy*,[26] and added to it the obligatory *ta'sīs*, *ridf* and *k̲urūǧ* for further clarification, and to assure the lengthening of the line and the raising of the voice in the rhyme, as these letters (*alif*, *wāw*, *yā'*) indicate the lengthening and softening of the voice. They wanted to trill and prolong the voice with melody, which is what differentiates poetry from speech and which is to the poem what the finish-line is to the race.[27]

And:

> They designated these letters (*alif*, *wāw*, *yā'*) as *waṣl* because the poem is composed for singing, driving the camels by melody, and for the trill. Their trill often comes at the end of the line, and the voice is only tuned by the letters which indicate a long vowel: quiescent *wāw*, *yā'*, and *alif*. Therefore, they added [these letters] to complete the line, and assigned them with this role, because the voice is tuned by them [...]. They did not permit the alternating of the *waṣl*-letters so that the voice would not change, because the voice which is tuned by a *wāw* is not like the voice which is tuned by an *alif*. In this way they adjusted them, just as they adjusted the letters of the *rawiyy* (that is,

---

[26] The word is *qāfiya*, but Ibn Kaysān consistently uses this word to indicate the *rawiyy*; he does not use the word *rawiyy* at all (see note 16).

[27] *wağamīʿu hād̲a aḥsanu ʿindahum min taġyīri 'l-qawāfī li'anna 'l-qawāfiya hiya 'l-latī faṣalat bayna 'l-kalāmi wa'š-šiʿri li'annahu qad yaqaʿu 'l-waznu 'l-lad̲ī yakūnu šiʿran fī 'l-kalāmi walā yusammā šiʿran ḥatā yuqaffā falid̲ālika ḥaraṣū ʿalā īḍāḥi 'l-qāfiyati wa'alzamūhā mā atbaʿūhā mina 't-ta'sīsi wa'r-ridfi wa'l-k̲urūği ziyādatan fī 'l-bayāni waḥirṣan ʿalā iṭālati 'l-bayti warafʿi 'ṣ-ṣawti bi'l-qāfiytai bimā fī hād̲ihi 'l-ḥurūfi mina 'l-maddi wa'l-līni li'annahum arādū 't-tarannuma bid̲ālika wamadda 'ṣ-ṣawti bi'l-ġinā'i 'l-lad̲ī yubayyinu 'š-šiʿra mina 'l-kalāmi wahuwa li'š-šiʿri ka'l-miḍmāri* (Ibn Kaysān 1859:60-61, and also 53-54).

they determined that the same letter would repeat throughout the entire poem, just as the same *rawiyy* repeats throughout the entire poem).[28]

2.4. *Components of the* qāfiya *and their manifestations in language*

The fact that the Arabic theory of rhyme uses written signs (i.e., letters and vowels-marks) to describe the *qāfiya*, which is actually a combination of sounds, has a double significance:

(a) The letter acquires a theoretical status. It serves as a term which indicates both a component of the *qāfiya* and its location within the *qāfiya*. The *qāfiya*, for instance, is defined as including six letters and five vowels, "letters" signifying abstract "components," rather than their specific realizations; and the *rawiyy* is defined as "the letter on which the *qaṣīda* is constructed, and one which must appear in every line in a fixed location" (see 2.2.1.1).

(b) It is always indicated which character of the Arabic alphabet can function as what 'letter' (in the abstract sense) of the *qāfiya*. Actually, only the *rawiyy* is a consonant (and so, also, is the *waṣl* if followed by a *k̲urūǧ*), while all the other components—*ta'sīs, ridf, waṣl* (not followed by a *k̲urūǧ*)—are signs indicating long vowels. Hence, the discussion of the *qāfiya*-components focuses mainly on the letters indicating long vowels: it specifically states that only *alif* can be a *ta'sis*, while *alif, wāw, yā'* can all be a *ridf*, with *wāw* and *yā'* rhyming together; that *alif, wāw, yā', hā'* can be a *waṣl*; and that *alif, wāw, yā'* can also be a *k̲urūǧ*. However, these very same letters are also used to indicate consonants. In order to distinguish between situations in which the letters indicate consonants, and those in which they indicate long vowels, the Arabic rhyme treatises provide a list of all the possible instances in which these letters are not pronounced but merely serve to indicate various morphological functions.

The morphological aspect of the letters acquires special significance in the discussion of the following question: when can the letters indicating consonants, which may be both root and morpho-

---

[28] *wa'innamā waṣalū bihād̲ihi 'l-ḥurūfi li'anna 'š-šiʿra wuḍiʿa li'l-ġinā'i wa'l-ḥudā'i wa't-tarannumi. Wa'akt̲aru mā yakaʿu tarannumuhum fī āk̲iri 'l-bayti. walaysa šay'un yağrī fīhi 'ṣ-ṣawtu ġayra ḥurūfi 'l-līni 'l-yā'i wa'l-wāwi 's-sākinatayni wa'l-alifi, fazādūhunna litamāmi 'l-bayti wa'k̲taṣṣūhunna li'anna 'ṣ-ṣawta yağrī fīhinna ... walam yuğīzū ḥurūfa 'l-waṣli baʿḍahā maʿa baʿḍin karāhiyata an yak̲talifa 'ṣ-ṣawtu li'anna 'ṣ-ṣawta 'l-lad̲i yağrī fī 'l-wāwi laysa ka'ṣ-ṣawti 'l-lad̲ī yağrī fī 'l-alifi. fasuwwiya baynahā kamā suwwiya bayna hurūfi 'r-rawiyyi* (Ak̲faš 1970:12 -13, and also 78, 105; 114; Tanūk̲ī 1970:112).

logical, function as *rawiyy*? Such, for instance, is al-Tanūḵī's treatment of the question, "which letters can be *rawiyy*":

> All the letters of the alphabet can be *rawiyy*, except for the weak letters, of these:
>
> *alif* indicating the dual in the past and future tenses, as in: *qām**Ā**, lam yaqūm**Ā***.
>
> *alif* added on to the root, lengthening and clarifying the vowel of the preceding *rawiyy*: *iḍrib**Ā**, iḏhab**Ā***.
>
> *hā'* indicating the feminine gender in a noun (=*tā' marbūṭa*), as in: *ṭalḥa(**H**), šağara(**H**)*.
>
> *tanwīn*
>
> *alif* substituted by *nūn* in the *waṣl*, as in: *lanasfa'a**N***.
>
> *tanwīn* substituted by *alif* at the end of a line: *ra'aytu zaid**Ā*** instead of *zayd**AN***.
>
> *yā'* indicating the feminine gender in the imperative mood: *iḍrib**Ī**, kul**Ī***.
>
> *alif* clarifying that the vowel preceding it is *fatḥā*: *an**Ā***.
>
> *hā'* assuming the same clarifying function: *gulāmi**H**, yā aba**H***.
>
> *hā'* indicating third person pronoun singular; it is *rawiyy* when preceded by a quiescent letter: *min**HŪ**, wada'**HŪ***; but when preceded by a movent letter, it is not *rawiyy*, rather *waṣl*: *ku**LLUHŪ**—uḵi**LLUHŪ**, qida**MUH**—ḥuma**MUH***.
>
> The same applies to *hā'* which indicates a third person singular pronoun of the feminine gender: *ḏā'i**QUHĀ**, ša**DDAHĀ**—ra**DDAHĀ***. In these examples the *hā'* is not *rawiyy*, but it can be *rawiyy* if preceded by a quiescent letter: *nabnī**HĀ***.
>
> The *alif* which follows *hā'* in a third person feminine pronoun: *lah**Ā**, 'indah**Ā***.
>
> *tā'* indicating third person feminine of a past tense verb: *marra**TI** wḥağğa**TI** 'lmar'atu*, can be *rawiyy*, despite its being a pronoun, because it is strong.
>
> *kāf* indicating a second person pronoun, feminine or masculine, can be *rawiyy* despite its being a pronoun, because it is strong (similar to the status of *mīm* and *nūn*, which too represent [also indicate] consonants that sometimes have a morphological function). Similar to *hā'*, it is *rawiyy* if preceded by a quiescent letter. If preceded by a movent letter, there is a difference of opinion as to whether or not it can be *rawiyy*; some believe that it can only be *rawiyy* if it rhymes with a root *kāf* (unlike morphological *hā'*, which is not considered *rawiyy* if it follows a movent letter).
>
> *tā'* indicating the first person of a past tense verb can be *rawiyy*: *akal**TŪ**—šarib**TŪ***.
>
> *wāw* indicating third person plural in a verb (*fa'alŪ*) is not *rawiyy*. But if it follows a movent letter, it is *rawiyy*: *'aṣa**W**—rama**W***.
>
> *wāw* is *rawiyy* when it is the third root letter in a verb in the future tense (even though it is quiescent): *yağz**Ū**—yad'**Ū***

> movent *yā'* is always *rawiyy*. When *yā'* is the third root letter of a verb in the future tense then it would preferably be *waṣl*. This also applies to *yā'* which indicates first person in a possessive pronoun: *'ik̲watĪ—bĪ; nafsĪ—mit̲LĪ—qabLĪ*. The examples demonstrate that it was rhymed as *rawiyy*.
>
> *yā'* which was originally accented, yet the accent is not pronounced, can be *rawiyy*: *'l'alĪ—'lmaṭĪ* (originally *'l'aliyy—'lmaṭiyy*).
>
> The same applies to *yā' al-nisba*, when it is not pronounced as accented: *'lyat̲ribĪ—'lǧamalĪ—dīni 'alĪ* (instead of *'lyat̲ribiyy—'lǧamaliyy—dīni 'aliyy*).
>
> However, in the ambiguous cases of whether a letter can be *rawiyy* or not, it is preferable that it function as *waṣl* (Tanūk̲ī 1970:75-82; For a comprehensive discussion, see Damanhūrī:84-86).

Every one of the letters which function as components of the *qāfiya* is similarly discussed, but being an intersection for a wide variety of phenomena, the discussion of the *rawiyy* is both the most lengthy and intriguing in Arabic rhyme theory.

An analysis of the discussion on the *rawiyy* reviewed here, reveals that the Arabic accounts of the *qāfiya*-letters are actually based on two fundamental oppositions. Together these oppositions organize the relationship between the sound and its morphological function:

(1) an opposition of substance, between consonant and vowel (in the medieval terms, between 'quiescent letter' and 'movent letter'; 'strong letter' as opposed to 'weak letter').

(2) an opposition of function, between the function of a root and that of a morphological element.

The discussion of the question "which letters can be *rawiyy*?", can now be summarized in the following table:

Table 1
RAWIYY

	consonant	**vowel**
root	all the letters of the alphabet indicating consonants	*alif, wāw, yā'* according to norm
morphological	*hā', tā', kāf, nūn, mīm* when rhyming with root consonants; otherwise according to norm	

As a matter of fact, only eight letters are actually presented here as *qāfiya*-letters: those which are "problematic" with regard to the two oppositions: *alif, wāw, yā'* (and sometimes *hā'*), which indicate both consonants and vowels; and *tā', kāf, nūn, mīm, hā'*, indicating consonants which may be both root and morphological. The position of each of the eight letters with regard to the two oppositions and, consequently, its possible role within the *qāfiya*, are outlined in the following table:

Table 2

	movent root letter	**quiescent root letter**		**movent morphological letter**	**quiescent morphological letter**	
***tā'* (*marbūṭa*)**	A. *rawiyy* B. *rawiyy* alternating with root *tā'*	*rawiyy*		A. "*waṣl*"—N^{3} B. *rawiyy* alternating with root *tā'* C. *rawiyy*—N^{1}	"*waṣl*"	
kāf	*rawiyy*	*rawiyy*		A. "*waṣl*" B. *rawiyy*—N C. *rawiyy* alternating with root *kāf*	A. "*waṣl*"—N^{1} B. *rawiyy*—N C. *rawiyy* alternating with root *kāf*	
mīm	*rawiyy*	*rawiyy*		A. "*waṣl*"—N B. *rawiyy*—N$^{1-2}$ C. *rawiyy* alternating with root *mīm*	A. "*waṣl*" B. *rawiyy*—N C. *rawiyy* alternating with root *mīm*	
nūn	*rawiyy*	*rawiyy*		A. *rawiyy*—N^{1} B. "*waṣl*" C. *rawiyy* alternating with root *nūn*	A. "*waṣl*" B. *rawiyy*—N C. *rawiyy* alternating with root *nūn*	
hā'	A. *rawiyy* B. *waṣl* alternating with morphological *hā'*	A. *rawiyy* B. *waṣl* alternating with morphological *hā'*		A. *waṣl* B. *rawiyy* alternating with morphological *hā'*	A. *waṣl* B. *rawiyy* alternating with morphological *hā'*	
		as consonant	as vowel		as consonant	as vowel
alif	*rawiyy*	*rawiyy*—N^{1}	A.*rawiyy*—N B.*waṣl*—N	—	*waṣl*—D	*ta'sīs*,*ridf* *waṣl*,*kurūǧ*, *rawiyy*—N$^{1-2}$
wāw	*rawiyy*	*ridf*—N$^{1-2}$	A.*rawiyy*—N^{1} B.*waṣl*—N	—	*rawiyy*—N^{2} *ridf*—N^{1}, *waṣl*—N^{2}	*ridf* *waṣl* *kurūǧ* *rawiyy*—N
yā'	*rawiyy*	*ridf*—N$^{1-2}$ *rawiyy*—D	*rawiyy*—N$^{1-2}$ *waṣl*—N *ridf*	—	*rawiyy*—N *ridf*—N *waṣl*	*ridf*, *waṣl*, *kurūǧ* *rawiyy*—N$^{1-2}$

Explanatory notes for Table 2:

(1) Since *alif*, *wāw* and *yā'* indicate both consonants and vowels, it was necessary to divide the corresponding columns of the quiescent letters into two sections.

(2) The table reflects the information which is described in the treatises on rhyme, and not necessarily the actual situation in poetry. The shaded areas represent that which is according to the theory, yet, somehow was not referred to in the rhyme treatises.

(3) N = norm; "*rawiyy*—N" meaning that a certain letter functions as *rawiyy* according to the accepted norm, but not according to the rule. The word "norm" has three meanings here:

> N^1 the common—or rare—usage by poets, as indicated in the treatises on rhyme.
> N^2 the usage recommended or decreed by the rhyme theorists.
> N^3 the usage by poets of a certain period, and non-usage by poets of another period (such as "early" and "modern" poets)—again, as stated in the treatises on rhyme.

Based on the remarks in the treatises on rhyme, I have attempted to indicate in the table the number of adequate norms; however, as the Arabic references are incidental and sometimes contradictory, the above outline is necessarily incomplete.

(4) D = dialect. The reference is to a certain tribe's linguistic usage, if this is explicitly stated in the treatise on rhyme.

(5) "*waṣl*" (in quotation marks) = a morphological consonant located after the *rawiyy*, in the position of *waṣl*. The rhyme theorists assigned the name *waṣl* only to the letters *alif*, *wāw*, *yā'*, and *hā'*, and did not consider the possiblity of other morphological consonants assuming the same function.

2.5. *Rhyming norms*

The table clearly reflects the difference in application of the rule, as opposed to the norm, in the rhyming theory. The rule applies to all the components of the *qāfiya*, while the norm applies principally to the *rawiyy* (and to the *waṣl* which supplements it: according to the norm, whatever is not *rawiyy* must necessarily be *waṣl*). This is because the *rawiyy* is an intersection of all the possible combinations which are created by the two fundamental oppositions mentioned above. It is these two oppositions which determine the meaning of "rule" and "norm" for the eight letters represented in the table:

(a) the opposition of function ("root" vs. "morphological") determines the meaning of "rule" and "norm" for the letters *tā'*, *kāf*, *mīm*, *nūn*, *hā'*. The rule is that every root letter is *rawiyy*; every morphological letter is *waṣl*. The norm is that morphological letters can be *rawiyy*.

(b) the opposition of substance ("movent" vs. "quiescent") determines the meaning of "rule" and "norm" for the letters *alif*, *wāw*, *yā'*. Every movent letter is within the scope of the rule: a movent root letter is *rawiyy*, and a movent morphological letter is either *ta'sīs*, *ridf*, *waṣl*, or *ḵurūǧ*. The norm: all of these letters, when quiescent (whether indicating a consonant or a long vowel), may be *rawiyy*.

Apart from the norm which refers to letters functioning as components of the *qāfiya*, the rhyme theorists list additional norms, which they bring together under the title "the rhyme faults" (*ʿuyūb al-qawāfī*). The list is not identical in all treatises on rhyme, and there are conflicting opinions on the names of some of the "faults," nevertheless, this basically includes:

(1) *iqwā'*: an occasional change in the vowel of the *rawiyy* within one poem, that is, the rhyming of the vowels **i** and **u**, and both of these with **a**. For example:

(95) 's-saw**ĪqŪ**—s**ŪqĪ**—tar**ŪqĀ**

(2) *ikfā'*: an occasional change in the letter of the *rawiyy* within one poem; the letter of the *rawiyy* is substituted for letters which are phonetically similar. For example: (The examples are quoted from Tanūḵī 1970:117-137).

(96) šu'**ŪNUHĀ**—yastad**ĪMUHĀ**
(97) ṣudu**Ǧ**—ṣuqū
(98) li**ṢṢŪ**—yaʿta**SSŪ**—ba**SSŪ**
(99) aqb**ĀḌĪ**—'r-rad**ĀDĪ**—wiǧ**ĀDĪ**

(3) *badal*: a substitution of the letter of the *rawiyy* in a rhyming word in order to adjust its sound to the sound of the previous parallel consonant:

(100) 's-saʿl**ĀTĪ**—'n-n**ĀTĪ**—aky**ĀTĪ**
instead of: 's-saʿl**ĀTĪ**—'n-n**ĀSĪ**—aky**ĀSĪ**

(4) *sinād:* any occasional change in the letters preceding the *rawiyy:*

— a *qāfiya* with a *ta'sīs* rhyming with a *qāfiya* without a *ta'sīs:*
(101) ṯumm**MA 'S**la**MĪ**—**SAM**sa**MĪ**—'l-**'Ā**la**MĪ**.[29]

— a change in the vowel of the *daḵīl:*[30]
(102) –ub**ĀdiRŪ**—'l-muẓ**ĀhaRŪ**

— a *qāfiya* with a *ridf* rhyming with a *qāfiya* without a *ridf*:
(103) –**tūṢIHĪ**—**ta'ṢIHĪ**

— a change in the vowel of the *ridf*:
(104) –ḵam**ŪŠĀ**—qur**AYŠĀ**
(105) –'l-luğ**AYNĪ**—'**INĪ**

— a change in the short vowel preceding the *rawiyy*, when the *rawiyy* is a quiescent consonant. This is not considered a "fault" if the *rawiyy* has a vowel.

(5) *īṭā'*: a repetition of the same word at the ends of lines. The lesser the distance between the lines in which the same word rhymes, the greater the fault. If the word repeats with a different meaning, that is, if there is a maximum of sound similarity and the difference shifts from sound to meaning, then it is not considered to be a serious fault.

(6) *taḍmīn*: enjambement. The Arabic rhyme theorists include the enjambement among the faults of rhyme, even though it is not a function of the rhyme itself, but rather of a discrepancy between the syntactical units and the line endings. Among the common examples of *taḍmīn*, there is one case in which the enjambement occurs consecutively throughout six lines; it is evident that the poet turned this "fault" into an embellishment. Ibn Kaysān was aware of this possibility, and he writes:

> The intentional *taḍmīn* is not of the number we have mentioned, as it was employed purposefully, and we must not consider it a fault insofar as the poet is concerned: the fault is rather in he who strains to make his lines appear like maxims, every maxim standing on its own and not leaning on others (Ibn Kaysān 1859:58-59).

A study of the list of the "rhyme faults", and the table outlined above, lead to the following conclusion: Since all the *qāfiya*-components are

[29] There is an attempt to settle the prosodic discrepancy here by claiming that in a certain dialect, *'ālam* was pronounced as *'a'lam*, that is, as a consonantal *alif* (see Aḵfaš 1970:27; Tanūḵī 1970:130; Ma'arrī 1971:1, 14-15).

[30] See various opinions on this: Aḵfaš 1970:21; Mubarrad 1973:11; Ibn Kaysān 1859:51; Ibn 'Abd Rabbihi 1965:5, 496; Tanūḵī 1970:87; Ma'arrī 1971:1, 8-9, 18; Ibn Rašīq 1972:1, 161).

obligatory and their combinations fixed and closed to normative variations, the possibility of variation shifts to other spheres related to the *qāfiya*. For instance, the realization of the *qāfiya*-components in the specific linguistic material, and the range of sound uniformity of the rhyme members. This may vary from a minimal change of the *rawiyy* alone, to a maximal repetition of sounds resulting from rhyming with the same word; in this particular case, the distinctive feature betweem the rhyme members, a *sine qua non* for the very existence of rhyme, is thus transferred from sound to meaning.

2.6. *Treatises on rhyme and their historical significance*

The Arabic theory of rhyme is undoubtedly distinguished by the description of the *qāfiya*-components by means of the letters. There are several possible explanations for this practice:

(1) Although the Arab grammarians collected oral texts, they had written texts before them when they developed their hypotheses on rhyme and, therefore, formulated their opinions in terms of letters.

(2) Lacking, apparently, theoretical conceptualization by which to describe all six types of "letters" in the *qāfiya*, they thus discussed every occasion in which the letters indicate consonants or long vowels, or, the affiliation to a certain root or declension.

(3) The Arab prododists were not interested in developing a theory of rhyme for its own sake; they had a practical interest in composing treatise on rhyme, namely, to provide poets with a manual for rhyming, which would specify the rules and illuminate certain issues, such as what is permitted and forbidden in rhyme, what is considered beautiful and what is considered flawed. They preferred to describe the rules of rhyme from the practical point of view with regard to words and the letters as their components. The need (or, perhaps, demand) to produce guide-books on rhyme is in itself characteristic of a changing of periods in the history of Arabic poetry. This represents a stage of transition from the composing of oral poetry, in which the laws of rhyme are part of the inherited poetic repertoire,[31] to the creation of written poetry by an intellectual social élite,

---

[31] Cf. anecdotes told by al-A<u>k</u>faš, which show that the Bedouins, from whom the grammarians heard the poems, were not familiar with letters, nor even with the term 'letter' (A<u>k</u>faš 1970:1-2). Also of relevance in this context is the anecdote about the poet <u>D</u>ū al-Rumma, who spent much of his time among the Bedouins and concealed his knowledge of reading and writing, claiming that this

fully aware of the artistic and aesthetic aspects of their composition.

---

was a disgrace among the Bedouins (see Iṣbahānī 1963:18, 20); he probably did this in order that his credibility as a poet would not be doubted.

PART THREE

RHYME IN RHYMED PROSE

3.1. *Historical Background*

The origins of the *saǧʿ*—the Arabic term for rhymed prose—are rooted in the pre-Islamic period, emerging in religious and ceremonial practices. Prophets and soothsayers[32] expressed themselves in *saǧʿ*, thus Ǧāhili prayer formulas which were preserved in medieval Arabic sources are usually in the form of rhymed prose.[33] After the rise of Islam *saǧʿ* was apparently suppressed, partly because it was marked as a Ǧāhili practice and partly because the Koran itself was written in *saǧʿ*. A massive effort was dedicated to emphasize the uniqueness of the Koran and protect it from competing imitations.[34] Approximately 130 years after the rise of Islam, toward the end of the Umayyad period (mid-eighth century), the *saǧʿ* regained its previous prestigious status. In this period it reappeared in official speeches and in the epistles of court scribes, but only about fifty years later, in the days of Hārūn al-Rašīd, did the *saǧʿ* again become widely used. The rhyme of rhymed prose during this period is not yet complete: it does not encompass all rhyme members, and has no fixed rules. In time rhyming became elaborate, and penetrated almost every field of writing, beginning in the ninth century (with the writings of Ibrāhīm al-Ṣābī, Abu Bakr al-K̲awārizmī, al-Q̲āḍī al-Fāḍil etc.), and reaching its ultimate development in the eleventh century, in the *maqāmāt* of al-Hamad̲ānī and later of al-Ḥarīrī.

Although intriguing, the historical perspective of the *saǧʿ*—its apparent disappearance during the first century of Islam (although it was no doubt preserved orally), its reemergence and subsequent penetration into most of Arabic literary writings—is beyond the scope of our discussion here, which is focused on the rhyming norms in rhymed prose, and the function of the rhyme in the prose-text.

[32] cf., e.g., the story of Šiqq and Saṭīʿ (Ibn Hišām 1859:10-12).

[33] For *ṭalbiyāt* formulas see Ibn al-Kalbī 1924:7; Ibn Ḥabīb 1942:311-320.

[34] In accordance with the conception of *Iʿǧāz al-Qurʾān*. On the tarditional Arabic attitude towards the problem, see, for instance, ʿAskarī 1952:266-268; Ǧāḥiẓ 1932:1, 234-238; Bāqillānī 1981; K̲alafallah and Sallām 1968. See also ch. 7, note 12.

3.2. *The rhyming scheme of rhymed prose versus that of poetry*

The most conspicuous difference between poetry and rhymed prose with regard to rhyme is that in poetry a single rhymeme is retained throughout the poem, whereas in rhymed prose the rhymeme changes after every few (usually two to four) rhyme members. It may seem easier to maintain the rhyming rules when they are applied to a few rather than to many rhyme members; however, we discover that poetry adheres to the rules with strictness and severity, whereas rhymed prose observes these rules with a considerable flexibility. Although the basic conditions determining the structure of the rhymeme in poetry equally apply to the rhymeme in rhymed prose, it appears that the writer's freedom to frequently alter the rhymeme also affects his choice of the rhymeme structure. Unlike poetry, the employment of rhymeme in rhymed prose is much more a matter of norms than of rules, and it changes from one period to another and from one literary genre to the next.

Let us examine several types of *sağʿ* texts from different periods:

3.2.1. *Rhyme in the Koran*

It is well known that in the *sağʿ* of the Koran the rhymemes are located at the ends of verses (*āyāt*). The Koranic rhymemes follow the basic classical Arabic rhyming scheme, which defines five different types of rhymemes according to the arrangement of syllables within it (see 1.2). All five types are presented in the Koran;[35] the most common rhymeme is the one encompassing a long open vowel before the *rawiyy*; in this event, too, the long vowels ***ī*** and ***ū*** rhyme together, but not with the long vowel ***ā***. This rhymeme is characteristic of the long *sūra*s, but is found in most of the short *sūra*s as well. The other rhymemes are less prevalent, but they all do appear in the Koran, mostly in the short *sūra*s. Examples follow of the most common rhymeme:

(106) tufliḥ**ŪN**(a)[36]—muntah**ŪN**(a)—'l-mub**ĪN**(u)—
'l-muḥsin**ĪN**(a)—'al**ĪM**(un)

(5:90-94)

[35] Verse 125 in *Sūra Ṭaha* (20): *qāla rabbi lima ḥašartanī aʿmā waqad kuntu baṣīran* is exceptional because it is found within a group of verses with a different rhymeme. It is possible that the last three words are actually an old commentary-note inserted into the text.

[36] At the ends of the rhymes there are certain sounds which were not pronounced: the sounds indicating the cases in their different positions and the *tā'*

(107) ʿaẓ**Ī**m**Ā(N)**—saʿ**Ī**r**Ā(N)**—ḥak**Ī**m**Ā(N)**—ẓal**Ī**l**Ā(N)**—baṣ**Ī**r**Ā(N)**— ta'w**Ī**l**Ā(N)**

(4:54-59)

Examples of other rhymemes are:

(108) Law**Ā**ḥid(un)—'l-maš**Ā**riq(i)—'l-kaw**Ā**kib(i)—m**Ā**rid(in)—ǧ**Ā**nib(in)—w**Ā**ṣib(un)

(37:3-9)

(109) 'l-bayyin**A**(**T**u)—muṭahhar**A**(**T**an)—qayyim**A**(**T**un)—'l-bayyin**A**(**T**u)—'l-qayyim**A**(**T**i)—'l-bariyy**A**(**T**i)

(98:1-6)

(110) ʿah**DA**(**N**)—far**DA**(**N**)—ʿiz**ZA**(**N**)—ḍid**DA**(**N**)—'az**ZA**(**N**)—waf**DA**(**N**)—wir**DA**(**N**)

(19:78-86)

(111) 'l-bala**D**(i)—wala**D**(a)—kaba**D**(in)—'aḥa**D**(un)—luba**D**(an)—'aḥa**D**(un)

(90:2-7)

The situation is different with regard to the consonant combination of the rhymeme. Here, there are several deviations from the classical rule:

(A) *A change of status of the rawiyy*. The *rawiyy*, which is defined as "the only consonant of the rhymeme which is both necessary and sufficient for the existence of the rhymeme" (see 1.1.1), becomes here only an *optional* component, although desirable. A rhymeme constructed solely on the fixed location of its open syllable, with no *rawiyy* at all, is a common phenomenon of the Koranic rhymeme:

(112) qar**Ā**r(in)—yaš**Ā**'(u)—'l-baw**Ā**r(i)—'n-n**Ā**r(i)—k̲il**Ā**l(un)—'l-'anh**Ā**r(a)

(14:26-31)

(113) mat**Ā**b(i)—'l-mīʿ**Ā**d(a)—ʿiq**Ā**b(i)—h**Ā**d(i)—w**Ā**q(in)—'n-n**Ā**r(u)

(13:29-35)

The alteration of the *rawiyy* after every two to three rhyme members, usually with a phonetically similar consonant, is also widely used:

(114) 'l-ḥak**ĪM**(u)—'l-ʿaẓ**ĪM**(i)—'r-raḥ**ĪM**(u)—biwak**ĪL**(in)—'s-saʿ**ĪR**(i)—naṣ**ĪR**(in)—qad**ĪR**(un)

(42:2-9)

---

marbūṭa indicating the feminine gender in nouns and adjectives. In the transliteration these sounds were enclosed by parentheses.

(B) *A change in the status of the morphological suffix.* A certain deviation occurs from the classical rule, which states that a morphological suffix alone cannot be considered a rhymeme (see 1.1.2). We find that the most common rhymeme in the Koran is *ūn(a)*, or *īn(a)*, i.e., a rhymeme constructed on the morphological suffix indicating plural forms:

(115) yu'min**ŪN**(**A**)—'ẓẓālim**ŪN**(**A**)—taẓum**ŪN**(**A**)—mušrik**ĪN**(**A**)—yaftar**ŪN**(**A**)—'l'awwal**ĪN**(**A**)—yaš'ur**ŪN**(**A**)—'lmu'min**ĪN**(**A**) (6:20-28)

The rhyme **V CV** (1.1.4.1) is usually formed by words terminating with this particular suffix, thus its rhyming consonant is a one of a morphological nature; but when this rhymeme is retained throughout long units (such as the long *sūras*), it is alternately formed by words in which the rhyming consonant is a root consonant. In theory, it would seem that there is no deviation here from the classical rule, which does permit the rhyming of a morphological consonant with a root consonant. In practice, however, since the function of *rawiyy* was not always fulfilled by the same consonant, on occasion there might occur words whose root consonant was not *n* but another consonant, usually similar to it phonetically, rhyming in this rhymeme within the same text unit:

(116) yataḏakkar**ŪN**(a)—'l-mutaṭahhir**ĪN**(a)—'l-mu'min**ĪN**(a)—'al**ĪM**(un)—ḥal**ĪM**(un)—raḥ**ĪM**(un) (2:221-226)

There is no deviation from the *rawiyy*-rule with the other morphological suffixes; these are usually added to a root-consonant *rawiyy*.

(C) *A change with regard to the vowel of the rawiyy.* This vowel is no longer fixed in all the rhyme members, but changes according to the syntactical function of the rhyming word. This is of no real significance, however, as the vowel of the *rawiyy* is not pronounced, except in the indefinite, accusative case, in which instance the vowel is retained in all the rhyme members (see examples 100, 103).

These deviations from the classical rhyming scheme indicate a tendency in the *sağ'* of the Koran to minimize and obscure the phonetic repetition of the consonants in the rhymeme. Yet an opposite tendency, that of adding consonants (even if nonconsecutive) to the rhymeme, in a similar way to poetry (see 1.4.2) is also noticable:

(117) ā**MĪN**(un)—**M**ub**ĪN**(un)—ta**RǦ**i**MŪN**(a)—**M**u**ǦR**i**MŪ N**(a)—**M**uttabiʿ**ŪN**(a)—waʿuy**ŪN**(in)—**K**a**RĪM**(in)—fā**K**i**HĪN**(a)—**M**untaẓi**RĪN**(a)—'l-**M**u**HĪN**(a)

(44:18-30)

(118) **K̲ĀWIYA**(**T**in)—**BĀ**q**IYA**(**T**in)—**B**i'l-**K̲Ā**t**I'A**(**T**i)—**RĀBIYA**(**T**an)—'l-ǧ**ĀRIYA**(**T**i)—**WĀʿIYA**(**T**un)—**WĀḤIDA**(**T**un)—**WĀḤIDA**(**T**an)—'l-**WĀ**q**I'A**(**T**u)—**WĀ**h**IYA**(**T**un)

(69:7-15)

The preceding discussion shows that only with regard to the organization of its syllables does the rhymeme of the Koranic *saǧʿ* strictly adhere to the basic scheme of rhyming. The organization of consonants is more open and flexible, permitting many possible combinations concerning the number and order of the consonants.

We have already mentioned the difference between the long and short *sūra*s in rhymeme employment: while in the long *sūra*s the same rhymeme is usually retained throughout all (or most) of the *sūra*, the short *sūra*s employ a variety of rhymemes, which alternate within the *sūra*. Yet another distinction between the long and the short *sūra*s is that the verses (*āyāt*) of the long *sūra*s are quite lengthy and include an average of about twenty words each (many verses are even longer). In the short *sūra*s, the verses are short, including an average of about five words each. This fact has a marked effect on the syntax: while the rhyme members in the long *sūra*s very often include several sentences, every rhyme member in the short *sūra*s forms one single sentence, or only a part of a sentence. This explains the alternation of the rhymemes: in order to create a framework of rhymed prose for the lengthy multi-sentenced rhyme members, it seems necessary to retain the same rhymeme throughout the whole text-unit (the *sūra*). Without that, the framework would have been obliterated and a text of regular prose would have resulted. On the other hand, when the rhyme members are short, often several of them must be grouped together to form one complete sentence; the effect of a rhymed text is easily created and retained in this case, and the rhymed prose can be varied by the alternation of rhymemes.

The creation of a framework of rhymed prose in the long *sūra*s is actually more complex and achieved in several ways. The most prominent method is, as stated, the retention of one rhymeme throughout the entire *sūra*, and, even the employment of the same rhymeme in most of the long *sūra*s. This leads to two additional phenomena of opposite character. First, a certain flexibility exists in following the basic rhyming scheme with regard to phonetic and morphological composition of the rhymeme. We find, for example, a rhymeme of the morphological suffixes **ĪN(A)** and **ŪN(A)**, or a *rawiyy* which is realized in a rhymeme not by one, but by several consecutive consonants, usually phonetically closed. Such flexibility acts undoubtedly to reduce the rhyming effect, especially if measured against the poetic norm, where the rules are meticulously followed even in *qaṣīdas* exceeding 100 lines.

In opposition, we encounter an opposite trend: that of strengthening the effect of rhyming by distinctly enlarging the rhyming-unit. Syntactically, the phrases are characterized by a regular syntactic pattern, or, more precisely, several basic syntactic patterns, which repeat regularly with only a change in the words: either all the words occasionally change from one ending phrase to another, or only some of the words change. In many instances, the verses of the long and medium-length *sūra*s terminate in a short phrase, usually of two to four words, which is, in fact, an independent syntactic and semantic unit; the last word of this phrase carries the rhymeme.[37] In this sense, the ending phrases behave—and probably also function—as the formulas of the oral text (see Lord 1974:47). Semantically, the ending phrases are characterised by having a general unspecific meaning, which enables them to be both easily attached to different verses and to conform to almost every context; their meaning modifies each time to the particular context. For example:

(119) *'inna 'llāha ʿalā kulli šay'in qadīrun*: "Indeed God can do all things"
(120) *wa'llāhu sarīʿu 'lʿiqāb*: "And God is quick to punish"
(121) *in kuntum taʿlamūn/tu'minūn*: "If you will know (if you had known); or, if you will believe"

[37] See Bell's discussion (Bell 1953:69-70) on these phrases. Bell considers only phrases of this type in which the subject is Allah. His approach is also different from the one presented here. He recognizes that the function of these phrases is to create the possibility of rhyme, yet he does not explain why an entire phrase is needed for this purpose. Bell also points out that there are certain groups of verses, such as verses 12-14 in *sūra* 23, from which, if the last phrase is omitted from each verse, one finds a passage of rhymed prose rhyming with a different rhymeme. This fact proves, in his opinion, that the original unit in the Koran is the short passage and not the sūra. Bell touches upon these questions in the framework of his discussion on the structure of the Koran. His interest in the Koran's structure is an historical one, and his general claim is that an analysis of the Koran's structure proves its eariy editing, perhaps even by Muhammad himself (*ibid*.:82-97).

(122) *falahu ʿadābun ʿalīmun*: "And a painful torture (is in store) for him"
(123) *walā yahtadūna*: "And they do not walk in the straight path"

Such independent units appear with great frequency only at the end of verses. Nevertheless, ending units which are more semantically dependent on their preceding ones, even to the degree that they cannot be semantically replaced, also appear at the end of verses. For example:

(124) *ʾūlāʾika ḥabiṭat ʾaʿmāluhum wafī ʾn-nāri hum k̲ālidūn*: "Those—their works have failed them and in the fire they shall dwell forever" (9:17)
(125) *wayaʾba ʾllāhu ʾan yutimma nūrahu walaw kariha ʾl-kāfirūn*: "and God refuses but to perfect his light though the unbelievers be averse" (9:32)

We find in the Koran a strong tendency to establish such semantically and syntactically independent units in positions of the rhyme. Where these units repeat—whether completely or only partially—they help to intensify the effect of the rhymeme by adding other dimensions of repetition to that of sound, which is no doubt lost in the long verses: the repetition of syntactical structure and of meaning. The common rhymeme of the long verses is particularly sound-poor, and the distance between two rhyming words is so great that the element of sound repetition in the rhymeme loses its impact. Increasing the rhyming unit proportionately to the length of the rhyme members (the verses), rather than adding more consonants and vowels to the rhymeme, seems an unusual solution to the problem of creating a rhyming effect in a prose text which strives to distinguish itself as unique.

It must be emphasized again, however, that what we have described so far is no more than a Koranic trend, certainly not the rule of the Koran, and, further, that this trend applies chiefly to the medium and long *sūra*s, in which the same rhymeme is retained throughout. The formulaic sentences can also be detected in short rhyme members and sometimes even constituting the entire rhyme member (as in *sūra* 15, for example). The rhymeme itself in such cases is ample enough to create the effect of rhyme. The short *sūra*s, by contrast, do not retain one rhymeme throughout, but rather alternate them after every irregular number of rhyme members. The question of what exactly determines the alternation of the rhymemes still remains to be answered; the answer, however, should address the semantic relationships between the rhyme members. These relationships will be discussed in the section on the *maqāmāt*, the most sophisticated form of rhymed prose in Arabic literature.

3.2.2. *Rhymed prose in the early Abbasid period*

The rhymed prose of the Koran remained a unique phenomenon in Arabic literature. Composing rhymed prose became a common literary habit with court clerks and men of letters in the Abbasid period, but they were not supposed to look to the Koran as their model. The famous theological idea of *Iʿǧāz al-Qurʾān* (which stated that the Koran is inimitable both in content and style), intended to protect it against imitations, indeed served to lend it a supreme, exemplary theological status. But at the same time this idea also served to push the Koran outside the literary arena, by preventing it from being an inspiration for actual literary production. Writing in the style of the Koran could only be considered in a context of an "imitation" of the holy book, and therefore necessarily be condemned as an act of heresy. Only few dared to try and do so, and then apparently as an act of challenging the supreme theological status of the Koran, rather than the literary options it could offer for writing.[38]

The *saǧʿ* of the Abbasid priod is therefore remote from that of the Koran, certainly of its medium and long *sūra*s, and closer in style to that of the Ǧāhili *saǧʿ*. The Abbasid period witnessed the flourishing of the formal use of rhymed prose for religious sermons (*k̲uṭab*) as well as for secular purposes, such as official correspondence, prefaces to books, and short monographical treatises. The material to be discussed here is primarily from the time of Hārūn al-Rašīd (d. 809) and his sons Amīn and Maʾmūn (d. 833). This was in fact the formative period for the rhymed prose of classical Arabic literature; those characteristics which further developed and intensified in subsequent periods are already expressed at this time.

[38] The well-known examples of al-Muk̲tār, al-Mutanabbī, al-Ḥallāǧ, should apparently be referred to in a political, religious, or ideological context and not in a literary context. Ibn al-Muqaffaʿ, however, did seem to challenge the *faṣāḥa* of the Koran, and so also the Andalusi Yaḥyā b. Ḥakam al-Ġazāl (and even al-Maʿarrī, if indeed the accusation is true that he attempted to imitate the Koran) (Suyūṭī 1970:1, 243-244; 1951:2, 119).

The rhymemes of this type of *sağʿ* are located at the end of the syntactical unit—a sentence or phrase—and they alter after every two and sometimes three rhyme members. Yet the rhyming system is not comprehensive, as there are non-rhyming members occurring between groups of rhyme members. The rhyming scheme is very flexible as compared not only with that of poetry, but even with that of the Koran:

Vowels: The obligatory order of the syllables and vowels, which determines the five types of rhymemes in the Arabic rhyming scheme, is only applied here as a general framework. All the rhymemes do appear, and are usually retained, although not necessarily. The rhymemes tend to preserve long open syllables before the *rawiyy* (rhymemes **V CV** [1.1.4.1], **V** cv **CV** [1.1.4.3]) more frequently than long closed syllables (rhymemes **vc** **CV** [1.1.4.2], **vc** cv **CV** [1.1.4.4.]), or short vowels (rhymeme cv cv **CV** [1.1.4.5]). We find rhymemes such as:

(126) 'ẓ-ẓafa**R**(a)—bi'n-naṣ**R**(i) (Ṣafwat 1937:3, 99)
(127) 'l-k̲i**BR**a(**TI**)—'t-tağ**R**i**B**a(**TI**) (*ibid.*:3, 135)
(128) dāk̲i**LA**(**N**)—muqbi**LA**(**N**) (*ibid.*:2, 410)

Consonants: The particular arrangement of consonants within the rhymeme is not subject to any binding rule, as is the case in poetry. There is no regularity in the number of consonants participating in the rhymeme, nor in their location or morphological composition. The rhymemes usually have a *rawiyy* which is a root consonant, but additional consonant arrangments also appear:

(A) Occasionally the determinig element in the rhymeme (1.1, 1.1.1) is not the *rawiyy*, but rather the grammatical pattern of the rhyming words, which determines a certain syllabic arrangement. A *rawiyy*-consonant may appear in some of the rhyme members, not necessarily in all of them. The grammatical pattern is the minimal condition for the existence of the rhymeme in such a case:

(129) biʿilmih(i)—bi'amrih(i)—ḥaqqih(i)—d̲ikrih(i) (*ibid.*:3, 97)
(130) rağul**A**(**N**)—sayf**A**(**N**) (*ibid.*:3, 99)
(131) ẓul**MA**(**N**)—ṣan**MA**(**N**)—ḥaqq**A**(**N**)—munkar**A**(**N**) (*ibid.*:3, 99)
(132) 'l-'ak̲l**Ā**k(I)—li's-sad**Ā**d(I) (*ibid.*:3, 135)
(133) 'l-ʿaqab**A**(**TI**)—'l-hiğr**A**(**TI**)—'ṣ-ṣuff**A**(**TI**) (*ibid.*:3, 197)

(B) In some rhymemes the location of the recurring consonants is not fixed; or else the recurring consonant is not the third root-consonant in all the rhyme members, as is the rule for the *rawiyy*:

(134) muta**F**arriqa(**TIN**)—muḵtali**F**a(**TIN**)—mu'tali**F**a(**tin**) (*ibid.*:3, 99)
(The additional rhyming consonants ***m***, ***t***, in this example are morphological, the consonant ***l*** is a root consonant.)
(135) bifa**Ḍ**l(**IN**)—biba'**Ḍ**(**IN**) (*ibid.*:3, 121)
(136) k**ĀS**ida(**TUN**)—ḵ**ĀS**i'a(**TUN**) (*ibid.*:3, 189)
(137) ḥab**Ā**'ilu**H**(**U**)—ḍam**Ā**'iru**H**(**U**) (*ibid.*:3, 188)

(C) Some rhymemes have more than a single root-consonant, but none of these root-consonants is necessarily the third one:

(138) 'l-ḵa**SF**(a)—bi'l-'a**SF**(i) (*ibid.*:3, 99)
(139) **M**ab**SŪ**ṭA(**TIN**)—**M**aq**SŪM**a(**TIN**) (*ibid..*:3, 121)
(140) 'r-ra**ǦĀ**'(u)—'l-wa**FĀ**'(u)—**Ǧ**a**FĀ**'(in) (*ibid.*:3, 177)
(141) 'l-'a'**RĀB**(i)—**R**ik**ĀB**(in) (*ibid.*:3, 197)

(D) In some rhymemes only morphological consonants (one or two) rhyme:

(142) biqudra**TIH**(**I**)—maši'a**TIH**(**I**) (*ibid.*:3, 98)
(143) kaṯura**T**—ǧalla**T** (*ibid.*:3, 176)
(144) qulūbu**H**u**M**—fī**H**i**M**—min**H**u**M** (*ibid.*:3, 197)

The framework of the rhymed prose rhymeme is thus quite flexible, and allows for a variable sound-identity within a range in which only the minimum and maximum are fixed. The minimum is produced by the mere selection of repeated syllable-arrangement, and the maximum—by engaging all but one consonant in the rhymeme (in which case the rhymeme would encompass a word and even two, while in poetry it encompasses only a part of a word). This freedom to choose the measure and arrangement of sounds within a rhymeme is autonomous for each individual rhymeme, so that sound-poor rhymemes may exist side by side with sound-rich rhymemes in the same text.

3.2.3. *The* maqāmāt *of al-Hamadānī and al-Ḥarīrī*

Rhymed prose, exercised and developed in the writings of the court scribes at the height of the Abbasid period (late eighth, early ninth century), continued to be widely used during the following two centuries in most fields of abstract writing. In the eleventh and in the beginning of the twelfth centuries rhymed prose was combined with a new literary model of fiction to create the genre of the *maqāma* (ch. 1).

The rhyming scheme of the *maqāma* is basically an elaboration of that found in the earlier Abbasid rhymed prose, in the sense that it adheres to more rigid sound arrangements in the rhymemes, and allows for less freedom of choice within the range of possibilities from minimum to maximum. The trend toward a firmer organization of the rhymeme—in contrast with other facets of the rhymed prose—is expressed in a fuller adherence to the classical rhyming norm. The syllable organization of the rhymeme is totally preserved, all five types of rhymemes appear, and they are mutually exclusive, as in poetry. As regards consonants, the classical norm is strictly followed in al-Ḥarīrī's work, and almost completely in the work of his predecessor al-Hamaḏānī. There is also a clear tendency to add extra consonants (root or morphological) to the *rawiyy* in al-Hamaḏānī's work, while there is almost no rhymeme without at least two consonants (usually root) in al-Ḥarīrī's work. The additional consonants before the *rawiyy* have no fixed location. The rhyming scheme in the *maqāma* demands a maximum of sound similarity in the rhymeme, which is much more than is demanded by the basic rhyming scheme of poetry, but similar to that of *waṣf* poems (1.4.2); this similarity in sound is certainly more than what the rhyming scheme of the earlier rhymed prose demanded.

The freedom to choose the measure and arrangement of sounds for each individual rhymeme is followed in the *maqāma* as well; here, too, sound-poor rhymemes appear side by side with sound-rich rhymemes, without any restrictions.

3.3. *The basic rhyming norm of rhymed prose*

The three examples of rhymed prose discussed thus far represent its major appearances in classical Arabic literature. An examination of these examples shows that unlike poetry, in which a restrictive rhyming scheme dictates set rules, the norm of rhymed prose leaves the choice of how to organize the sounds in the rhymeme up to the writer, setting an extremely wide range of possibilities. Only the boundaries are fixed: they are the minimum and maximum sounds a rhymeme can hold, beyond which there can actually be no rhyme. The minimum of sounds in the rhymeme is a set arrangement of syllables, with no recurring consonants (and in an extreme case, without even a recurring short vowel); whereas the maximum of sounds is the recurrence of all the consonants and vowels of the rhymeme (a word and beyond), the difference being shifted to the semantic or morphological domain:

(145) **Ṭ-ṬĀQATĪ—'Ṭ-ṬĀQATI** "window—capacity" (Hamaḏānī 1962:127)

(146) **BARQAʿĪD—BARQA ʿĪD** "*Barqa ʿīd* (name of a place)"—"shine crescent of moon indicating the beginning of the feast" (Ḥarīrī 1929:60)

Within this flexible norm, some rhyme systems are more bound to rules than others. The rhyming system of the Koran is more strict than that of early rhymed prose (seventh-ninth century) but less so than that of the *maqāma*. Adherence to each particular rule also varies among the different occurrences of rhymed prose. The rhyming system of the Koran is stringent mainly with regard to the long vowels and less so with regard to the consonants, whereas the rhyming system of the *maqāma* is stringent in its vowels and consonants alike, and particularly in its consonants. Historically speaking, the later the period, the closer the adherence to the rules of rhyme, or the stricter the application of the norm.

3.4. *The principle of rhymeme alternation in rhymed prose*

As it was stated at the beginning of this chapter, the major difference between the rhyming scheme of poetry and that of prose is that poetry retains a single rhymeme throughout a poem, whereas the rhymemes of rhymed prose changes after every few rhyme members. In Western poetry, the alternation of rhymemes is part of a well-established poetic tradition, in which the order of the rhymemes as well as the number of rhyme members in each rhymeme are dictated by pre-set patterns (ABAB, ABBA, CDDC, and so forth). In Arabic rhymed prose no pre-set patterns of alternation exist, and nothing is therefore regular—neither the number of rhyme members within the same rhymeme, nor the number or order of rhymemes which may appear in a text.

What then determines the alternation of the rhymemes in the Arabic rhymed prose? Whereas in Western poetry the patterns of rhymeme alternation are imposed by poetic tradition, regardless of the semantic structure of the text, in Arabic rhymed prose the alternation is determined by semantic principles, which actually create the sequence of the text.[39] My contention is that any group of rhyme members which share the same rhymeme constitutes not only a single rhyming unit, but also *a unit of meaning*, in which the rhyme members are joined together according to semantic principles. Thus any unit of meaning added to the sequence of the text would necessarily rhyme with a separate rhymeme.

This would be best illustrated by a text from the *maqāmāt*, which is structured upon narration rather than upon an outline of ideas. Phrases whose endings are marked by the same rhyme ("rhyme members") are joined together to form a unit of meaning on the basis of two semantic principles:

(A) *The repetition principle.* Every two or more successive phrases which are syntactically homogeneous and semantically synonymous (that is, convey the same information in different formulation) form a unit of meaning marked by a common rhymeme. Any additional phrase will always repeat the information already conveyed in the previous phrase(s) in the unit. The impression is that of redundancy, which perhaps serves a rhetorical or ornamental function, but takes no part in furthering the narration. The following examples are taken from *al-maqāma al-maḏīriyya* of al-Hamaḏānī:

(147) *daʿānī baʿḍu ʾt-tuǧǧāri ilā maḏīratin waʾanā bibaġdāda* ***walazimanī mulāzamata ʾl-ġar*****ĪM(I)**
waʾl-kalbi liʾaṣḥābi ʾl-raq**ĪB(I)**
ilā an aǧabtuhu ilayhā waqumnā faǧaʿala ṭūla ʾṭ-ṭarīqi ***yutnī ʿalā zaw*****ǦATIH(I)**
wayufaddīhā bimuh**ǦATIH(I)**
wayaṣifu ḥidqahā fī ṣanʿti**HĀ**
wataʾannuqahā fī ṭabḵi**HĀ**
One of the merchants invited me to porridge when I was in Baghdad, **and he stuck to me like a creditor**
and like the dog to the sleepers of Ephesus[40]
until I accepted [his invitation], and we went [to his home]. All the way **he was praising his wife**

[39] Rhyme may function as an organizing principle of a poetic text also in modern poetry. In that case, this function is a reaction against the exclusively embellishing function of rhyme in the poetry of the earlier generations.

[40] An allusion to the legend of the seven sleepers of Ephesus, cf. Koran, *sūrat al-kahf* [18], verse 9.

and laying his life down for her
and describing her talent in her work
and her cleverness in cooking.
(Hamaḏānī 1962:123-124)

This passage comprises three units of meaning, each composed of two phrases and marked by its own individual rhymeme. Each phrase in the first unit contains a simile of the same subject: the extent of the merchant's clinging to the hero of the *maqāma*. In the second unit the two phrases are synonymous, and their common meaning is the merchant's praising of his wife. The two phrases of the third unit are also synonymous, and in both of them the merchant describes his wife as a woman of valor, who is talented in cooking. The second and third units are similar in that they both speak in praise of the wife, yet they constitute two separate units of meaning, because the third unit adds more specific information, which is highly relevant to the narration: The wife's cooking skills are important because the merchant invites his guest to eat porridge in his home, and the two are on their way to the meal.

(B) *The complementation principle*: Every two or more consecutive phrases which complement each other in the information they convey, form a unit of meaning. The phrases are usually syntactically heterogeneous, and each phrase adds new information to that given by the previous phrase, or qualifies it in some manner. The complementation can be based on a variety of metonymic relations: causality, concatenation, space and time shifts, part and whole relation. When phrases join together on the basis of the complementation principle, they form a single continuity of meaning and often of syntax as well, so that if one of the phrases is omitted, the result would be a lack of information or elliptic syntax. For example:

(148) *kam tuqaddiru yā mawlāya unfiqu ʿalā kulli dārin minhā?* ***qulhu takmĪN(AN) in lam taʿrifhu yaqĪN(AN)***
How much do you estimate, sir, that I spent on every room [of the house]? **Give an estimation**
if you do not know with certainty. (*ibid.*:126-127)

(149) ***fa'akaḏtuhu minhā ikḏata K̲alS(IN)***
wa'štaraytuhu biṯamanin baK̲S(IN)
I took [the necklace] from her slyly
and [so] I bought it at a low price. (*ibid.*:132)

(150) ***wanaʿūdu ilā ḥadīṯi 'l-maḍĪRA(TI)***

> ***waqad ḥāna waqtu 'ẓ-ẓah*ĪRA(TI)**
> **Let us return to the story of the porridge**
> **because the noon hour has already arrived**. *(ibid.*:134)

It should be emphasized that the complementation principle works here to link phrases into a *unit of meaning*. Any information added by a phrase therefore remains within the boundaries of the one unit of meaning. Only the conjoining of the *units* of meaning creates the text continuity and contributes to advance the narration. Moreover, information which advances the narration is often given by a single sentence with no rhymeme, or by a long sentence of which only the last part constitutes a rhymed phrase within a unit of meaning (example 147).

These two semantic principles which function to build a unit of meaning, or, in other words, to bring several rhyme members under the same rhymeme, are not mutually exclusive. A unit of meaning can be clearly constructed on the basis of one principle or the other, but often enough we can find both principles working together, with various degrees of dominance over one another. Both the repetition and the complementation principles are in fact manifestations, in a very specific field (i.e., the influence of meaning on rhyme) of the two basic principles which serve to form practically any sequence of the language: the principle of equivalence and the principle of contiguity (or the metaphorical and metonymic principles as termed by Roman Jakobson [see Jakobson 1956:55-82]).

The principles of repetition and complementation function in fact not only on the level of linking several rhymed phrases into one unit of meaning, but also on the level of linking units of meaning into an entire text. The making of the text continuity in the *maqāmāt* is beyond the scope of this discussion on rhyme; suffice it to say that the extent to which one principle or the other is employed in the creation of the text continuity can serve as a reliable indication of stylistic differences between the two great creators of Arabic *maqāmāt*—al-Hamaḏānī and al-Ḥarīrī.

In general, al-Hamaḏānī tends to make more use of the complementation principle, whereas al-Ḥarīrī prefers the repetition principle. This observation is based on their respective use of the principles on two textual levels: the "lower" level, of linking rhymed phrases into a unit of meaning, and the "upper" level, of linking units of meaning to form the text continuity. On the level of forming units of meaning, al-Hamadānī uses both principles, with a slight preference for the complementation principle. On the level of linking units of meaning into a text, he uses rather exclusively the complementation principle. Al-Ḥarīrī too makes use of both principles in the "lower" level of the joining of rhymed phrases, but in the "upper" level he prefers the repetition principle. In fact, he usually makes a double use of the repetition principle, as he tends to split the rhymed phrases by creating internal or sub-rhymemes in the following ways:

(A) A complementation group is split, and each of its phrase is joined with additional phrases to create a repetition sub-group:

(151) ***falammā 'ḍṭaramat bimaḥḍarihi 'š-šahaw*ĀT(I)** /
*waqarimat ilā maḵbarihi 'l-lahaw***ĀT(I)** /
*wašārafa an tušanna 'alā šarbihi 'l-ġār***ĀT(I)** /
*wayunādā 'inda nahbihi yā la'ṯ-ṯār***ĀT(I)** //
***našaza abū zaydin ka'l-mağ*NŪN(I)** /
*watabā'ada 'anhu tabā'uda 'ḍ-ḍabbi mina 'n-***NŪN(I)**
And when they became inflamed with desire at the sight [of the goblet] /
and their tongues hungered to experience it /
and their ranks were about to raid it /
and shouts were raised in the midst of their plunder—Oh! vengeance!
Then Abū Zayd sprung up like a madman /
and moved far from it, like the lizard is far from the whale.[41]
(*al-maqāma al-sanğariyya*, Ḥarīrī 1929:170-171)

The overall unit of meaning (built upon the complementation principle) is: "...and when the goblet was brought—Abū Zayd sprung up and moved far from it." This unit is split into two distinct units, whereby each one is built upon the repetition principle with its own rhymeme. In this example, the repetition principle functions on the level of linking rhymed phrases into a unit of meaning.

(B) Each phrase of a repetition group is split to create a complementation sub-group:

(152) ***familtu li*MUğĀWARATIH(I)**/ ***ilā* MUḥĀWARATIH(I)**
*wa'ġtarartu bi***MUkĀŠARATHI(I)**/ *fī* **MU'ĀŠARATIH(I)**

[41] An allusion to the Arab proverb, "When the lizard approaches the whale"—referring to two things which are impossible to bring together (see *Ğāḥiẓ* 1968:2, 434).

wa'stahwatnī kudratu **DiMNATIH(I)** / *limu***NāDaMATIH(I)**
wa'ağratnī kud'atu **SiMATIH(I)** / *bimunā***SaMATIH(I)**
I was inclined to be in his company /
in order to converse with him
and I was tempted into joking with him /
while I was in his company
and I was deceived by his appearance /
into being his drinking partner
and his majestic look deluded me—/
into whispering secrets with him (*ibid.*:172)

The overall unit of meaning here (built upon the repetition principle) is: "I was tempted to become friendly with him." This breaks down into four units of meaning of two rhymed phrases each, which are built on the complementation principle. In this example, the repetition principle functions on the level of linking units of meaning to create the text continuity.

Structurally speaking, al-Ḥarīrī relies upon the repetition principle on both levels of text continuity. Historically speaking, what al-Ḥarīrī actually accomplished was to break down al-Hamaḏānī's units into smaller units, which sometimes have minimal rhymed phrases consisting of just one word.

The differences regarding the use of the two principles in the writings of both authors can be displayed in the following diagram:

	al-Hamadānī	**al-Ḥarīrī**
Principle used to join rhymed phrases	repetition complementation	complementation repetition
Principle used to join units	complementation (mainly)	repetition (mainly)

As stated, al-Hamaḏānī makes more use of the complementation principle whereas al-Ḥarīrī resorts mainly to the repetition principle. More specifically this means that al-Hamaḏānī uses predominantly the *complementation principle* on both levels of the text continuity, but mainly on the "upper" level; whereas the later al-Ḥarīrī resorts predominantly to the *repetition principle* on both levels of text continuity, and again, mainly on the "upper" level. As the complementation principle functions through juxtaposition, while the repetition principle functions by way of similarity, the dominant use of each of the two principles has significant effect upon the style and structure of each author's *maqāmāt*. Al-Hamaḏānī's *Maqāmāt* thus display a better structure of plot (a typical metonymic pattern) than that of al-Ḥarīrī's *Maqāmāt*, where we find an emphasis on a variety of eloquent expressions (founded on metaphoric patterns).

These differences, and especially the fact that the repetition principle was favoured by al-Ḥarīrī, the later and more popular of the two, have a significant implication on the development of fiction in classical Arabic literature. They offer a new perspective on the often discussed question of why did fiction in classical Arabic literature fail to gain a level of prestige and development comparable with that of fiction in European literature (cf. ch. 1, section 4).

PART FOUR

CONCLUSIONS AND PERSPECTIVES

4.1. *The aesthetic norm of rhyming*

The institution of rhyme, that is, the arrangement of linguistic material according to sound-characteristics, is intrinsically dependent upon an aesthetic norm which determines what sound-arrangement is to be considered "pleasing", or "euphonic" to the listener. The classical Arabic rhyming system has its own characteristic aesthetic norm. A close examination of the diachronic changes in this norm, in both poetry and prose, reveals that they occurred exclusively in connection to consonants: in their quantity, arrangement, and morphological origin (more specifically, belonging to a root or a declension). The structure of the syllables, and the implications of this structure on the long open vowels, is the one consistent element of the rhyming system throughout all the classical period. The conclusion of Part One of this chapter (presented in section 1.3) concerning the aesthetic norm is thus strengthened: the basic effect of classical Arabic rhyme is created by the regularity of the syllables (and by the location of the long vowel in the rhymeme). This effect is intensified by the repetition of grammatical forms. The regularity of the syllables is more relevant to the rhyming effect than is the quantity of identical sounds in the rhymeme (determined by the consonants), which varies according to the literary genre and the time period.

4.2. *The relationships between the formal elements of the rhymed text—rhyme, metre, repetition of syntactical structures—in poetry and prose*

The repetition principle was defined in Part Three as "a manifestation in a very specific field—that of the influence of meaning on rhyme—of a more general principle which serves to form practically any sequence in language ... the principle of equivalence" (3.4). The principle of equivalence, which combines several linguistic elements into a sequence provided that they are equivalent in meaning, functions on the non-semantic aspects of the language as well, as demonstated in the discussion on rhyme. Other non-semantic manifestations of this principle in the rhymed text are metre, and repetition of syntactical structures within the rhymed phrases. These non-semantic manifestations of the equivalence principle maintain a "balance of power" relationship in poetry and rhymed prose, which can be described as follows:

Rhyme. The manifestations of rhyme are discussed in the first and third chapters, and may be summarized aas follows:

The rhyming norm in poetry is fixed and stringent: 1) One rhymeme is sustained throughout the poem. 2) The permissible minimum and maximum of sounds in the rhymeme are clearly determined; apart from a few exceptional cases, the minimum is exactly equivalent to the maximum. 3) Almost no diachronic change occurs; the same rhyming norm exists in a large corpus of poetry throughout the classical period.

By contrast, the rhyming norm in rhymed prose is rather flexible: 1) The rhymemes alternate after every few rhyme members. 2) The rhyming norm applies to the widest minimal and maximal range of sounds permitted by the structure of the Arabic language. 3) The rhyming norm is subject to diachronic changes, as observed in the three examples considered in Part Three—the Koran, the seventh-ninth century rhymed prose, and the *maqāmāt.*

Metre. The metre is an obligatory condition upon which a classical text is to be defined as a poem. The metric system of poetry is a fairly fixed one; even its deviations are predetermined. In rhymed prose, on the other hand, there is no metre.

Repetition of syntactical structures. In poetry: because the vowel of the *rawiyy*, which is a syntactical indicator, is included in the rhymeme, one may assume that this would influence the order of words in a verse. For example, a *rawiyy* having the vowel ***u*** indicates that the rhyming word functions as the subject or the predicate in the sentence; and since the rhyming word is the last word in the verse, a sentence is formed in which either the subject or the predicate are located at the line-end, whereby its other parts are placed before. It is an obvious assumption that in such a case, an elliptic syntax would result. Yet, there are almost no discernible instances of distortion in the syntactical order due to rhyme. When the order of the words does change,[42] these changes are all within

---

[42] For instance, Abū Huwās's verse,
faǧā'at bihā ka'š-šamsi yaḥkī šu'ā'uhā

the framework of the general phenomenon in the classical Arabic language referred to by Bloch as "Sperrung" (see Bloch 1946:114-153): the separation of words, or word phrases, where syntax obligates them to remain together. Such cases are not frequent however, at least not in those particular cases where it is clear that the separation is due to rhyme. Through syndetic and asyndetic structures, Arabic syntax allows for the formation of new complete sentences at the ends of lines, in proximity to the place of rhyme. Poetry exploits this option, and thus cases of elliptic syntax are avoided.

In rhymed prose, however, the syntax is highly bound, and the same syntactical structure tends to repeat in all the rhyme members which share a common rhymeme. This tendency is especially common where rhyme members are joined together on the basis of the repetition principle. Al-Ḥarīrī seemed to even value this as a poetic quality, as he attempted to repeat syntactical structures as often as possible. Yet a repeating syntactical structure is sometimes found where rhyme members are joined together on the basis of the complementation principle as well. The repetition of the same syntactical structure leads to a repetition of grammatical forms, thus creating a certain occasional "metre", due to the repetition of the same syllabic arrangement. A more detailed discussion on these matters is, however, beyond the scope of this study.

The relationships between the formal elements in poetry and in rhymed prose can be summarized in the following table:

	rhyme	**metre**	**repetition of syntactical structures**
poetry	fixed norm	set	free syntax
rhymed prose	flexible norm	none	fettered syntax

We may well conclude that these three non-semantic manifestations of the equivalence principle maintain a "balance of power" of two

šuʿāʾa ʾṯ-ṯurayyā fī zuǧāǧin lahā ḥusnā
"She [the wine-selle] brought the wine shining in its glass container like a sun whose rays imitate in their beauty the rays of light comong from a glass lamp"(Abū Nuwās 1962:49. see chapter 3, example 4). The syntactical unit which is split is: *yaḥkī šuʿāʾuhā šuʿāʾa ʾṯ-ṯurayyā ḥusnā*: "whose rays imitate in their beauty the rays of light coming from a glass lamp". Into this unit the following unit was inserted: *fī zuǧāǧin lahā*: "in its glass container," and the word *ḥusnā* "in their beauty" was moved to the place of rhyme. See additional examples: *Sībawayhī* 1881:31.

against one: in poetry, when two of such manifestations (rhyme, metre) are fixed, the third (repetition of syntactical structures) is variable; and in rhymed prose, when the third manifestation is fixed, the other two are variable, to the point of non-existence.

CHAPTER FIVE

STAGNATION AND RECOVERY: THE INTRODUCTION OF ARABIC LITERARY MODELS INTO TENTH CENTURY JEWISH LITERATURE *

The Methodological and Conceptual Framework

The contacts of Jewish literature with Arabic between the tenth and the thirteenth centuries, when the centres of Jewish culture in the East, North Africa and Spain were under Arabic rule, are notable in the history of Jewish literature. Today, after more than one hundred years of study, they are considered to be common knowledge both by professionals and educated laymen. Yet, despite their salience, during this period the contacts have never been a central issue in medieval Jewish literary research.

There are three main reasons for this:

First, ever since the beginning of scholarly interest in ancient and medieval Jewish literature in early nineteenth century, scholars were largely occupied with editing the gradually emerging texts: at first texts that were found in European collections and libraries, then later those that were discovered in the Geniza. Establishing the corpus of Jewish literature was an essential stage, prior to which it was impossible to hypothesize about any premodern Jewish literature.

Second, scholarly activity concerning medieval Jewish literature sprang up and developed in a cultural context characterized by a romantic and nationalistic spirit, resulting in an ideological attitude towards the question of Arabic influence over Jewish, mainly Hebrew, literature. Modern Jewish interest in ancient and medieval Hebrew texts was part of the awakening of nationalist feelings, in which Hebrew texts were considered to be national literary creations written in the language of the nation, Hebrew.

* This chapter summarizes some of the main hypotheses and arguments presented in my Hebrew book (Drory 1988). The reader will find there an extensive account of the material on which these arguments are based, and a comprehensive bibliography.

Within this ideological framework, there was naturally no interest in demonstrating which Arabic models were involved in the creation of the Hebrew texts, apart from the recognition of basic "Arabic influence". Again, this scholarly activity was carried out in the environment of Romanticism, when everything "original" was heavily praised, while all "influence" was condemned. It was no great honour for a text, not to mention a whole body of literature, to be exposed as "influenced," rather than being considered "original." These views played a large part in the general lack of interest in discovering or pointing out contacts with Arabic literature.

Third, the only research methods available until very recently (the historical-philological and comparative literature approaches), did not provide an adequate theoretical framework for a fruitful discussion of the contacts between the two literatures. The research methods available for dealing with "literary influence" merely compared, on the basis of certain similarities, simple and homogeneous units, or distinct topoi, etc., usually regardless of their literary and historical context. Such approaches supplied neither the theoretical framework, nor the practical methods, for discussing the issues of literary contacts in a broader context than the individual text. The historical-philological method even developed a clear dislike for units larger, or more complex, than the individual text, and thus avoided generalized hypotheses.

These factors made it impossible for the subject to receive the attention it deserved. Over the last century, many details relating to contact of Jewish literature with Arabic were assiduously collected and published, but in the absence of a theory that could give significance to such research by providing basic concepts of dealing with inter-literary contacts, the collected information has remained largely unused. It has not contributed significantly to our understanding of the role that Arabic literature played for Jewish literature of that period.

It is time for this situation, in which widespread awareness of the contacts between Jewish and Arabic literature exists alongside very limited professional interest, to be corrected. First, today there is finally a large corpus of both medieval literatures. Second, in recent years new literary theories have developed based on structuralist and functionalist thinking, which provide us with conceptual and theoretical frameworks to re-evaluate the contacts between the two literatures. In particular, the polysystem theory, and within it, the concept of interference of inter-cultural relations, have made possible new approaches to the contacts between Jewish and Arabic literatures. These methods help to clarify what caused Jewish literature of the period to seek out contact with Arabic, and how these contacts were manifested; in other words, what role did such contact play in the development of Jewish literature. The answer to these questions will no doubt contribute to a more complete understanding of this chapter in the history of Jewish literature.

One of the first questions that arises when re-examining the contact between the two literatures is: when did it begin? The earliest surviving Spanish Hebrew texts (written in the second half of the tenth century by Menaḥem ben Sarūq, Dunaš ben Labraṭ and their disciples), already show clear indications of Arabic literary models, while Hebrew texts written in the Moslem East only a short time earlier (in the first half of the tenth century, e.g., by Saʿadya Gaon) hardly show any such readily identifiable signs of Arabic models. Why are such models conspicuously absent in Jewish literature of the Moslem East, where Jews had lived among Arabic culture for three hundred years (during two hundred years of which there was a fully developed Arabic literature), while the models were so prevalent in Spain?

When and where can the first contacts with Arabic literature actually be found? In Spain, where the impact of Arabic literature is visible from the inception of Jewish literature there, indicating, so to speak, an advanced stage of contact, or rather in the East, where there are hardly any such Arabic signs in the Hebrew texts? Such questions call for a re-examination of the accepted view of medieval Arabic-Hebrew literary contacts, and demand new consideration of the earlier stage of Jewish literature under Muslim rule in the East.

Studies seeking to understand the beginnings of Jewish-Arabic literary contact in the East tend to work on the assumption that trends similar to those found in the Spanish Golden Era will be revealed, only in embryonic (that is, in simpler and more restricted) forms. A different framework of reference could show that the Eastern Jewish contacts with Arabic manifested themselves in an entirely different manner than in Spain.

Also, the method usually employed in studies of Spanish Jewish literature tends to examine distinct, relatively homogeneous units, such as a single poem, a genre (wine, panegyrics), or isolate modes like metre, rhyme, imagery for discussion. I propose to deal instead with larger and more heterogeneous literary aggregates—"literary systems"—of which the production of texts is only one aspect.

My work concerning Arabic interference with Jewish literature stems from the "polysystem theory," developed by Itamar Even-Zohar (1990), which offers a highly sophisticated conceptual framework for working with broad and heterogeneous bodies of literature—that is, not only a whole corpus of texts, but also various literary activities of which the production of texts is only one. Thus it enables one to regard literary interference in a context far broader and diverse than that of traditional "comparative literature," rooted in romanticist thinking.

The polysystem theory allows for the consideration of all literary productions of the period, including productions that were traditionally not considered part of the contemporaneous Jewish "literature," and were subsequently ignored in literary studies, or discussed in the field of Judaic studies separatly from literature. Its conceptual framework makes it possible to see all the various texts as inter-related parts of a system rather than as separate aggregates of literature. In other words, it replaces taxonomical thinking with the structuralist-functionalist approach.

The new hypotheses resulting from the adaptation of the polysystem theory necessarily broadens the literary field under investigation. Research in the last few decades was restricted to texts that were "literary" in the most conventional sense of the term. This refers to texts that evinced clear "poetic" elements, such as rhyme and metre. Such restriction narrowed down the scope of what was considered Jewish literature to a relatively small portion of the total sum of writings in Jewish languages. The present study, in contrast, examines all tenth century Jewish writings, including *halakha*, *midrash*, Esoteric wrtitings and Karaite literature, as well as texts written by Jews in other languages such as Aramaic, Judeo-Arabic and Judeo-Persian, as integral entities of the Jewish literary (poly)system. In fact, this inclusive view is quite close to the broad definition of Jewish literature implicit in the literary research of the late nineteenth and early twentieth centuries, which did include these texts. The difference is that while the earlier scholars granted all works equal status in an all inclusive reservoir of texts, I tend to regard the literature of the period as a *system* with a hierarchically structured literary repertoire.

Working with the hypothesis that the question of when contacts between Jewish and Arabic literatures began requires an examination of large bodies of literature and their inter-relations, it seems necessary first to reconstruct the Jewish Literary *System* (=JLS) at the first half of the tenth century, and the hierarchical relations between the various literary models within it. However, space limitations preclude a full description of the whole JLS. I will therefore say only a few words about the major opposition upon which the JLS was constructed and its basic hierarchy of genres before moving to the main subject, which is the Jewish repertoire of literary models, and the introduction of Arabic literary models into it. This discussion, I believe, will help us understand why Jewish literature did not draw upon Arabic literature for over three hundred years of Jewish life in Muslim culture; at what point conditions within the JLS changed so as to initiate appropriation from Arabic literature; and the nature of that appropriation.

1. *Canonized vs. non-canonized: Rabbanite vs. Karaite literature*

Literary systems are founded on the opposition between what is held to be "canonized" and what is held to be "non-canonized" (Even-Zohar 1990:15-17). In the first half of the tenth century, this opposition divides the corpus of Jewish literature into two: Rabbanite literature, consisting of the texts written or transmitted in Rabbanite circles (mainly in Mesopotamia, but also in Palestine and other peripheral Jewish centres), and heretic literature, or rather what Rabbanite circles considered to be "heretic" (*kitve minīm*), consisting mostly of the texts written in Karaite circles, and in some other heretic sects. While this opposition obviously reflects contending ideologies, the distinction made here is purely literary, between two bodies of texts that differ in age, in their repertoires of literary models, in the hierarchy of their genres, and in their relation to each other. These differences imply that the two aggregates of literature are two distinct literary *systems*, each with its own independent dynamics. Nonetheless, since each claimed to be the "real" Jewish literature, each should also be considered part of one larger system, a polysystem ("system of systems"), that in fact constitutes the Jewish Literature of the period.

Rabbanite Judaism was the established ideology governing the centre of this Jewish polysystem in early tenth-century. Rabbanite literature was created to give expression to this ideology, and thus took on canonized status in the Jewish literary polysystem. At the centre of the Jewish literary polysystem were the literary models of the dominant Rabbanite literature; at the periphery, another body of texts developed, which clearly opposited the canonized Rabbanite centre both in ideology and models. This was Karaite literature. Since Karaite literature viewed itself as an alternative to Rabbanite literature—hoping to replace the Rabbanite models with its own and acquire canonized status in the eyes of the entire Jewish public—it can be regarded as the non-canonized part of the Jewish literary polysystem. While Karaite literature defined itself in opposition to Rabbanite literature and constructed literary models that were explicitly distinct from the Rabbanite ones, Rabbanite literature—with the exception of Saʿadya Gaon's writings—ignored the Karaite models and did not deign to recognize the existence of Karaite texts. It should be emphasized, that the terms "canonized" vs. "non-canonized", "centre" vs. "periphery" refer to *relations* between members of a system and to the positions each occupies within the system according to those relations, not to some fixed *attributes* of given bodies of texts.

By the beginning of the tenth century, Rabbanite literature was already 800 years old. It was a highly established system with a clear hierarchy of genres: with *halakha* at the top of the hirarchy (studying the *Talmud* and producing texts of religious law), *midrash* and *piyyuṭ* (liturgy) next, and finally esoteric writings (*sifrut ha-nistar*). A system in itself, Rabbanite literature was also structured upon a major opposition between "canonized" and "non-canonized." Here the opposition is between *halakha*, *midrash* and liturgy as the canonized genres on the one hand, and the various types of esoteric and mystical literature, the non-canonized genres, on the other. The Bible is conspicuously and perhaps surprisingly absent from this scheme. In fact, the Bible was neither an object of literary preoccupation in early tenth century Rabbanite literature, nor a living source for literary models. It did serve liturgical functions in the synagogues on Sabbath and holidays, and was used as teaching material for young children, but as a sacred canon, it was actually pushed of Rabbanite literary activity.

Karaite literature was much younger—its earliest texts, like *Sefer ha-mitsvot* of ʿAanan, were no more than a hundred and fifty years old—and the tenth century was a period of construction and development. It was not as established as Rabbanite literature, and one cannot yet observe a clear hierarchy of genres. Its repertoire of genres consists of Biblical commentaries, writings of religious law based on the Bible alone (*sifrei mitsvot*, as opposed to the Rabbanite *halakha*, which is based on the *talmud*), linguistic treatises focused on the Hebrew of the Bible, refutations (*hasagot*), addressed mainly to the Rabbanites, and some religious poetry. What is most salient is the major preoccupation with the Bible, which was the goal—as well as the basis—for the whole Karaite literary activity.

In sum, the fundamental opposition structuring the JLS of the early tenth century was between the Oral Law, and the Bible. The centre of the system was occupied by Rabbanite literature, while at the periphery of the system lay the non-canonized literary activities of the Karaites (as well as secondary Jewish centres not mentioned here). Within the Rabbanite system, writings and other activities connected with the Oral Law were at the pinnacle of the hierarchy, with the Bible and literary activities connected with it relegated to a lower position. In contrast, the hierarchy was reversed in the Karaite system at the margins of the JLS, with the Bible taking top place. Here a new repertoire of literary genres was developed around the Bible and replaced the traditional Rabbanite repertoire based on the Oral law.

2. *The major literary models of early tenth-century JLS*

Let us now look at the major literary models that produced the Rabbanite and Karaite texts. First, the Rabbanite literary models.

2.1. *Univocal literary models: the Rabbanite models*

Rabbanite literary production of the time contains an enormous amount of Halakhic letters, responses on questions concerning religious law and regulations addressed to the Babylonian academies. However, this body of literature notably lacks books on the subject of *halakha*: there is practically almost no one authoritative composition on Halakhic subjects. How this omission be accounted for?

The answer involves the status of writing in Rabbanite literature. In the early tenth century the most important and prestigious field of Rabbanite literature was still dominated by oral composition and transmission, the official norm of Halakhic activity since the second century CE. Religious law was studied and transmitted orally, and the few Halakhic books that can be recognized as belonging to that period are of the nature of *megilat setarim* ("concealed scroll"), which consists of private, unofficial notes taken by a student during lessons, or written by the teacher himself for his own purposes. The long dominance of oral tradition in Rabbanite literature and the relegation of written communication to "private," unofficial purposes, created an atmosphere that was not conducive to writing, and prevented the development of official Rabbanite writing models. So when the need for official writing arose in connection with the rise of hegemony of the Babylonian academies over the Jewish world, it created a real problem for the Rabbanite literature. The answer was found in the epistolary model. Although this model had a long history in Rabbanite literature, it was traditionally considered "non-literary," in that the usual rules of "literature" were not applied to it. In the Rabbanite context, "non-literary" was "non-sacred" and already in the *Talmud* we find indications that the *igeret* (letter) was considered "non-sacred," in clear opposition to the canonical sacred Scriptures. Being "non-literary" in this sense of "non-official," the epistolary model was a viable option for writing in place of the missing official writing models. It conveyed the message of the Babylonian *halakha* without contradicting the official literary norms of oral transmission. Consequently, the period witnessed the proliferation of *responsa*, based on that model. The most prestigious section of Rabbanite literature was thus functioning with the help of a model which was expressly marked by its non-official status. This situation is a clear symptom of literary impasse.

In the second major section of Rabbanite literature— *midrash*— a classical model dominated, whose norms and items had been fixed hundreds of years earlier. Its literary ideal was strict adherence to classical forms, dedicating most of its creative energies to their perpetuation. Accordingly, compositions in the classical model were presented as works of the classical Rabbibic period and every effort was made to conceal their contemporaneity. They were attributed to earlier figures, usually from the *Mishna* or *Talmud*, or were published anonymously in the form of a collective message. Every indicator of time and place was disguised or obscured, substituted for the traditional items of the classical Rabbinic repertoire.

The classical model was highly established in this period, a situation that expressed itself in a set repertoire. The model was so entrenched that new material could make its way in only after it was restructured, with new items replaced by ready-made classical ones. This reduced ability of a major Rabbanite literary model to stay dynamic is also a sign of stagnation.

Preference for well-established classical models also characterizes the production of liturgical poetry (*piyyuṭ*)—the third major genre of the Rabbanite literature of the period.

This short sketch of the Rabbanite literary models shows quite clearly that in the early tenth century, Rabbanite literature was evidently entering a state of stagnation.

2.2. *Univocal Literary Models: The Karaite Models*

Rejecting Rabbanite ideology, the Karaites also abstained fron using Rabbanite literary models, as those were identified with the ideology they were made to serve. The Karaites were thus inclined to create their own literary options in place of Rabbanite one. Their choice of the Bible as the focus of their literary activity illustrated the traditional dilemma of Jewish literature: the choice between the Bible and the Oral Law. As the Oral Law was strictly Rabbanite, the Karaites selected the option that was currently available, that is, not necessarily marked as Rabbanaite. However, their repudiation of the canonized Rabbanite models left a void which demanded both organizing principles for a new literary repertoire and new models for writing, in order to produce the texts in which to develop the Biblical option. The Karaites sought to fill the vacuum with new texts and formulate a new *halakha* to replace the Rabbanite one they had rejected. Their need for new literary models generated some interest in dormant Hebrew models from centuries earlier, such as the Dead Sea Scrolls *pesher* model of Biblical exegesis. Such Hebrew models, however, had never gained wide acceptance, either because there were not enough texts available to provide sufficient literary models or because what they did provide seemed alien and remote. Thus, the Karaites eventually turned to the models they found in Arabic literature, accessible to them in the surrounding Muslim culture.

The Karaites first adopted the basic Arabic principle of organizing the literary repertoire around one sacred text—the Koran. This principle had played a major role in the crystallization of Arabic literature about two hundred years earlier. Aided by the Arabic religious-literary ideology of *i'ǧāz al-Qur'ān*,[1] and the *faṣāḥa* of the Arabic language and of the Koran, Arabic literary activity focused on the holy book and gave rise to literary genres whose highest purpose was to explain and justify the superior status of the Koran in the literary system. This included not only Koranic exegesis, but also various linguistic and lexicographic activity in search of "pure," "authentic" Arabic, and the collection and interpretation of ancient Arabic poetry. All this was done ideologically if not always practically, in the name of the understanding and reconstructing the pure, authentic language and meaning of the Koran.

An examination of the Karaite literary repertoire (Biblical exegesis, Halakhic writings, linguistic studies, polemics) reveals that this Arabic principle was involved in the construction of the Karaite literary system around the Bible. While parts of the Karaite repertoire, such as *mizvot books*, developed out of the need to distinguish between Karaite and Rabbanite Judaism, other parts, such as linguistic studies and the verse-by-verse model of Biblical interpretation—as well as some of the writing models—must be understood as the influence of the more abstract organizing principle taken from Arabic literature. However, Karaite borrowing from Arabic literature was not all-inclusive. The Karaites took no interest in substantial parts of the Arabic repertoire, such as Arabic poetry and the historical literature connected with it, or the Arabic poetics and rhetorics that had developed around both poetry and the Koran. Karaite borrowing was determined by the needs of the developing literary system in its opposition to Rab-

[1] Cf. ch.4, 3.2.2.

banite literature and by the specific options available in the JLS at the time for carrying out the borrowed functions.

In addition to the Arabic organizing principle the Karaites borrowed the most basic writing model in the Arabic literary system, along with certain more specific models. Karaite writing was founded on the model of the Arabic treatise, but its specific literary features were largely determined by its domestic context, which was the need for a literary model that would be clearly distinguishable from the Rabbanite one. Thus, the individualist literary ideology behind the Karaite model, known as "search and request," emphasized individual questioning and inquiry rather than the Rabbanite total acquiescence to authority. This domestic context also explains the model's most prominent features: the attribution of compositions to their real authors, the use of the authorical first person, and the mention of contemporary reality-items like names of places, dates, political and personal events, and customs (particularly Rabbanite social customs, which the Karaites would mock). As a result Karaite writings have enormous value for historians, who will find information on Jewish and Rabbanite everyday life, which cannot possibly be found in the corresponding Rabbanite literature produced in the classicist model.

Thus, for instance, Karaite literature holds very interesting testimonies to Rabbanite social intermingling with Muslim society, which the Karaites sharply criticize. Those testimonies shed light upon Rabbanite behaviour otherwise unknown to us, as it could not have been reflected in Rabbanite literature. Judging solely from Rabbanite sources about Jewish life within Muslim society, lead to very misleading perceptions about this world. The remotness of Rabbanite literary models from the actual Rabbanite realia of the time is another telltale sign of ossification.

Another borrowing from Arabic literature was the concept of a written text intended for readership and not simply for private, unofficial use. This concept was new to Jewish literature, and was first introduced by the Karaites (and eventually by Saadia Gaon). The Karaite text was no longer a mnemonic device for oral, official transmission, nor a means of preserving an oral text in writing. It was a literary unit with independent existence and value. The new official status of the written text required that it be edited differently from unofficial texts, and demanded attention to its literary form. The new textual model had a systematic structure, with a methodical introduction and chapters arranged logically by content.

Along with the penetration of Arabic literary models, a new type of writer emerged who, after the Arabic example, wrote in a range of genres rather than restricting himself to one. Ibn Qutayba, or Abū al-Farağ al-Iṣbhānī, are typical contemporary Arabic examples. Thus, the Karaite author Salmon ben Yeruḥim wrote a Bible commentary, a religious law treatise, a linguistic treatise, refutations and religious verse. All the other known Karaite authors from that period and even earlier—such as Binyamin al-Nahāwandī, Yaʿqūb al-Qirqisānī, and Sahl ben Maṣliaḥ—wrote in more than one genre.

Let us examine more specifically the Karaite model of Biblical exegesis. Here, too, the official status of the written text and the impact of that new status on writing patterns stand out. Karaite Biblical exegesis was no longer an oral homiletic interpretation connected to the weekly portion of the Bible read in the synagogue, like the Rabbanite *derasha*, but a written, verse-by-verse commentary of entire Biblical books, often accompanied by a methodological introduction. An entire pattern of communication was actually replaced, with all the implications for the arrangement of information in the text, and its editing.

In the first half of the tenth century, there were two distinct models of Biblical exegesis in Karaite literature. The first was the *pesher* model, which may be a derivative of the exegetic model of the Dead Sea Scrolls' *pesharim*. It involved allegorical interpretation of the Bible. The second was a domesticated adaptation of an Arabic model of Koranic exegesis, which I have therefore called the "Arabic" model, and it was this one that ultimately took over. This "Arabic" model was appropriated selectively, taking on the one hand basic elements, like the formal arrangement of text and the general conception of exegesis, and on the other, highly specific terms and ideas, or even lists of exegetic rules, that had originally been part of a complete programme. Apart from these appropriations, the "Arabic" model contained a whole range of interpretative methods and ideas not necessarily related to the original Arabic exegetic model. They grew up out of Karaite domestic needs to distinguish Karaite from Rabbanite literature, as described earlier.

It is possible that the Arabic source for this model was not the canonized model of Koranic exegesis, as in al-Ṭabarī's *Tafsīr*, but rather a non-canonized model of exegesis, which served the Muʿtazila, that was involved here. The Muʿtazilites developed Koran exegesis in circumstances quite similar to those of the Karaites: the need to defend their beliefs from their opponents' attacks led them to base their thinking on the Koran, and they specialized in Koranic interpretation. In the ninth and tenth century they wrote many whole Koranic commentaries (*tafāsīr*), as they usually used writing rather than oral transmission. Muʿtazilite sources, like Ibn al-Murtaḍā's *Ṭabaqāt al-muʿtazila*, provide evidence of a vast amount of *tafāsīr* production in Muʿtazitilite circles, but due to their non-canonized status, only a small number survived. However, references and quotations from these commentaries found in Muʿtazilite polemic literature and other similar Muʿtazilite texts (e.g., al-Rummānī's *Masāʾil*), indicate that their literary form was closer to the Karaite "Arabic" model than any other exegetic model in Arabic literature. I further suggest that the Syriac model of Biblical exegesis may also have played a role in the creation of the Karaite model. These suggestions are based on evidence of three-way cultural contacts between Jews on the periphery of Jewish life and non-orthodox Moslems and Christians.

3. *Ambivalent literary models: Masoretic activity*

Both Rabbanite and Karaite literary models held a univocal status within Jewish literature: each model clearly belonged to only one literary system, either the Rabbanite or Karaite. The literary features of texts created according to those univocal models allowed audiences to identify the texts as either Rabbanite or Karaite definitively. During the first half of the tenth century, a Rabbanite Jew would refrain from writing in a model identified as Karaite, and vice versa. The univocal status of these models, then, determined the borders of the two literary systems for their audiences. Alongside the univocal models, other models existed in Jewish literature whose status was ambivalent: they could belong simultaneously to both the Karaite and the Rabbanite systems, even though the two were contradictory and their repertoire enabled each to consider the texts created according to these models as either Karaite or Rabbanite as desired. Their ambivalent status made it possible for these models to play a role in the literary contacts with Arabic literature. Arabic functions were introduced into Jewish literature through the ambivalent models, which were accepted by both canonized and non-canonized literatures, yet were not subject to the rigid Rabbanite norms which prevented innovation in the Rabbanite repertoire. This can be demonstrated by the ambivalent model found in the Tiberian *Masora* (i.e., the correct reading of the Bible).

An accepted view among scholars ever since the publication of Paul Kahle's works (1902; 1913; 1927-1930) is that by the end of the ninth century three systems for the punctuation of the Bible were in use in the Jewish communities of the East: the Babylonian, the Palestinian and the Tiberian systems. Along with other Masoretic material, they testify to the existence of three distinct traditions of the Bible reading. We have indications that the Babylonian system was the most widespread. Al-Qirqisānī says in the first half of the tenth century that the Babylonian reading was in use throughout the entire Eastern Islamic world, from Syria to China and down to Yemen (al-Qiqisānī 1939-1943:I, 135). Several hundred Biblical fragments with Babylonian punctuation have survived, yet we have very few copies or fragments of Tiberian, not to mention Palestinian, punctuated Bibles. This corresponds with all the other data attesting to the domination of the Babylonian center over the Eastern Jewish world at the time.

Yet, during the first half of the tenth century we note a process of canonization whereby the Tiberian reading acquires priority in the Jewish world, and becomes the authoritative reading of the Bible—a status it has preserved until today. As a result, the other two systems were forgotten and eventually disappeared. Obviously, the successive Jewish settlement in Tiberias, the long tradition of Biblical study and teaching there, Tiberias's Masoretic activity, and the development of a sophisticated punctuation system, jointly played a significant role in the ascendance of the Tiberian reading, and in the concomitant decrease in the status of the other reading traditions. But these facts do not explain per se the need to choose between various reading traditions that arose at this particular time, or why the final choice turned out to be a considerably less widespread reading than others. Neither do they explain the basic principle on which the choice was actually made.

The question of which reading tradition to choose evolved within a non-canonized Jewish group, the Karaites. Engaged in creating a separate non-rabbinic Jewish ideology, the Karaites wished to establish their own institution of "the Holy Book," the Bible, which would be distinct from the Rabbinic. They sought a "true," authoritative reading, and the Tiberian was suitable because it was not identified with any particular Rabbinic establishment, yet it was inveterate and established enough to function as the "true original reading." But could that reading be regarded as more "original" than, for instance, the Babylonian one? There are a number of contemporary statements about the Tiberian reading, most of which are found in Karaite texts. These construct an ideology which promotes the Tiberian reading as "the authentic and original reading of the Bible." It speaks of the purity of the Tiberian Hebrew articulation, the beautiful and correct Hebrew tongue of the Tiberians, and portrays them as the loyal guardians of the authentic reading of the Bible.

An analysis of these statements clearly shows that the ideology was structured upon an Arabic model (Drory 1988:138-149). It is the same model that served, about one century earlier, to build up the exemplary status of the Koran's language and the status of the desert tribes (*aʿrāb*) as the true preservers of pristine Arabic. The basic concept is that a certain group within a community, whether ethnically or otherwise determined, is considered to preserve the "pure, original" stratum of that community's language in its speech. Thus, scholarly activity pertaining to the community's language should center on the speech of that particular group. The concern of Abbasid grammarians (like al-Aṣmaʿī) with the Arabic of the Bedouins is a well-known example, which needs no elaboration (Blachère 1950).[2] This fundamental Arabic paradigm was transferred to the Jewish world and applied to the Hebrew of the people of Tiberias, and the Tiberian Bible reading. Its actual effect on scholarly activity is revealed in a fragmental Judeo-Arabic text published by Nehemia Allony, in which a contemporary Hebrew scholar describes his work methods in passing. He recounts that after giving certain linguistic problems considerable thought and thoroughly studying the Bible and the language in use (*al-kalām al-mustaʿmal*) in search of answers, he finally put his ideas to the test by matching them with findings collected through

[2] Cf. ch. 4, 2.2.

time spent in the streets and squares of Tiberias, listening to the speech of simple people:

> I have dedicated a great deal of thinking and research [to this problem], and searched throughout the Bible and the spoken language, and after a laborious effort and considerable trouble it became clear. I checked and compared [my results regarding this matter] with [the usage of Hebrew] in the Bible and within the spoken language. *I used to spend a lot of time sitting in the squares and streets of Tiberias, listening to the speech of the simple and common people in the marketplace, while observing the rules of their language, in order to verify whether my formulation were correct* when compared to the spoken Hebrew and to the different types of Aramaic, that is, the "targum" and other types, which are similar to Hebrew [...]; all my findings turned out to be true and correct.[3]

A mid tenth-century Karaite exegesis of the biblical verse concerning Jacob's blessing of his son Naphtali: "נפתלי אילה שלחה הנתן אמרי שפר"—'Naphtali is a hind let loose; he giveth goodly words' (Genesis 49:21), states: "אמרי שפר mean *aqāwīl ḥasana*, beautiful speech, by which God gave special distinction to the people of Tiberias; that is, eloquence and articulate speech."[4]

But perhaps the most Arabized formulation of this idea about the special qualities of Tiberian Hebrew is found about a half a century later, in Ibn Ǧanāḥ's *Kitāb al-luma'*, where he says: "as the Tiberians are the best of all Hebrew people in terms of the beauty of their tongue and their eloquence."[5]

It is not just an isolated theme that was borrowed from the Arabic and adapted into the Jewish cultural system, but rather a full ideological paradigm, which controls the form and status of the most prestigious Book of the community, and from which a complete strategy of scholarly activity derived.

The first expression of the concept of the exemplary status of the Tiberian tongue and Tiberian Bible reading appear in Karaite writings and in writings of uncertain religious affiliation, but in

[3] *wakuntu uṭīlu 'l-ǧulūs fī sāḥāt ṭabariyya wašawāriihā a[st]ami'u kalāma 'l-sūqa wa'l-'āma wa abḥaṯu 'ani 'l-luġa wa'uṣūli[hā] anṭuru hal yankasiru šay mimmā aṣaltu aw yanfasidu šay mimmā ẓahara lī wafī mā nuṭiqa bi[hi mina] 'l-'ibrānī wa'l-siryānī wa'anwā'ihi a'nī luġata 'l-targūm waġayrahu fa'innahu muǧānis lil'ibrānī (...) fakaraǧa ṣaḥīḥ muḥarrar* (Allony 1970:98-100).

[4] *wakaṣṣa biḏālika ahla ṭabariyya wahuwa ḥusnu al-luġa wa'l-manṭiq*. David ben Abraham al-Fāsī, *Ǧāmī al-alfāẓ* (Skoss 1936:2, 699).

[5] *iḏ hum (ahl ṭabariyya) afṣaḥu al-'ibrāniyyīn lisānan wa akṯaruhum bayānan* (Derenbourg 1886:29).

which the Karaites showed considerable interest, namely Masoretic Grammar. At the same time, there is evidence that this concept also made its way into marginal Rabbanite literature. It was quite likely that the imposition of this concept on Masoretic activity, an accepted element in Rabbanite Judaism, contributed to its subsequent absorption into canonized Rabbanite writings.

The Karaites also gave impetus to the copying of the Bible in the form of a codex (*maṣḥaf*). The Karaites recognized the authority of the Masoretes of Tiberias and chose the Tiberian reading of the Bible as the only legitimate one. They ordered proofread and authorized Bibles in the form of codices, with vocalization and accentuation, from the Tiberian Masoretes, for personal and liturgical use. In this way, they created a new Biblical format. The ready acceptance of literary activity encouraged by the Karaites (whether or not it was actually developed by them) in the Rabbanite world demonstrates that it was not identified as an exclusive Karaite model. It contained traditional Rabbanite elements preserved in Tiberias, namely the *Masora*, on which the new functions appropriated from the Arabic were imposed during this period. This imposition of new functions on traditional elements created the ambivalence that allowed the model's admittance into both Rabbanite and Karaite literature.

4. *Sa'adia Gaon's role in the contacts with Arabic*

As stated, the models appropriated from Arabic entered Jewish literature mainly through non-canonized sections, such as Karaite literature. These were completely different from Rabbanite models and served an anti-Rabbanite ideology, factors which might well have led Rabbanite Jewry not to use them and should have prevented them from penetrating canonized, Rabbanite, literature. Yet from the middle of the tenth century, these models penetrated Rabbanite literature so deeply that certain Rabbanite texts can only be identified and distinguished from Karaite ones by their ideological message.

For this change to have taken place in Rabbanite literature, the appropriated Arabic models had to be transferred from the non-canonized to the canonized literature. One remarkable person made this transfer possible—the Rabbanite Sa'adya Gaon (882-

942). Saʿadya Gaon combined a unique personality and special cultural circumstances which made him a vehicle for introducing the new literary models into Rabbanite literature. Saʿadya fought the Karaites' ideology with their own tools: he wrote in the same models that served the Karaites. He thus removed the "Karaite label" from these models turning them into "neutral" models that could acquire Rabbanite identity and be accepted into Rabbanite literature. He provided Rabbanite literature with the option of using writing models adopted from Arabic, which had been taboo when only the Karaites used them. Their rapid absorption in Rabbanite literature shows just how needed a new repertoire of literary models was.

Saʿadya Gaon introduced several new literary models into Rabbanite literature. The first one consisted of both a restructured Rabbanite literary system, in which the Bible is newly placed at the upper level of the literary hierarchy and becomes the focus of literary interest, and the new repertoire that Saʿadya created around the Bible. The second model was the concept of the Bible as a literary and linguistic exemplar. This was accomplished by imposing on the Bible the Arabic *faṣāḥa*. The third was a revitalized Hebrew liturgical poety on which the status and functions of Arabic poetry had been imposed. Saʿadya Gaon created a liturgical canon based on norms appropriated from classicist Arabic literary criticism. The fourth model he introduced was the elevation of the written text, along with its basic writing models, to official status. The fifth and sixth were new Judeo-Arabic and Hebrew prose writing models. Saʿadya Gaon's attempt to create a model for eloquent Hebrew prose based on the Bible was especially interesting, although unsuccessful.

Connecting Saʿadya Gaon's literary activities with those of the Karaites does not constitute a claim that the Karaites preceded Saʿadya Gaon, that he "imitated" their writings, or that they were more "important" than he. Saʿadya Gaon was a contemporary of Karaite writers, but most Karaite literature was actually written in the generations following him. Moreover, his writings show greater, and more varied, signs of contact with Arabic literature than do Karaite writings. I have sought to draw attention to a fact whose importance is generally underestimated and often ignored: Saʿadya Gaon's literary activities cannot be understood without the context of the Karaites.

5. *Conclusions*

I hope to have clarified the circumstances that caused the emergence of literary contacts with Arabic, and why it is difficult to trace those contacts in Eastern Jewish literature. The long dominance of oral transmission resulted in a lack of official writing models in the most prestigious genre of Rabbanite literature. Combined with the exclusive dominance of rigid, highly established classicist models in other Rabbanite genres, Rabbanite literature—the canonized centre of Jewish literature—fell into a state of stagnation. In contrast, non-canonized Karaite literature, which developed in plain opposition to Rabbanite literature out of a desire to oust and replace it with its own alternatives, demanded new literary models that would be distinct from the Rabbanite ones. This demand for "free" models brought the Karaites to the large reservoir of Arabic literature. What led them to turn to Arabic literature as a source of literary repertoire was thus their situation in the peripheral sections of Jewish literature rather than an admiration of Arabic literature, which was the case later in Spain.

Jewish literature therefore tended to appropriate only the particular functions it needed from Arabic literature, imposing them on elements already extant in Hebrew. It did not appropriate of complete and detailed literary models or select models according to their status in Arabic literature. Eastern Jewish literature borrowed principles, general concepts and patterns of literary activity from Arabic literature, and used them to reorganize elements within its home system. It made no attempt to create new items to carry out these foreign functions, as would frequently be done later in Spain. This explains why tenth-century Jewish literature contains so few "visible" and readily identifiable Arabic elements. For such elements to be visible, they would have had to be whole models appropriated from Arabic, imposed on new elements created especially for them.

An examination of models appropriated from Arabic literature shows two borrowing procedures. The first was the appropriation of fundamental concepts and organizing principles, which served to reorganize the JLS. These were most basic in Arabic literature already two hundred years earlier, when it crystallized. Their prestige in Arabic literature made them familiar to anyone living in Muslim culture, and available when needed even to people who were not versed in Arabic letters. The second was the appropriation of Arabic writing models. Here, in contrast, no contact was made with the official Arabic Literary System, but rather with its non-canonized sections, especially the *muʿtazila* and *kalām* literature.

Arabic literature was not the only alternative to Rabbanite models that arose in the search for new literary models. This search also led to a renewed interest in the Hebrew literary repertoire and its appropriate models, namely those that were not canonized or actively used during that period. But the attempts to use ready-made Hebrew models for new tasks did not succeed. The Hebrew models served for a short time alongside the Arabic models. But whereas the domestic version of Arabic models lasted and were ultimately admitted to Jewish literature of this period, the ready-made Hebrew models were eventually abandoned.

The greatest contribution of Jewish contact with Arabic literature was that it made possible the growth and development of Jewish literature. It enabled a literary system whose canonized section had reached an impasse, and whose active models were beginning to ossify, to progress forward. This contact provided Jewish literature with two new options, which opened up the way to its continued development:

(1) Contacts with Arabic literature turned the alternative option to the Oral Law that lay dormant in Jewish literature, namely the Bible, into a viable possibility for literary production.

(2) Those contacts eventually enabled writing to gain official status by undermining the norm of oral transmission in Rabbanite literature. Writing gained legitimacy, and new models desighed for writing rather than for the preservation oral transmission were introduced into Jewish literature.

This was the "Eastern phase" of contact with Arabic: it began, developed, and ended in the East. Nevertheless, by providing an alternative to the traditional Rabbanite literary system, this phase laid the groundwork for the more advanced "Spanish phase." It provided a legitimate option for a JLS that differed from the Rabbanite tradition in its structure, fundamental literary conception and repertoire. But in order for this alternative to undermine the prime status of Rabbanite literature in the JLS and become the driving force in a restructuring of canonized Jewish literature, the literary centre of the JLS had to be relocated in another part of the globe—Muslim Spain—where different cultural conditions prevailed.

CHAPTER SIX

THREE MAJOR KARAITE CONTRIBUTIONS TO TENTH CENTURY JEWISH CULTURE*

Any paradigm reaches a stage at which a reexamination of its fundamental assumptions and theoretical concepts becomes necessary. The need to deal satisfactorily with new questions, no longer answerable within the traditional framework, sometime leads to a reevaluation, and ultimately reorganization, of the entire field of research. The study of medieval Hebrew literature, I believe, has reached this stage. Studies of medieval Hebrew literature published since the 1960s, for example, are implicitly based on the assumption that only texts distinguished by unequivocally "poetic" signs—meter, rhyme, metaphor, and other traits generally identified as "literary"—deserve to be classified as Hebrew "literature."[1] Thus the term "tenth century Hebrew literature" encompasses mainly poetry (sacred and secular), and, to a certain extent, also *midrash*. All other texts written at that time, in fact, the bulk of Jewish literary output, are implicitly assumed to be beyond the pale of "literature"—that is, not worthy of consideration in literary research. As long as the "literariness" of selected texts is dealt with as a self-contained issue, such a definition of "literature" might be sufficient; but when one is concerned with the historical and cultural context of those same texts, i.e., with the processes of development and change in Hebrew literature—it soon becomes clear that the old basis is no longer adequate. It constrains the scholar to confine attention to a limited segment of the contemporary literary production, without any guarantee that that particular segment was indeed the scene of the

* The following is an attempt to draw an overall picture and propose a general thesis. For that reason I have dispensed with examples and references. In my Hebrew book (Drory 1988) the reader will find an extensive account of the material on which these general remarks are based, together with a comprehensive bibliography.

[1] This is the underlying conception of the leading contemporary scholars in the field, such as Schirmann, Pagis, Fleischer, Levin and their disciples (for example, Schirmann 1979; Pagis 1976; Fleischer 1975, 1984; Levin 1968, 1977). The conception is faithfully reflected by the structure of the departments of Hebrew literature in Israeli universities and in the subjects of the courses that they offer.

most significant historical events. As a result, there is a real danger that central cultural processes will be ignored, and crucial questions left unanswered. When questions are asked that cannot be answered adequately within the framework of an established paradigm, the time has come for reexamination and reevaluation.

One question that cannot be tackled within such a limited concept of "literature" concerns a process that had perhaps the most crucial impact on tenth century Jewish culture: the emergence of Arabic-Hebrew literary contacts. This question cannot possibly be addressed on the sole basis of Hebrew liturgical poetry (*piyyuṭ*), scanty secular poems, and some aspects of midrashic literature. By what token can it be claimed that this corpus alone constitute the "genuine" Hebrew literature of the time, while all the rest of its variegated literary output must be left "beyond the pale," as it were, relegated to other fields of scholarship ("Judaic studies")? Is the accepted scholarly definition of "Hebrew literature" adequate for the structure of the Hebrew (or rather, Jewish) literary system of that era? In order to understand what was happening in tenth century Eastern Hebrew literature, it is necessary to examine everything that survives of the large corpus of texts written by Jews for Jewish audience, which surely transcends the narrow bounds of the traditional literary conception. As a matter of fact, the broad conception of literature proposed here has essentially provided the basis for scholarly occupation with medieval Hebrew literature up until the middle of the present century.[2] For the scholars who established the corpus of medieval "Hebrew literature" there was no real differentiation between texts treating *halakhah*, *midrash*, esoteric literature, Bible exegesis, refutations, grammar, liturgical or secular poetry—whether written in Hebrew, Aramaic, Arabic or Persian. They were all part of one corpus. The difference, however, is that unlike earlier scholarship, rather than treat "literature" as an undiscriminated inventory of texts, the conception proposed here considers "literature" as a *system*, that is, as a structured and heterogeneous complex of activities and products pertaining hierarchic relationships (like center versus periphery; official, prestigious, versus unrecognized, unofficial status).

---

[2] See, for example, Steinschneider (1902), Pinsker (1968 [1860]), Mann (1972 [1931]), Ginzberg (1929), and the later work of Scheiber and Habermann, to mention only a few.

The Eastern Jewish texts that can be dated to around the beginning of the tenth century may be divided into two large bodies: (1) orally transmitted or written texts from Rabbanite circles (whether in Iraq, Palestine or other, peripheral regions)—"Rabbanite literature"; (2) texts written in Karaite circles in basically the same area—"Karaite literature." This distinction between Rabbanite and Karaite literatures reflects a distinction not between religious ideologies, but between literary institutions; that is to say, the two bodies of texts differ in their repertoires of literary genres, stocks of literary models, historical ages and behavior toward one another. In all these respects Karaite and Rabbanite literature constitute separate, independent literary systems (up to the time of Saʿadya Gaon). Nevertheless, they were not entirely unconnected. As each considered itself the sole "genuine" literature of the Jews and competed with the other for the recognition of the entire Jewish public, they may be justifiably seen as two subsystems of a single system—the "Jewish literature" of the era.

Thanks to the Rabbanite hegemony over the Jewish community, the texts that had been produced to express Rabbanite ideology (*halakhah*, *midrash* and liturgical poetry) received a canonical status in Jewish literature, and the literary models on which they were based became official (though not exclusive) models of Jewish literature. Disregarding, momentarily, the literary activity of Saʿadya Gaon, which was quite exceptional and by no means characteristic of the Rabbanite literature of the time, the state of affairs regarding Rabbanite models was as follows. In the most prestigious Rabbanite field, that of *halakhah*, the official norms were oral production and oral transmission of texts. Due to their long-term powerful domination (from Second Temple time), with writing confined to "private," unofficial needs, Rabbanite literature did not evolve official models for writing. When, while establishing their political power in the Jewish world, the Babylonian academies had to recourse to writing as a means of long-distance communication, the unofficial model of the letter was selected for this purpose. This model had traditionally been considered "extraliterary" (in Rabbanite terms, lacking sanctity). Thus it was found a readily available tool for communicating the Oral Law (*halakha*), as laid down in Iraq, to the rest of the Diaspora, without violating the official norms of oral composition and transmission. This explains the proliferation of *responsa* at this time—the *responsum* being a form of letter—in contrast to the scant number of halakhic monographs.

In the field of *midrash* too, classicist models, also originated in oral activity (as surviving written exemplars indicate), prevailed. Its norms and repertoire of items had been established centuries earlier. Its poetics dictated absolute acceptance of the literary paradigm created in previous generations; literary creativity was exclusively confined to the reproduction of that paradigm. Accordingly, every effort was made to conceal a work's contemporariness, presenting it as written in antiquity. Texts were therefore ascribed to ancient personae (usually Mishnaic or Talmudic: *Pirke de R. Eliezer*, *Tanna de bei Eliyahu*, *Alfā Betā de Ben Sīrā*). Alternately, works were left anonymous, conveying as it were a collective, superpersonal and supertemporal message by obscuring or concealing any detail that might disclose the work's time or place of writing: realia, place-names, indications of time, etc., were omitted or replaced by old, ready-made items.

The Rabbanite models were at this time highly established. No new literary material could be admitted in a Rabbanite text unless it would be moulded after the classical models, and make use of items from the traditional repertoire. Rabbanite literature thus displayed the definite symptoms of stagnation. This is why no contacts can be discerned between the canonical (that is, Rabbanite) Jewish literature, and Arabic literature: any sign of such contact could only be introduced through the classicist models, and thus necessarily be disguised as part of the genuine Jewish tradition. In other words, it would be practically invisible.

A new body of texts was emerging, however, alongside the established Rabbanite literature: this was Karaite literature, motivated by a complete negation of Rabbanite ideology and a desire to supplant its entire literary institution. This state of affairs is typical of the relationship between an official and an unofficial bodies of literature: Rabbanite literature did not recognize the existence of Karaite literature and never referred to the literary models that it has established (Saʿadya Gaon was the rare exception). Karaite literature, on the other hand, defined its identity in blatant opposition to the Rabbanite paradigm, and designed its literary models to be palpably distinct from the Rabbanite models. In contrast to the old, institutionalized Rabbanite literature it was relatively young: the earliest extant texts, from Anan ben David and later from

Benyamin al-Nahawāndī, were at most 100-150 years old. By mid tenth century this young literature was vigorously flourishing.

Inspired by the need to create an alternative to Rabbanite literature, the Karaites resorted to the traditional alternative to Oral Law within Jewish literature; namely, the Bible. In order to actualize this option and create a full-fledged literary system, they needed literary models that would enable them to build a new repertoire based on the Bible, and to produce new texts expressing their ideology. For the Karaites, the Rabbanite models were totally identified with Rabbanite ideology, which they had rejected; these models were therefore abstained. The quest for fresh, unused models led them to the large repertoire of Arabic literature, which was readily accessible in their culture. They actualized their alternative to Rabbanite literature, basing it on the Bible, by actively employing literary models borrowed from Arabic culture.

Thus, the recourse to Arabic literature as a source of literary models began at the periphery of Jewish literature, in its non-canonized sections, driven by a need for literary models to replace the official, canonized ones. It was a readily available solution to an internal problem of Jewish culture; it did not by any means represent a desire to imitate Arabic literature as supposedly superior to the Hebrew one, as would be the case some generations later in Spain. In fact, the Karaites were avowed opponents of any contact with Arabic culture. Some of the very Karaite authors who themselves took up Arabic literary models (Daniel al-Qūmisī, Salmon ben Yeruḥim and Sahl ben Maṣliaḥ) spoke out explicitly against Jews imitating any element of Arabic culture, adopting Arabic customs or studying the Arabic sciences (offenses which they attributed to the Rabbanite Jews).[3]

1. *First contribution: introduction of an option for change in Jewish literature*

Thus Rabbanite literature, the center of the Jewish literary system, was progressively stagnating, its creative models showing signs of

[3] See Daniel al-Qūmisī, cited in Mann 1972 [1931], II, 77-78; Salmon ben Yeruḥim, in Neubauer 1866: 109-110; Pinsker 1968 [1860], II, 134; Sahl ben Maṣliaḥ, in Pinsker 1968 [1860], II, 32; Harkavi 1970²: 201. These declarations originated among the Palestinian Karaites. Al-Qirqisanī, who lived in Iraq and was more acclimatized to Arabic culture, held a different view.

ossification. At the periphery of the system, however, among Karaites, conditions were emerging that would permit new models to enter the system. The introduction of this option for change and renewal in Jewish literature was the first major contribution of Karaite literature to the Jewish culture of the early tenth century. In Karaite literature the foundations were laid for a new repertoire of literary models that would enable Jewish literature—if it learned how to utilize that repertoire—to break out of its impasse and evolve.

But was the mere appearance of a new option for change enough to actually generate the change? The Jewish literary system of the early tenth century was characterized by an extreme polarization between official (Rabbanite) and unofficial (Karaite) texts. The mere fact that models appropriated from Arabic literature had entered through Karaite literature was sufficient to brand them as "heretical," and thus disqualify them for use by Rabbanite authors. Nevertheless, beginning in the second half of the tenth century, Arabic models made massive advance into Rabbanite literature and were rapidly assimilated there. Credit for the admission of these identifiably "Karaite" models to Rabbanite literature should go primarily to the literary activity of Saʿadya Gaon (882-942), which mediated between Karaite and Rabbanite literature. Saʿadya Gaon disputed Karaite ideology and fought to refute it, using to that end the very same writing models as the Karaites themselves. He thus disengaged the models from Karaite ideology, eradicating their identification by Rabbanite readers as "Karaite" (and therefore ipso facto unusable); instead, they became neutral writing models, suitable for expressing Rabbanite bodies of knowledge and ideas. In so doing Saʿadya Gaon offered Rabbanite literature the option of using reworked writing models taken over from the Arabic—an option that had been blocked to the Rabbanites as long as these models had been used exclusively by the Karaites. Their rapid assimilation into Rabbanite literature after Saʿadya's activities demonstrates how urgent the need was for new writing options.

Chronologically speaking, Saʿadya Gaon wrote around the same time as some of the Karaite authors; the bulk of Karaite literature even developed in later generations. Moreover, Saʿadya's use of the Arabic repertoire of literary models seems often more elaborate and varied than that of the Karaites. Yet the significance of Saʿadya's literary activity cannot be understood apart the context of Karaite literary activity, for it was against that background that his own literary efforts were undertaken. Saʿadya Gaon is so valued in Jewish culture that he is usually regarded as the inaugural figure of his time, initiator of every innovation, from literary form to scholarly enterprise. He ought to be evaluated, however, in the overall context of his era, not as remembered in our Rabbanite-biased historical memory. It should not be forgotten that while his literary and scholarly activities were quite exceptional in the Rabbanite community of his time, they were actually very similar to those of contemporary Karaites scholars. Many of the new options Saʿadya Gaon introduced into Rabbanite literature were prepared in the framework of Karaite literature.

2. *Second contribution: introduction of writing as an official mode of text production*

The second major Karaite contribution to Jewish literature in the tenth century was the introduction of writing as an official mode of text production. As mentioned, Rabbanite literature had basically maintained the ancient tradition of oral production and transmission of texts, while avoiding the institutionalized writing of literary works. Copious evidence in Rabbanite literature show that oral transmission was an indication of the canonical status of a text, and that written texts were considered inferior in status to orally transmitted ones. The Bible enjoyed, indeed, the official status of a written text, but its sacredness prevented it from serving as a source for productive writing models in Rabbanite literature. The unsystematic unscrupulous structure of most of the surviving Rabbanite texts of the period clearly testify to their unofficial status and prove them to be intended for private rather than public use (e.g., *megillot setarim*, "concealed scrolls"); They look like mnemonics aids for orally transmitted matters, or draft versions of texts whose official presentation was oral (e.g., anthologies of *midrashim* meant for oral delivery as sermons). The inferior status of written versus oral production was probably the main reason for the lack of coherent writing models in pre-Saʿadyan Rabbanite literature, and the scarcity of Rabbanite books.

The number of Karaite works, counting texts that survived both in their entirety or in part, or that are mentioned by name in the sources, is far greater than the number of contemporary Rabbanite works (not including, again, the works of Saʿadya Gaon); Further, each major Karaite author of the period may be credited with multiple works. There were several reasons why written production was legitimized and achieved official status in Karaite literature:

(1) Unlike the Rabbanites, Karaites had no rooted inhibitions concerning writing. They did not have a long abiding tradition of oral study and transmission, which was by this time so completely identified with the texts it carried, that it became itself sacred and therefore inviolable.

(2) The Karaites lived in a highly developed culture of literary production in writing. Although Arabic culture had great respect for oral transmission, in the tenth century the predominant norm in practice was writing.[4] The Arabic literature of the period was already a literature of written texts. A great cultural heritage, that had been accumulated and transmitted by word of mouth (poetry, *ḥadīṯ*), was now transmitted in writing; and new texts were immediately committed to writing.

(3) As a separatist sect struggling to establish their identity, the Karaites were avid polemicists. Their eagerness to polemicize created pressure to produce new texts; The void left by their rejection of Rabbanite models led them to adopt a readily available option in their culture, that is, writing, as their official mode of producing these texts.

Once the written text had been accorded official status with the Karaites, a new norm for the structure of such works was established. As already pointed out, the (few) Rabbanite written texts were characterized by their lack of a coherent, systematic structure and a display of oral transmission. Karaite texts, however, established a new model of literary production: a written text intended for a reading public rather than for personal use. No longer a mere instrument structured for memorizing an oral performance, the written text became its own performance: a thematic piece following the logic of reading, systematically divided into chapters and topics and headed by a methodological introduction, written in first person and attributed to its real author. The Karaites utilized this official writing model to build up their literature as an alternative to

[4] See, e.g., Goldziher's discussion (1971:II, 175-180) of the evolution of the term *iǧāza* in Arabic culture.

Rabbanite models. Since Saʿadya Gaon also made use of the literary alternative established by the Karaites, it came to be identified specifically with his literary output and lost its Karaite identification. The immediate acceptance of the model by the Rabbanites after Saʿadya Gaon again demonstrates the great Rabbanite need for such a model and the readiness to adopt it once it was made available.

3. *Third contribution: preparation of language-setting for the new writing models*

The third major contribution of Karaite writing to the Jewish culture of the tenth century was the preparation of language-setting for the new literary models; i.e., the establishment of a division of function between Hebrew and Arabic as the languages of writing for Jewish literature. Essentially, the traditional Hebrew/Aramaic diglossia in the written language was replaced by a Hebrew/Arabic diglossia, with Arabic replacing Aramaic. This process was by no means "natural," or "self-evident." The rejection of Aramaic as a language of writing, mainly by the Karaites, disrupted the traditional Jewish language-setting, allowing the various available linguistic options to compete for the status of "written language." Thus, at a relatively early stage in Karaite literature, one finds Binyamin al-Nahāwandī offering the option of using solely Hebrew for writing (and even, apparently, for speaking!);[5] The option was ultimately rejected. Daniel al-Qūmisī, born in Persia and active in Jerusalem in the first half of the tenth century, still wrote most of his works in Hebrew, judging from the surviving fragments. However, Salmon ben Yeruḥim and Sahl ben Maṣliaḥ, who were active in Jerusalem about one generation later, wrote some of their works in Hebrew and some in Arabic. One generation later Yefet ben ʿAlī was writing all his works (of those extant) in Arabic, as did the later Karaite authors.

Despite some attempts, Hebrew did not become the exclusive language of writing in Karaite literature. Gradually it was abandoned in some fields of writing and supplanted by Arabic. Hebrew could not be made into a language of writing without building up a set of linguistic and stylistic registers, to meet the writers' needs. The use of Hebrew faced various constraints, such as the Karaite's

[5] See on this issue ch. 7.

reluctance to make any use of Rabbanite language, which could have offered, at least in the halakhic field, ready registers; and the state of Biblical Hebrew as a dead, classical tongue. Based on these constraints, it was apparently easier to construct linguistic registers for some literary needs than for others. Wherever it was more difficult to construct, in a short time, a suitable Hebrew register than to use a readily available Arabic one, Hebrew was dropped in favor of Arabic. Such was the case in Karaite Bible exegesis. Daniel al-Qūmisī's Hebrew commentaries clearly illustrate the great difficulties involved in creating a Hebrew register for exegesis and the considerable degree of Arabic interference in the Hebrew text. One generation later, Karaite Bible commentators no longer used Hebrew, preferring instead to write in Arabic.

Finally, a division of labour was established between the two languages: Arabic was accorded the communicative function of language, while Hebrew was granted the festive-ceremonial one. An Arabic text was supposed to render clear, understandable meaning; an Hebrew text was expected to make the reader marvel at the beauty and sophistication of wording. During an intermediate phase before this division of labour was consolidated, the same texts were often written in two versions, Hebrew and Arabic (e.g., the genre of refutations, written by both Karaites and Saʿadya Gaon). The two languages competed here for the same body of literature, each fulfilling a different function of the written language. The competition is mostly apparent in Karaite writings. Saʿadya Gaon also made his contribution, of course, but the tendencies evident in his works are different from those of Karaite literature.

The question of the tenth century Jewish contacts with Arabic literature in the East exemplifies the difficulties in discussing Jewish cultural history without considering the entire literary output of the period and its intra-relationships. This must encompass *all* Jewish output (not only its supposedly "literary" corpus), including both Rabbanite and Karaite literature. Karaite literature in particular presents the arena in which the events most significant for the evolution of Jewish literature in this period took place. In Karaite literature the conditions necessary to maintain the dynamics of Jewish literature were created at a time when the center of the literary system had begun to stagnate. Karaites brought in literary models appropriated from Arabic, legitimized writing as an official mode of literary production, and prepared the division of labour between the two languages of writing employed in Jewish culture for centuries to come.

CHAPTER SEVEN

"WORDS BEAUTIFULLY PUT": HEBREW VERSUS ARABIC IN TENTH-CENTURY JEWISH LITERATURE

Introduction

The first half of the tenth century was a period of growth and development for Jewish literature under Islamic rule. This era witnessed the first signs of contact with Arabic, which was to bring about a major change in the Jewish literary system. New models for writing were introduced, both in Rabbanite literature (mainly through the literary activities of Saʿadya Gaon) and in its Karaite equivalent.

The introduction of new writing models into Jewish literature raised the question of which language to use for them. This was no simple question, as the Jews lived in a complex multi-lingual situation. In the urban centres their spoken language was Arabic, while in the rural areas of Mesopotamia they still spoke Aramaic (Blau 1962:181-82; Blau 1981²:19-20).[1] Three languages, however, served them in writing: Aramaic, Hebrew, and Judaeo-Arabic. While Aramaic at that time still preserved its status as the principal language of writing in Rabbanite literature, based mainly in the Babylonian centre, Hebrew was also used: Mishnaic Hebrew served together with Arabic in prose writings (perhaps in Palestine more than in Babylonia), liturgical poetry (*piyyuṭ*) developed its own Hebrew poetic language, and Karaite literature created a kind of "non-Rabbanite"[2] Hebrew to fulfill its writing needs, which was used together with Judeo-Arabic. The use of Arabic as the language of writing penetrated Jewish literature and gradually spread, especially in Karaite literature, but also on the periphery of Rabbanite liter-

[1] Morag (1960:220-21) even claims that in Babylonia Aramaic was the main language spoken.

[2] This does not mean a language entirely devoid of all elements of Rabbinic Hebrew, and indeed this was not entirely the case with Karaite Hebrew (see Goldenberg 1973-74:132). But the Rabbinic elements, even where present, were never dominant in Karaite Hebrew, and in any event, it was considered non-Rabbinic Hebrew by those who used it.

ature (such as in the writings of Saʿadya Gaon[3]). For Rabbanite literature this was only the beginning of a process whereby Aramaic was replaced by Arabic as the official language of writing (Blau 1962:282-83; Blau 1981² :20-22; Rabin 1981:23-24).

This was, therefore, a period of flux and change in the Jewish language scene of the East—mainly regarding the language of writing, since the major transition in spoken language from Aramaic to Arabic had apparently already taken place. The triple language situation prevailing in writing at this time was thus actually only temporary, as Arabic encroached upon Aramaic and replaced it. It was an intermediate stage between the previous situation, in which Aramaic and Hebrew had divided up the functions of the written language, and the future situation, when Arabic and Hebrew would divide those functions, although not necessarily according to the same divisions as in the previous situation. This process reveals a basic diglossic pattern in the Jewish linguistic system, within which two languages functioned simultaneously as the language of writing: Hebrew, the "original national language," and a second, "foreign" language acquired through many years of coexistence—first Aramaic (which, as time went by, also acquired the status of a "national language") and later Judeo-Arabic.[4]

---

[3] The description of Saʿadya Gaon as being on the periphery of Rabbanite literature is based on the literary models he used, and not on the ideology he expressed. Although Saʿadya Gaon has remained in our historical memory as the most important figure in Rabbanite literature of the early tenth century, the writing models he used were most unusual in contemporary Rabbanite literature, and at the same time very similar to those used in Karaite writing, which indeed was on the periphery of the Jewish literature of the time.

[4] Interestingly, despite the fact that both Aramaic and Arabic were originally "foreign" languages whose use was the result of long Jewish co-existence with other nations, the two have been ascribed unequal status today. Because of the canonization of the Talmud and later Halakhic and Midrashic literature, Aramaic is considered a holy tongue "naturally" suited to Jewish religious literature; while Arabic, which was used for the same purpose and almost for the same genres, (such as Halakhic writings, Responsa and Midrash, not to mention Biblical commentaries) is considered a foreign language, whose deep encroachment into all genres of Jewish writing is somehow puzzling. For example: "It has often been asked why the Jews so readily gave up their inherited language and became, in a relatively short time, almost completely absorbed into the linguistic culture of their Arab masters. How did it happen that ... they employed an Arab vernacular *even in commentaries on the Bible and tracts of law*?" and "... The readiness to turn to Arabic is so evident that one cannot but wonder how it came about that the latter had almost superseded Hebrew and Arabic *even in the most sacred matters of Judaism*" (Blau 1981² :19-20. My emphases; see also Blau 1962:282).

1. *Hebrew/Aramaic diglossia*

In this diglossia situation, each of the languages fulfilled different functions in writing. Let us consider briefly the "Hebrew/Aramaic" diglossia in Babylonia preceding any contact with Arabic, according to the most characteristic examples of each of these two languages. It appears that Aramaic was used for both Halakhic and economic communication with the various Jewish communities, and in fact for all informative writing. Its function was one of reportage, of conveying information. Hebrew, on the other hand, was used mainly for liturgical poetry, a literary model in which the informative function held very low priority. The themes were fixed by the weekly portion of the Torah; the emphasis was on revealing the expected contents, that is, on poetic language and its non-semantic aspects (such as alliteration, rhyme, strophics, alphabetical and name acrostics and others). In other words, Hebrew was used in a literary model that gave great preference to the poetic and festive functions of the language, largely at the expense of comprehensibility (Fleischer 1975:269-72).

It appears that what was natural in Aramaic seemed "foreign" and suspect in Arabic. This feeling is sometimes even attributed to the Jews of the period. When Goitein talks, for example, of the Aramaic translation of the Torah and Hafṭarot being read in the synagogue while the Arabic translations of the Bible and prayers were not ("the Arabic language was not permitted in the synagogue rites"), he says: "There was a clear feeling: *Aramaic had been the national language for fourteen hundred years and it was sacred*, while Arabic, for all its familiarity, and despite the fact that most of the people spoke it ..., was considered *a foreign language* and was not admitted into the congregation" (Goitein 1962:48, my emphases). On this point, there seems to be some confusion between the sacred status of a text and the sacred status of a language. The Aramaic translation of the Torah was read in the synagogue because that specific text had been canonised as a ritual text; this does not necessarily mean that the Aramaic language itself held sacred status.

The wonder at the supercession of Arabic "even into the most sacred matters of Judaism," as Blau puts it, is not a wonder at all, if one distinguishes between the status of *texts* within Jewish literature and the status of the *language* in which they were written, and if one looks at the language in the context of the function it fulfilled in the literary system. Blau himself does so when he offers his explanation for that "wonder": "... the reason should be sought in the function of the language which was pushed aside by Arabic in the Fertile Crescent, that is, Aramaic." (Blau 1962:282); "The very fact that Aramaic, used in both everyday vernacular and religious writing, was supplanted by Arabic in oral communication almost automatically entailed the use of Arabic in religious works as well." Blau 1981[2]:21-22). Arabic then, replaced Aramaic by taking upon itself the functions which Aramaic had previously fulfilled.

This division of functions between Hebrew and Aramaic, according to which Hebrew primarily served the poetic function, while Aramaic served to communicate, definitely did not apply in the same way and with the same clarity to all sectors of the Jewish literary repertoire. The differences in the use of Hebrew in Babylonia and Palestine have already been mentioned, and the facts regarding other peripheral communities, such as Persia and North Africa, indicate similar situations there. This represents a common relationship between the two languages of Rabbanite literature, in the canonized centre of the Jewish literary system. The situation was neither new nor alien to Jewish culture. Perennial existence in a diglossic reality had created an awareness of the use of different languages for different needs. This situation recalls Rabbi Yonatan's statement: "It is befitting that the world use four tongues: the foreign tongue [*laʿaz*, i.e. Greek] for singing, the Roman tongue [Latin] for military affairs, Syriac for lamentation, Hebrew for speech" (Yerushalmi, Meg., I, 71b; see also Kutscher 1972:59). Regarding the Rabbanite use of Hebrew at the beginning of the tenth century, we might even claim that the more it served ceremonial purposes, the more stylistically distinct it became from Aramaic and even from Mishnaic Hebrew; whereas the more it was used for informative or professional purposes (usually, Halakhic purposes), the more it resembled Mishnaic Hebrew and Aramaic in style.

For example, in the Hebrew letter of Ben Meir, Head of the Palestinian academy, to the Babylonian Geonim concerning intercalation (ca. 921, Bornstein 1904:45-56), one can distinguish three different registers of Hebrew, which interchange according to the subject matter: the exalted rhymed opening and ending are close in style to that of prayer and liturgical poetry (46-47); in the section dealing with its writing circumstances, which mentions Saʿadya Gaon in a negative light (that is, the section that refers to "the real world"), the letter contains a relatively large number of calques (loan translations) to Arabic (50); and the discussion of the intercalation itself is written in Mishnaic style, in the professional register ready for this purpose (51-55).

2. *Hebrew/Arabic diglossia*

The advent of Arabic into the Jewish repertoire of written languages in the East was described above as the process of Arabic replacing Aramaic. Although this description is correct from a historical perspective, it should be emphasized that this process did not entail Arabic gradually easing out Aramaic of its functions in order to fulfill the same functions. The penetration of Arabic was only one of many wider contacts between Jewish and Arabic literature, during which numerous new functions, writing models and literary genres entered the Jewish literary system, while some of the old were rejected. The entire literary system was therefore different from the one in which Aramaic had functioned. Moreover, the exchange of Aramaic for Arabic was not monolithic in all sectors of the Jewish literary system, and did allow for Arabic to gradually spread into the territory of Aramaic.

If Arabic penetrated Rabbanite literature through rivalry with Aramaic, in Karaite literature the situation was entirely different. Karaite Judaism dispensed with Aramaic long before Rabbanite Judaism did so. Apart from the writings of Anan ben David, which predate this period by approximately one hundred and fifty years, there are no Karaite texts written in Aramaic; the Karaites seem to have identified Aramaic with the Rabbanite world. Arabic was therefore accepted by the Karaites as their written language not through rivalry with Aramaic, but by filling the vacuum left by their ideological refusal to use Aramaic. Nevertheless, the fact that Arabic became the written language of the Karaites should by no means be regarded as self-evident or "automatic," nor did it necessarily stem from the refusal to use Aramaic. On the contrary, it would appear that the rejection of Aramaic disrupted the established relations in the language system (like those between Aramaic and Hebrew), thus opening a cometition of all the linguistic options available to Jewish literature for the status of "the language of writing." Thus, in the earlier stages of Karaite literature (the first half of the ninth century) there arose yet another, non-Arabic, option for the language of writing: Hebrew. Further, it seems that the Hebrew option was put foreword not only for writing, but also for speech! This was suggested by Binyamin al-Nahawāndī, and I know of only one reference to it: a short remark, almost an aside, by al-Qirqisānī. In a discussion of whether vows containing the name of God are valid when taken in a language other than Hebrew, he says:

> And in this contention there is also an answer to Binyamin's claim *that we should speak nothing but Hebrew among ourselves*(!)[5] (my emphasis).

Whether Binyamin al-Nahawāndī indeed publicly voiced a call for the revival of Hebrew as a spoken language, and whether it was favourably received, we shall never know. The historical selection of documentation preserves testimony of his religious and theological opinions, but not of his views—or vision—concerning the Hebrew language. Nonetheless, the remains of his writings, which include fragments from a Book of Precepts, a Book of Laws, and some Bible exegeses, are all written exclusively in Hebrew. This perhaps testifies at least to Binyamin al-Nahawāndī's ambition to make Hebrew the only language of writing, if not to his much wider vision. The fragments of Ḥīwī al-Balkī's refutation on the Bible (Fleischer 1982, including further refs.), while somewhat more restricted, offer additional testimony to non-Rabbanite Hebrew writing in non-Rabbanite circles in the middle of the ninth century.

While the option to make Hebrew the exclusive written language of Karaite literature arose at an early stage, it was never accepted. Daniel al-Qumīsī, who was born in Persia and worked in Jerusalem in the first half of the tenth century, still wrote most of his works in Hebrew, if we are to judge from the extant fragments (assuming that their identification as belonging to Daniel is correct). These include Bible exegeses, a Book of Precepts, a propaganda epistle written entirely in Hebrew, and only one propaganda epistle (if it is indeed his) in Arabic. But Salmon ben Yeruḥim, who lived and worked in Jerusalem roughly one generation later, and Sahl ben Maṣliaḥ in the second half of the tenth century, wrote some of their works in Hebrew and some in Arabic. Yefet ben ʿAlī (yet one more generation later) wrote all his works (those that remain) in Arabic.[6] The remains of works by other Karaites of the

[5] *wafī hāḏā radd(un) ʿalā binyamīn fī qawlihi annahu lā yağūz(u) lanā an natakallam(a) fīmā baynanā illā biluġat al-ʿibrānī* (Nemoy 1939:4, 645).

[6] Yefet ben ʿAlī's existing Hebrew works are later translations from the original Arabic.

tenth and early eleventh centuries, such as Ibn Saqawayh, David ben Abraham al-Fāsī, Joseph Ibn Nūḥ, Abū al-Farağ Hārūn, and Joseph Ibn Bak̲tawayh, are also all written in Arabic as opposed to Hebrew. It should be emphasized that both exclusive and partial writing in Hebrew appears to emanate from Palestine Karaite circles, whose origins were in Persia. We have no testimony regarding the Babylonian Karaites language of writing apart from al-Qirqisānī's works, and these are written in Arabic. It is possible that the option of Hebrew never arose there at all, only that of Judeo-Arabic.

Hebrew thus did not become the exclusive written language of Karaite literature. After this option was introduced, there were attempts in Karaite literature to put it into practice, but it was gradually abandoned in certain genres, as Arabic took its place. The attempt to entrust to Hebrew all the functions of a written language, as dictated by the needs of Karaite literature, was unsuccessful: Hebrew, apparently, could not cope with all of them. Outside Rabbanite Hebrew, there was scarcely a solid and live stratum of Hebrew that could begin to function as a written language for the changing literary needs. To make Hebrew into the language of writing would have meant constructing a completely new system of linguistic registers to suit the dictates of the new literary models. The Karaites sought to avoid Rabbanite language (which could have offered, at least in Halakhic subjects, ready-made registers) and their knowledge of Rabbanite Hebrew was likely insufficient. Meanwhile, Biblical Hebrew was a dead language. For those reasons, it was apparently easier for them to construct linguistic registers for certain purposes than for others. Where it was more difficult to construct a suitable Hebrew register in a short time, and suitable Arabic registers already existed, Hebrew was abandoned in favour of Arabic.

This occured in the main genre of Karaite writing, Biblical exegesis. The Hebrew Biblical commentaries written by Daniel al-Qūmisī testify clearly to the lack of a suitable Hebrew register for such writing. These works demonstrate the difficulty in creating such a register, and the great extent of Arabic interpolation into Hebrew writing, even to the point of frequent dovetailing of Arabic words and phrases into a Hebrew text (see for example Markon 1957). A mere generation later, the Karaite Biblical exegetes Salmon ben Yeruḥim and Sahl ben Maṣliaḥ had given up writing in Hebrew entirely, and wrote their commentaries only in Arabic.

3. *The division of functions between Hebrew and Arabic*

In the case of refutations, another flourishing genre in Karaite literature, the exchange of languages was less drastic than with Biblical exegesis. Refutation literature was actually written by both Karaites and Rabbanites; but while most Karaite authors wrote refutations, very few Rabbanites are known to have done so, except for Saʿadya Gaon, who outwrote them all (Drory 1988:156-78). In the first half of the tenth century it appears that both languages were used. There are refutations written in Hebrew, as well as in Arabic. Is this a case of two languages fulfilling the same functions indiscriminately? If we had before us either Hebrew or Arabic texts, we would tend to describe the situation as a rivalry between the two languages over the status of the official language of writing, where the preference for one language over the other depends upon convenience, or the ideological stance of the writer. But in fact we have texts from this time that were written in two versions, one in Hebrew and one in Arabic. This raises a question, since it does not seem to be a matter of writing in two languages for two different purposes, but rather of writing in different languages for the very same purpose. In any event, in most cases we have only one version—the Hebrew—containing a declaration that the author intends to write a second, Arabic version; sometimes there is a testimony to the actual existence of the second version. Salmon ben Yeruḥim, in his refutation of Saʿadya Gaon entitled *The Book of the Wars of the Lord*, writes:

> And I will respond to him (i.e., Saʿadya Gaon) a suitable response
> In Hebrew and also in Arabic. (Davidson 1934:36)

And:

> Your (Saʿadya Gaon's) sharp spears and arrows
> Will turn back on themselves towards your words,
> ... I will refute them
> And do better than you...
> I will also write in the tongue of Ishmael [That is, in Arabic],

> And I will set [my refutations] out wisely and knowledgeably. (Davidson 1934:60)

We do not have the actual Arabic version of this refutation, but in his Arabic commentary of Psalms 104, xix, Salmon ben Yeruḥim comments: *kamā šaraḥt(u) fī kitāb al-radd ʿalā al-fayyūmī*, "As I explained in my response to Saʿadya Gaon" (Davidson 1934:7), and it is possible that this phrase refers to the Arabic version of the refutation.

Sahl ben Maṣliaḥ writes in his response to the refutation of Jacob ben Samuel, a disciple of Saʿadya Gaon:

> And you also wrote: "Your responses should be in the holy tongue" ... and since you said: "in the holy tongue," I have replied to you from beginning to end in the same order as you wrote. I have done as you requested, though I did not wish it nor is it fit in my eyes to write as you have done, for I desire that the reader may read it easily. *Perhaps I shall write this epistle in Arabic too, so that those who do not know the Jewish tongue (i.e. Hebrew) may also read it, as I cannot permit your severe accusation not to be accessible to all men. I therefore desire to write it in another language, so that all who hear it may reproach you when you write opinions inappropriate to the traditions of learned men, because you wrote to me a letter in the tongue of Ishmael* and I read in it harsh words. (Pinsker 1860:2, 25, my emphasis)

Sahl ben Maṣliaḥ is declaring here his intention to write an additional version of this refutation, in Arabic. He also implies that Jacob ben Samuel wrote to Sahl ben Maṣliaḥ both in Hebrew and in Arabic.

To those who wrote both in Hebrew and in Arabic, one must now add Saʿadya Gaon, who produced both a Hebrew and an Arabic version of at least two essays: the *Egron* (more accurately, the introduction to it, Allony 1969:19-22; see ch. 8) and the *Sefer hagalui* (Hebrew version: Schechter 1902:37-40, 44-47; 1903:4-7; Chapira 1914. Arabic version: Harkavy 1892:133-235; Lambert 1900; Malter 1912; 1921:387-94; Stern 1955). In addition, the Arabic title to *Essa mešali*: *al-radd ʿalā ben ašār ʿibrānī* ("A Response to Ben Asher, in Hebrew") possibly hints at the existence of an Arabic version (Lewin 1943:496; Klar 1954:281).[7]

---

[7] Wertheimer suggests, on the basis of an analysis of the sources, that Ḥīwī al-Balḵī also wrote his refutation in both Hebrew and Arabic (Wertheimer

Why did some authors feel the need to write their essays both in Hebrew and in Arabic? An answer could found by examining the differences between the Hebrew and Arabic introductions to Saʿadya Gaon's *Egron* (Allony 1969:148-163; Drory 1995), or his explanation in the Arabic introduction to the *Sefer hagalui* of his need to write a *tafsīr*, commentary, on the Hebrew version of the book (Harkavy 1892:161 ff.). Taking into account also Sahl ben Maṣliaḥ's previously quoted words, the authors seemed to feel that a Hebrew version was "inadequate," and therefore either explanations or a second version were necessary in Arabic. It is as if writing in Hebrew was not "authentic," not capable of expressing things "as they really are"; and that in order to communicate complex ideas accurately, one must write in Arabic.[8] Sahl ben Maṣliaḥ expresses this feeling in the above passage, when he says that he may write an Arabic version of his response to Jacob ben Samuel the Rabbanite, so that ben Samuel's harsh accusations and their grave significance would reach as wide an audience as possible (not only those who understand Hebrew); perhaps he felt the accusations to be insufficiently clear in Hebrew. Saʿadya Gaon describes the readers' incomprehension of the first Hebrew version of *Sefer hagalui*, and while he ascribes the lack of comprehension to their ignorance [*ǧahl*] (Harkavy 1892:161, 163, 165), this does illustrates how alien—and therefore how uncommunicative—the Hebrew register that he had chosen to use in this book actually was.[9]

If writing in Arabic satisfied the needs for precise expression which could be understood by all, what need was filled by writing the texts in Hebrew? What was demanded from Hebrew writing, which could not be satisfied by writing in Arabic? Again, specific references show that first and foremost, writing in Hebrew dem-

---

1925:22). What we have of his writings is, in any event, only in Hebrew (Fleischer 1982). There are also several short Arabic paraphrases of his words (Zucker 1959:14, 28).

[8] See also Cohen's remark regarding the pair of letters from 1039, one in Hebrew and one in Arabic, concerning the conflict over the Palestinian Gaonate: "Clearly they were intended to form a pair. [...] Perhaps the author of the Arabic letter, Shemarya ben Maṣliaḥ, wanted, simply, to make more explicit certain vague allusions incorporated into the more flowery, but less specific, rhymed-prose Hebrew epistle (the complicity of the Qayrawan notables, the malevolent of Nathan's Fustat relatives, the proposed diplomatic strategy)." (Cohen 1976:17); I thank Prof. M. Cohen for drawing my attention to his article.

[9] Cf. ch. 10, note 26.

onstrated ability, it gave the learned author an opportunity to show off his command of the language. Sahl ben Maṣliaḥ says, in his verse response (as opposed to his prose response) to Jacob ben Samuel:

> Remember the arrogance in your words
> When you said: "Let it be written in the holy tongue, as I did"
> Behold, my quiver is full of arrows, and I will teach you.
> And if you continue to provoke me,
> I will ply you with drink from the same cup and I will intoxicate you.
> (Pinsker 1860:2, 24; Nemoy 1972:162)

In other words: You challenged me to respond in Hebrew, as you wrote to me. I will show you that I can write as well as you and even better! Here, we cannot help but recall similar words found in the responses of Menaḥem ben Sarūq's disciples to Dunaš ben Labraṭ, in Spain[10].

3.1. *The commitment to the grammatical rules of Hebrew*

As writing in Hebrew was a sign of erudition, the writer often sought to display his command of its grammatical rules; Further, his writing was often appraised according to his level of success in mastering grammar. Thus Saʿadya Gaon, in his refutation of Daniel al-Qūmisī, opens his essay by criticising the standards of al-Qūmisī's Hebrew:

> I have found a book written by Daniel ben Moshe, known as al-Qūmisī, for the instruction of the people regarding their inheritance. I gave the book my attention, wishing to learn of its contents and its author, and when I began to read, I found that this Qumīsī has six faults ... showing inappropriate lack of knowledge. The first is that *he does not understand the holy tongue*... (Schechter 1903:42, my emphasis)

In his refutation of Ḥīwī al-Balḵī, Saʿadya Gaon says: "You know nothing about the language of the people and their [proper] ways of writing—so how do you dare raise accusations against them?" (Schirmann 1965:35)

An additional example can be found in the words of Sahl ben Maṣliaḥ: the first issue he sees fit to criticize in the epistles of Jacob ben Samuel, even before he begins his real argument, is Ben Samuel's mistakes in Hebrew grammar:[11]

---

[10] See ch. 9, section 4.

[11] Cf. also the apology for mistakes in Hebrew by Ṭubia ben Moshe, an elev-

> You also wrote in your letter to me: "You are anxious, and wish to warn and admonish the people and to testify from a place of prayer—ממקום קידה—and worship". You wrote קידה with a יו״ד, and this is incorrect as it comes from ויקד ארצה and the imperative of the causative is הקד, as in הקב, with no place for a יו״ד as you wrote. And if you say: "I wrote קידה meaning 'the place of the incense'," you should know that it should not be written with a יו״ד ... . *So far I have found nearly sixty errors in your letters, some of spelling, some of meaning; and he who wishes to argue with* בני מקרא *(may God protect and preserve them) cannot be someone like you for it is incumbent upon him first to learn before questioning, to save himself from shame.* (Pinsker 1860:2, 27, my emphasis)

Clearly, knowledge of the rules of Hebrew language was seen as a precondition to writing, at a time when those rules had not even been formulated, and grammar was not yet a formal discipline![12] However, there were no such demands when writing in Arabic. In Jewish culture, the idea that one should be aware of language and its rules, and preoccupy oneself with studying them, was associated only with Hebrew. Jewish Arabic writing reflects the level of Jewish knowledge of Arabic: Jews usually wrote in Middle Arabic, often straying from the classical normative grammar (Blau 1981²:23 ff). Apart from a lack of attention to the language itself, this indicates that Jews were not interested in Classical Arabic, the language of Arabic literature (Blau, *ibid.*). Further, they made no attempt in this period to adopt classical Arabic as the language of their writings, despite the prestige it enjoyed in Arabic culture (as indicated by the concept of the *faṣāḥa* related to it).

3.2. *The concept of the beauty of the Hebrew language*

The attention to language which we have seen with relation to Hebrew writing did not limit itself to the rules of grammar. Sahl ben Maṣliaḥ thus continues:

> It is written: "The heart of the righteous studieth to answer, but the mouth of the wicked poureth out evil things." [Proverbs 15, xxviii]. The interpretation: the Wise One says that the heart of a righteous

enth century Karaite, in the opening of his *Oṣar neḥmad*: "And you, my brothers, do not accuse me if you find mistakes in my language ... for from the tongue of Ishmael I have translated into Hebrew" (Poznanski 1897:167, n. 1).

[12] On the creation of official linguistic standards and the formulation of grammar for a classical language as testimony to its higher status in a diglossia situation, see Rabin 1985. Rabin brings examples of ninth century Latin, Greek, Arabic and Hebrew. See also Rabin 1981:25-26.

> man will always think deeply before answering his questioners with honest answers, and he will answer with *beautiful words* [ביופי מאמרו] and honest wisdom, for he will answer his disputant in righteousness and faith, as it is written: "The heart of the righteous studieth to answer." But the wicked man, when asked and has nothing to reply, will express wicked thoughts and utter curses and abuse to those who scorn him for his ready answers, as it is written: "the mouth of the wicked poureth out evil things." (Pinsker 1860:2, 27, my emphasis)

Sahl ben Maṣliaḥ emphasizes the contrast between the righteous and the wicked man, first from the point of view of the wisdom contained in the righteous man's answers (as opposed to the trivial "ready answers" of the wicked man). Next, he contrasts "the beautiful words"[13] of the righteous man to the lack of culture in the expression ("curses and abuse") of the wicked man. Weight is given here to the mode of expression, with emphasis on its aesthetic eloquece.

3.3. *The festive function of Hebrew as opposed to the communicative function of Arabic*

It becomes clear that writing in Hebrew was a mode of expression involving much attention to the language itself, as well as great awareness of its rules, its structure, and the stylistic options it offered the writer—Jews writing in Arabic had no interest in these aspects. Added to this the fact that Hebrew writing almost always used various prosodic and other complicated ornamental structures, a facet which was most apparent in the refutation literature (see

[13] Cf. the colophon of the Cairo codex of the *Book of Prophets* (whose date corresponds to 897 CE), where the beauty and eloquence of the words of the Prophets are no doubt emphasized: "וייסדום באמונתם בטעמי שכל בפירוש דיבור בחיך מתוק ביופי מאמר" (Gottheil 1905:639-41). There is, however, some disagreement as to the identity of those referred to in this colophon. Gottheil (*ibid.*) assumes they are the Masorites, but nevertheless also suggests the Karaites, a line of thought later developed by Wieder (1962:60, 85). To my mind, this being the colophon to the *Book of Prophets*, these are the Prophets themselves, who are believed to have transmitted—and maybe even to have written—the prophecies entrusted to them by God. One cannot but recall in this connection the Muslim view of the perfect style and beautiful literary form of the Koran [*iʿǧāz al-qur'ān*] (al-Ṭabarī 1957-1960:1, 10, 13-20; Ibn Fāris 1963:40-48; al-Bāqillānī 1981[5] :118, 302-303; al-Rummānī 1968[2] :75; al-Kaṭṭābī 1968[2] : 29-34; al-Ǧurǧānī 1968[2] : 118-119; ʿAbd al-Ǧabbār 1960: 304-315). Cf. also the words of Saʿadya Gaon in his introduction to the *Egron*: "ותלט עלגתם על שפר אמרינו ולא נכון כן" (Allony 1969:158). Hebrew is then, by nature, a language of שפר אמרים, words beautifully put.

Drory 1988:125-27). Thus, we can conclude that Hebrew writing did indeed serve a different purpose than writing in Arabic, even when used in apparently the same genre for the same subjects. While Arabic writing accommodated the communicative (or, rather, referential[14]) function of the language, Hebrew writing accommodated its festive and grandiloquent function. In the Arabic text, the author was chiefly concerned that his words be well understood; in Hebrew, the author's priority was that his words be beautifully put. In this way, he could both impress the reader with his command of the potential expressivity hidden in the Hebrew language, and also create text of festive nature.

The practice of writing both Hebrew and Arabic versions of the same text was not very widespread, and it appears to have come to an end around the middle of the tenth century. Nevertheless, it is highly significant for understanding the process whereby the functions of writing were divided between the two languages. It represents an important stage in that process—a stage at which the two languages competed for the same segment of literature, the refutation genre, with each fulfilling a different function.

Testimony to this state of affairs can be found in Saʿadya Gaon's second letter to the Jews of Egypt, following his appointment as head of the Sūra academy in Baghdad (928). As a letter of "warnings and rebukes" written in Hebrew, it clearly illustrates the conflict between the communicative and the festive functions in one text. Saʿadya Gaon's purpose in writing the letter to the Jews of Egypt was to establish his leadership. His rhetorics is structured on exhorting them to behave "righteously" in certain matters, both ethical and religious, which he detailed in his letter. He also desired to lend his letter an official, ceremonial, almost regal, complexion,[15] therefore he wrote the letter in Hebrew. But since Hebrew was associated with the festive function of the language, there was some risk that while the addressees might admire its wording, they would not pay close attention to its content. Therefore, he writes:

---

[14] To use Roman Jakobson's term in his well-known scheme. See Jakobson 1981:21-28. Jakobson addresses the basic functions of verbal communication in general; his definition of the referential and the poetic functions are applied in my discussion to written texts only.

[15] As in his first letter to the Jews of Egypt, in which he informs them of his appointment to the head of the Sūra academy (Abramson 1965:34-40).

> Children of Israel! *Do not praise the words of this letter and how beautifully they are put without obeying its contents.* For it is written `And lo, thou art unto them as a very lovely song of one that hath a pleasant voice, and can play well on an instrument: for they hear thy words, but they do them not' [Ezekiel 33,xxxii]. (Revell 1923:87, my emphasis)

It is hard to imagine that Saʿadya Gaon would have used this particular argument for his readers' obedience had the letter been written in Arabic.

As the division of functions between the two languages became firmly established and new models of writing crystallised, each of the two languages became identified with the writing-models it served. The incidence of writing twice, or at least the question of whether or not to do so, gradually disappeared. Arabic became the language of the writing-models—both Karaite and Rabbainte—that fulfilled the informative and communicative functions of Jewish literature (Bible exegesis, Halakha, philosophy, grammar, poetics, letters); Hebrew became the language of those writing-models whose purpose was to serve the festive and elevated functions of literature—mainly secular poetry, and later, artistic prose (of which the *maqāma* is one form).[16] The division of functions between the two languages becomes so clear-cut, that it is common to see in a text poems (or verses) in Hebrew ("the grandiloquent function") with

[16] During the early stages of Hebrew literature in Muslim Spain, before the clear division of functions between Hebrew and Arabic was consolidated, an attempt was made to impose this division of functions on Hebrew alone, with the functions being divided between poetry and prose. In the debates between Dunaš ben Labraṭ and his disciples and Menaḥem ben Sarūq and his disciples (see ch. 9), we see the same arguments duplicated, once in poetry and once in prose. Dunaš ben Labraṭ says in the introduction to his refutation to Menaḥem ben Sarūq: "I have written my refutation in verse / So that it will be an adornment / The rest I wrote in prose / Giving it the form of a letter / So that all learned men may read it" (Saenz-Badillos 1980:12*). The poetry here fulfills a decorative function, while the prose conveys the contents comprehensibly to anyone who may read it. This is the same argument that Sahl ben Maṣliaḥ uses to justify his writing in Arabic! The fact that Menaḥem ben Sarūq wrote his *Maḥberet*—the earliest linguistic work about Hebrew known to us in Spain—in Hebrew is further indication of the early deliberations over the division of functions. But those who came after Menaḥem ben Sarūq, such as Judah Ḥayyuǧ and his disciples, used Arabic for their linguistic writings. In Muslim Spain too, in the early stages of literary contact with Arabic, whereever it was difficult for Hebrew to cope with the challenge of the communicative function, it was finally abandoned in favour of Arabic.

their titles or words of introduction written in Arabic (the "communicative function").

3.4. *Why Jews did not write their secular poetry in Arabic*

The description of the division of functions between the two languages is the key to understanding why Jews did not write their secular poetry in Arabic, even though this was the language they used for every other kind of writing. The determining factor in the choice of Hebrew or Arabic as the language of writing was its *function* within the Jewish repertoire of languages, as opposed to the function of the other language, and not the *content* it was to express.[17]

This is proven by the incidence of writing twice, in Hebrew and in Arabic, to express the same issues. Here we witness the very process by which Hebrew acquired the status of a language fit for elevated and festive, rather than informative, expression. In the Jewish language repertoire of the time, Hebrew was already recognized as the language for elevated expression. Since in Arabic poetics language was first and foremost a vehicle for creating metaphorical worlds rather than for relating to reality (see ch. 3), Hebrew was found to be the appropriate language for secular poetry when Arabic poetics was introduced into Jewish literature. In Spain, where Jews were well-versed in classical Arabic, the language of Arabic poetry, and might well have chosen it as the language of their poetry, they intead chose Hebrew as the language of secular verse, in the second half of the tenth century. Their choice of Hebrew was not, then, determined by a lack of adequate familiarity with Arabic.[18] Rather, the Jewish poets of Spain took advan-

---

[17] On the distinction between the function and the element carrying it, see Tynjanov 1971[1929]; Bogatyrëv 1976).

[18] Blau (1962:283-84; 1981^2 :22-24) offers three explanations for the fact that Jews wrote their poetry in Hebrew: (a) the Jews spoke Middle Arabic, and "generally attained only a limited mastery of Classical Arabic"—which was the traditional language of Arabic poetry—certainly not enough for writing poetry; (b) the ideals of Bedouin society reflected in classical Arabic poetry "must have been quite alien to the world of Judaism" (1962:283), or to the "urban Jews" (1981^2 :23); (c) no religious poetry existed in Arabic, while there did exist a religious poetic tradition in Hebrew. To these Blau adds Stern's explanation (Stern 1963:254; Blau 1981^2 :223), that the Jews loved Hebrew, their holy tongue, and wished to adorn the new ideals of Jewish society with their national language. They considered themselves as serving Jewish, not Muslim, society.

tage of an existing option in the repertoire of languages available to them, a repertoire that had been prepared in the East during the first half of the tenth century: Hebrew serving only, or primarily, exalted and festive functions. The Jewish poets of Spain took

---

I would like to look at these explanations more closely, as, in my opinion, they are based on a fallacy that often appears in discussions about Hebrew-Arabic literary contacts, and which is rooted in confusion between the function of a language and the message it conveys.

Regarding explanation (a), while one may correctly claim insufficient knowledge of classical Arabic among Jews in the East, this was not so of the Jews of Spain. It is well known that the Jews of Spain were integrated into Muslim society, and this was also apparent in their Arabic education and command of the language. There is sufficient testimony to this in Hispano-Arabic literature. One anecdote related by Ibn Šuhayd (992-1035), tells of Yūsuf ibn Isḥāq al-Isrā'īlī, a Jew who studied Arabic poetry under him in Cordoba together with an Arab student. Yūsuf ibn Isḥāq outshined his Arab colleague in understanding ancient poetry and in his ability to compose a *qaṣīda* in Arabic (Ibn Bassām 1979:233-35). Following Blau's reasoning, one might expect that in Spain, Jews would write poetry in Arabic. And yet it was there, where the learned Jews knew classical Arabic, that almost all of the secular Hebrew poetry was written. In the East, on the other hand, where the Jews were indeed insufficiently versed in classical Arabic, almost no secular poetry was written (very little indeed compared to Spain). This means that it was not the poor command of classical Arabic that led to the writing of poetry in Hebrew and not in Arabic, but rather *that the very knowledge of classical Arabic brought about the writing of Hebrew poetry!* Arabic education, which included the study of classical Arabic, led to an acquaintance with Arabic verse, thus the Jews were exposed to new models of poetry. This exposure presented Hebrew verse with new functions previously foreign to it. The poetic functions of classical Arabic were grafted on to what was considered Biblical Hebrew. Stern's words in this respect seem to be most accurate: "They (i.e., the Jews) did not seek to address themselves to the larger Muslim public, *not because they would have been unable to compose poetry in Arabic*, but rather because they considered it their function to be at the service of their own particular Jewish society" (Stern 1963:254, my emphasis). Moreover, while there was Arabic poetry written by Jews in Spain, it was composed in the framework of Arabic, not Jewish, literature—as evidenced by the information and examples that have been preserved in Arabic, not Hebrew, works. Notable Jewish poets such as Samuel Ibn Negrella, Ibn al-Muʿallim (Stern 1963) and Joseph Ibn Ḥisdai (Ibn al-Qifṭī 1950:2, 237) wrote perfectly adequate Arabic poems. For other Jewish poets, writing Arabic verse was just one facet of total assimilation into Arabic society, an assimilation which even went as far as conversion to Islam. The case of Abū al-Faḍl Ibn Ḥisdai, the son of Joseph Ibn Ḥisdai from Saragossa, in the second half of the eleventh century (Ibn Bassām 1979:5, 457-94), is one such example. Ibrāhīm Ibn Sahl of Sevilia (d. 1251), who was considered an Arab poet (al-Maqqarī 1978:3, 522-27), is another. We also know of other Jews who were Arab poets (*ibid.* 522-30).

Regarding explanation (b), one may claim that Ǧahili poetry—which represented Bedouin ideals—although prestigious, was not the only accessible model of Arabic poetry. First and foremost, the Jews encountered the Arabic court poetry

up this eastern-born option, and bestowed upon Hebrew a new function: the expression new poetics adapted from the Arabic.

As Hebrew made contact with Arabic literature, its consolidation as an exalted language for festive functions was the result of several factors:

(1) Prior to the contact with Arabic literature, canonized Jewish literature had already established an opposition between festive and communicative functions of the two written languages, in which Hebrew answered to festive function (mostly in liturgy). During the early contacts with Arabic there existed, thus, a ready functional division of labour in the repertoire of Jewish languages. But that alone was not enough to make this particular division of labour the basic paradigm under the new circumstances brought about by the contact with Arabic literature. As stated, at an earlier stage the possibility had also been raised of making Hebrew the only language of writing. The new situation was also compounded by an additional factor:

(2) In the Muslim culture, classical Arabic enjoyed a prestigious status, and was conceived as having special literary qualities (the concept of the *faṣāḥa*, for example, and the *badī*ʿ theory which developed from it). Through the contact with Arabic culture, this paradigm of granting a prestige status to the classical language was adopted in Jewish culture and grafted onto the Hebrew language. Hebrew now received a tremendous boost to its previous function as a language for festive purposes. Moreover, the new borrowed function was not imposed in its entirety onto used, or "familiar" language-items (i.e., liturgical language), but rather onto unused, "new" items (i.e., Biblical language).

---

of their time; thus there was no gap between the world presented in poetry and the one in which they lived. Moreover, borrowing a literay model does not necessarily mean adopting its complete and homogenous whole; in the course of appropriation some of its elements may be totally rejected, while others may be substituted for their home equivalents.

Explanation (c) is irrelevant to the question of writing poetry in Hebrew, since liturgical poetry was not a matter of contact with Arabic literature. The problem of selecting a language for poetry arose with the *new* poetic models, which were introduced into Jewish literature following the contact with Arabic. These models had no existing tradition concerning which language should be used. This problem did not arise with regard to the old poetic models (the *piyyuṭ*), which had an established language tradition, and had no need, at this stage, to question it.

(3) A third factor, already mentioned, must also be taken into account: In Abassid court poetry (whose models were the first to be adopted by Jewish poets composing secular Hebrew verse) attention was paid to elegant and sophisticated imagery rather than to "realistic" presentation of reality (chapter three). Hebrew was suited to such poetics: owing to its status as an exalted language, weight had not been given to developing ways of conveying reality. In using it, emphasis was on its non-semantic aspects, or on those semantic aspects based on intertextuality, at the expense of developing semantic references to the world. That was the task of the other Jewish written language—Aramaic or Arabic. Hebrew was not a "concrete" language, and the designation of its words was often non-specific, even obscure (Even-Zohar 1970:291; cf. also Even-Zohar 1976); Arabic poetics opened the way to making this "non-concreteness" an aesthetic value.[19]

In summary, this division of functions between Hebrew and Arabic—Hebrew for the festive and exalted function; Arabic for the

[19] It is interesting to see how this norm still prevails some two hundred years later, in Hebrew rhymed prose, in whose creation the model of the Arabic *maqāma* was involved. One of the central poetic principles of the *maqāma* is fiction, the construction of a fictional world (see ch. 1). Although this principle crossed over into Hebrew rhymed prose, the Hebrew *maqāma* seems to have no interest in exploiting fiction to convey any significant massage about "the world". It concerns itself with fiction only insofar as it serves to demonstrate the author's verbal dexterity, not with fiction as a set of mimetic devices intended to create any kind of realistic illusion. The message itself is not nearly as interesting as the verbal artistry of its composition. One manifestation of this is, for example, the exclusion of reality-items from the text. On the other hand the Arabic *maqāma*, which is also written in ornate language and in rhyme, even though the verbal artistry is of central importance, still concerns itself (especially in al-Hama̱dāni's work) with "reality", even if only as a basis for parody and satire, and does provide us with much realistic information. If, however, one examines al-Ḥarīzī's adaptations of some *maqāmāt* by al-Hama̱dānī (Schirmann 1979:369-74), one can clearly see that in al-Ḥarīzī's *maqāmāt* (e.g. *A Meal with a Country Bumpkin*; *A Visit to a Wealthy Man*), all reality-items—food and furniture, for example—have been ousted. They are replaced by highly developed metaphorical descriptions, generally of one item of a representative and non-specific nature, composed of Biblical phrases or parts of verses. A comparison of the original Arabic version of *The Rooster Maqāma* (Stern 1946) with the Hebrew version, reveals a similar phenomenon—all the satirical elements dependent on reality are gone, replaced by the rooster's long speech, an example of verbal dexterity. Nevertheless, it should be mentioned that when al-Ḥarīzī really did wish to describe reality, he wrote his *maqāma* in Arabic and not in Hebrew (Ratzaby 1980; See ch. 10, note 26).

communicative function—was accepted not only because such functional opposition already existed in the Jewish repertoire of languages (in the division of functions between Hebrew and Aramaic); but also because Hebrew fit the new functions imposed upon it as a result of its contact with Arabic literature. Further, the possibilities of expression in the Hebrew language were appropriate to the poetics of the borrowed Arabic verse.

CHAPTER EIGHT

BILINGUALISM AND CULTURAL IMAGES: THE HEBREW AND THE ARABIC INTRODUCTION OF SAʿADYA GAON'S *SEFER HA-EGRON*

1. *Saʿadya Gaon as culture planner*

In his own perception, Egyptian-born Saʿadya Gaon (892-942 CE), who became the head of the Sūra academy in Baghdad, was the spiritual leader of the Jewish community in his generation. Displaying the acumen of a culture planner[1] and using political strategies, he managed to establish for himself a recognized cultural authority with which he was able to set up a new agenda for canonized Jewish literature (that is, its Rabbanite section), and restructure it in a way that was to completely change its face for generations to come. By introducing models of literary activity and writing which were innovative for the Rabbanite culture, but were staples of contemporary Arabic culture, and by acting to bring about their assimilation, his career radically altered the canonized Rabbanite literature.

Saʿadya Gaon introduced several new models of writing into Rabbanite literature, some in Hebrew and others in Arabic (using Hebrew script).[2] While the imprint of contemporary Arabic culture is discernible in all of them, either overtly or, in some cases, covertly, both the Hebrew and the Arabic models addressed Jewish problematics and were intended for the Jewish community. The texts that were produced according to these models dealt with issues that concerned the Jewish world of the time and became the subject of controversies among various groups, all of which considered themselves Jewish, but branded one another "heretical." Being well versed in contemporary Arab learning, its contents and its modes of expression, Saʿadya Gaon borrowed models of writing from the

---

[1] For the concept of culture planning see Even-Zohar 1994; 1997.

[2] See Drory 1988:156-178; ch. 5, section 4.

Arabic in order to express himself on Jewish matters, and insofar as he invoked aspects of Muslim learning, he did so by naturalizing them as part of the Jewish discourse.

The choice of languages for the new models of writing was not accidental: each of the two languages served for a different function of writing. As I have already argued in chapter 7 (especially 3.3), a clear-cut division of functions was being established in this period between the two languages. While Arabic served for the communicative function of the language, that is, for lucid, straightforward expression, Hebrew served for festive and grandiloquent writing (in no small measure at the expense of a clear and unequivocal message). The purpose of writing in Hebrew was to prove command of the language and to produce a text that would arouse admiration at its beauty and elegance; while writing in Arabic was intended to produce a clear and understandable text. From this respect Hebrew had a function similar (although certainly not identical) to that of unadulterated classical Arabic, which was expected to express distinctive aesthetic qualities. The difference between the Hebrew and Arabic functions is particularly striking in texts that were written in two versions, one in each language.

Nevertheless, to choose a language for writing was far from a simple, neutral decision, made according to convenience considerations, or one done solely on the linguistic level. Every language maintains its own repertoire of culturally constructed images and conceptions of "life." The choice of a language has therefore far-reaching implications for the basic cultural assumptions through which the writer delineates the cultural identity of his reading public and of himself as author. Writing in Hebrew or in Arabic suggested wholly different models of reality, and Saʿadya Gaon took full advantage of these options in the two introductions he wrote to his book *Sefer ha-egron*.

2. *Sefer ha-egron/al-Kitāb al-ǧāmiʿ*

At age twenty, while still in Egypt (in 902, according to the Hebrew introduction), Saʿadya Gaon composed a Hebrew-language lexicon for poets called Sefer ha-egron (*al-Kitāb al-ǧāmiʿ*), to which he prefaced an introduction in ornate, biblical-style Hebrew, vocalized and accented (Allony 1969). "Years later" (as he says in the introduction, without specifying how many), he prepared an expanded Arabic-language edition of the work,[3] preceded with an introduction, this time in Arabic. It is not clear whether he wrote the Arabic edition while he was still in Egypt, before embarking on his eastward journey in 915, or later, in Baghdad (i.e., after 922[4]). He followed the same pattern in one of his later works, *Kitāb al-ṭārid* ("Book of the exiled").[5] This treatise too was originally written in Hebrew (*Sefer hagalui*), but after some time the author felt the need to put out an Arabic edition in which he would explain everything that had not been understood, and indeed had aroused the readers' animosity, in the Hebrew text.[6]

The *Egron* is intended to be a handbook for poets writing in Hebrew. The first, Hebrew, edition, comprises of a Hebrew lexicon which is arranged according to two principles: first, alphabetical order according to the first letter of the word, to help build the acrostics; then, alphabetical order according to the last letter, to facilitate rhyming. A brief morphological discussion (part of which is missing in the manuscript) is included in the Hebrew introduction. The later, Arabic, edition preserves the dual alphabetical arrangement, while appending a discussion on some rhetoric and poetic matters. Saʿadya Gaon calls the acrostics *al-arkān al-awā'il* ("the initial pillars, or principles") and the rhyming *al-arkān al-awāḵir* ("the terminal pillars, or principles"), viewing them as the two "guardians" of the poem. The introduction to the Arabic edition suggests that he had noticed, since completing the Hebrew edition, that Hebrew poets needed guidance also in the practice of poetry, in matters which he called *al-awāṣiṭ* ("the middle [principles]"), for which he therefore dedicated a special discussion at the end of the lexicon.[7]

---

[3] In Arabic it is apparently called *Kitāb uṣūl al-šiʿr al-ʿibrānī*. See Allony 1969:16-19. He added to the acrostics and rhyming dictionary a translation into Arabic, and supplemented it with chapters on poetics.

[4] On the entire issuse see Allony 1969:23-25.

[5] Saʿadya Gaon wrote the Hebrew version between 931-934, after he had been removed from the gaonate by the exilarch David ben Zakkai; shortly afterward, in 935-6, he wrote the Arabic version, which was supposed to explain the Hebrew (Malter 1926:269).

[6] From the Arabic title of the Hebrew treatise *Essa mešali*: *al-radd ʿalā ben ašār ʿibrānī* ("A Response to Ben Asher, in Hebrew"), it can be inferred that this work, too, had two versions, in Hebrew and in Arabic, although the Arabic one is not extant (see Levin 1932:155; ch. 7, section 3).

[7] *wahāḏihi al-waṣā'iṭ 'llatī hiya nafs al-šīr wa'innamā al- ḥāšiyatayn lahā ka'l-ḥāfiẓatayn* (Allony 1969:154).

Following the custom in the Arabic literature of the period, both the Hebrew and the Arabic introductions are methodological in spirit, and both address two principal themes: an explanation of his reasons for composing the lexicon, and a description of the subjects covered by the work. This gives us common basis for comparing the two texts, which are supposed to explain the same point in two different languages. An analysis of the introductions shows that even when the two texts are aimed at the same target audience —an educated Jewish public interested in the Hebrew language, the Bible and the *piyyuṭ*—his choice of language caused Saʿadya Gaon to imagine in each case two completely different audiences, to project two distinct identity models on them, to address the two implicit audiences through dissimilar conceptual systems and means of persuasion, and to construct two different images of his own role vis-à-vis the audience. The choice of language led Saʿadya Gaon to create in each introduction a totally different image of his audience and of himself.

2.1. *The Arabic introduction*

The later, Arabic, introduction comes first in the treatise, before the earlier, Hebrew, one. The manuscript lacks the opening section of the Arabic introduction, which forms the beginning of the treatise. We do not know how much of the text is missing, but from the extant part it seems safe to assume that very little has been lost.

The extant part of the introduction begins by explaining why Saʿadya Gaon composed the *Egron*. The explanation revolves around the neglect of knowledge, which brings about its oblivion (*nisyān al-ʿilm*). His primary thesis is that the neglect of the Hebrew language led to its being forgotten, to the point that people can barely understand the Bible, not to speak of mastering the Hebrew vocabulary enough to exploit its richness in the practice of poetry. The *Egron* seeks to fill in such lacunas and to serve as a handbook for the study of the Hebrew language and the composition of poetry in Hebrew. Saʿadya Gaon elaborates on this line of argument by invoking a conceptual framework which was commonplace in contemporary philosophical and theological discussions, like those of the Muṭazilites and Kalām masters. Assuming that the universe is made of essences and occurrences (*uṣūl wa'aʿrāḍ*), he describes the relation between the individual and his knowledge in terms of the relation between essence and occurrence. Knowledge is occurrence, which depends on the essence, namely the individual person, for its existence. It is the property (*mulk*) of the individual, albeit a spiritual property (*nafsānī*), that is, acquired through the mind. Being a property, it is dependent on its carrier (*ğism*, or *ḥāmil*) and undergoes changes as he does.[8] The carrier of knowledge (*ḥāmil al-ʿilm*) must therefore cultivate it diligently, lest it be forgotten and lost. Saʿadya Gaon supports this argument with five verses from the *Book of proverbs* on the cultivation of wisdom,[9] including one that compares the cultivation of knowledge to a field which, if left untended, will sprout thorns. From the need to cultivate knowledge of the individual we may infer, according to Saʿadya Gaon, the need to do so within the community.[10] He cites two cases to illustrate a collective forgetting of knowledge. One is a personal testimony, in which he tells us that he heard many "disciples," or scholars (*talāmiḏ*), mentioning the oblivion which befell treatises on "the sciences based on tradition and logic."[11] The second case is a testimony of Muslims (*Banū Ismāʿīl*, "Ismaelites") on the early formulation of the rules of the Arabic language, which came as a reaction of a certain distinguished Arab figure towards a situation of neglect of the language.[12] The same situation exists among many Jews (*Banū Isrāʾīl*, "Israelites"), continues Saʿadya Gaon, who are not fluent in Hebrew, speak with mistakes, and, as mentioned, are insufficiently versed in the language to be able to exploit its richness in poetry.[13] Although Saʿadya Gaon does not state the name of the "distinguished

---

[8] Allony 1969:148, ll. 7-11.

[9] *Proverbs* 8:34; 29:18; 24:30-32.

[10] *wakamā yandarisu ʿilm al-farad min qillat al-tafaqqud kaḏālika yunsā ʿilm al-ğamāʿa bitarkihim taʿāhudahu* (Allony 1969:150, ll. 23-25).

[11] *ṯumma raʾaytu fī al-ğuzʾ min al-zamān ʾllaḏī šāʾa al-bārī ğall waʿazza ibtidāʾī fīhi talāmiḏ[an] kaṯīrīn yaḥkūn anna kaṯīran min al-ʿulūm al-ḵabariyya waʾl-qiyāsiyya ʾndarasa akṯaruhā waġabā (sic!) ʿan al-nās biğumla kitāb al-aṯqāl waʿulūm al-mabādiʾ wamā ašabaha ḏālika* (Allony 1969:150, ll. 25-29). It is not clear whether in these two examples he is referring to specific treatises, or to fields of scholarship (*ʿulūm al-mabādiʾ*= metaphisics?). A book by the name of *Kitāb al-aṯqāl* is not known. See Allony 1969:150, note 14.

[12] *wakamā yarwūn banī ismāʿīl anna baʿḍa ḵawāṣṣihim rāʾa qawman lā yufṣiḥūn al-kalām al-ʿarabī faġammahu ḏālika fawaḍaʿa lahum kalāman muḵtaṣaran fī kitābin yastadillūna bihi ʿala al-faṣīḥ* (Allony 1969:150, ll. 29-31).

[13] *kaḏālika raʾaytu kaṯīran min banī isrāʾīl lā yubṣirūn mursal faṣīḥ luġatinā fakayfa ʿawīṣahu waʾiḏā hum takallamū kān kaṯīr[an] mimmā yalfaẓūn bihi malḥūnan waʾiḏā hum šaʿarū kān al-mustafīḍ fī mā baynahum min al-arkān al-awāʾīl huwa al-qalīl, waʾl-matrūk huwa akṯar. wakaḏālika fī al-qawāfī, ḥattā sāra al-kitāb nafsuhu ʿindahum kaʾl-ġāmid min al-kalām waʾl-ġabbiyy min al-qawl* (Allony 1969:150-152).

figure" who was prompted to amend the corruption of the language, he obviously alludes here to the well-known anecdotes about Abū Aswad al-Duwalī and how he arrived at the idea of composing a grammar of Arabic.[14]

From this point, Saʿadya Gaon proceeds to describe the history of his lexicon. He recounts how he designed it, when he was twenty, to be compiled according to both the first letter of the word and the last letter (*al-qāfiya*), this "to facilitate accuracy in all things and to keep it in the memory, and so that the Hebrew language, with its difficult and simple words, will thus be preserved" (Allony 1969:152, ll. 45-46). He figured that a dictionary would meet the needs of anyone interested in writing poetry (*al-ṭālib*); but a few years later he realized that students of Hebrew poetry (*al-mutaʿallimīn*) needed more than this, that he had to expand on the very essence of poetic figures employed in poetry (*al-maʿānī anfusihā allatī fīhā yašʿurūn. Ibid.*, ll. 54-55), so he included these matters in the present edition. He specifies the subjects to be discussed, noting that he will quote examples from the early Hebrew poets, according to the principle (known of scholars and collectors of ancient Arabic verse) that antiquity determines the esteem in which a poet is held.[15] He concludes the Arabic introduction with a brief note on the order of the work, explaining that he decided to translate it into Arabic because "he saw the nation's need for this" and he hopes that God will reward him for having been useful to people.

2.1.1. *Comments on the Arabic introduction*

In the Arabic introduction, the speaker uses the first person, generally the singular. When he uses the first person plural, it is *pluralis majestatis*. Only twice the first person plural pronoun is used: "they taught *us* that diligence fights oblivion";[16] "the eloquence of *our* tongue",[17] denoting "the Jewish community" in general. But with these two exceptions, the discourse is that of an individual speaker

[14] See, for example, al-Zubaydī 1984:21-26; Abū al-Ṭayyib al-Luġawī 1974:24-30; al-Sīrāfī 1985:33-38.

[15] *ṯumma mā ra'aytu an astašhida ʿalayhi min qawl al-awwalīn yose ben yosse wayannai waelʿazar wapinḥas faʿaltu ḏālika. wa'ammā min qawl al-šuʿarā' al-aqrabīn falā taǧidunī aḏkur šay'(an) illā li'aḥmadi man kāna qawluhu marḍiyyan. fa'aqūlu walaqad aǧāda fulān fī mā qāla wa'adaʿu ʿaksahu an aqūla walaqad asā'a fulān fī mā qāla* (*ibid.*, 154, ll. 68-73).

[16] *ʿarrafūnā anna al-mulāzama tuqāwim ḥāl al-nisyān* (*ibid.*:148, ll. 14-15).

[17] *faṣīḥ luġatinā* (*ibid.*:150, ll. 33-34).

speaking in his own name and is very specific and definitive about his way in composing the book.

The image of the audience which Saʿadya Gaon is addressing emerges in this introduction in its broad definition as an audience of scholars (*talāmiḏ* [*ibid.*:150, l. 26], or *al-mutaʿallimīn* [*ibid.*:152, l. 52]) who are acquainted with scholarly knowledge (*ʿilm*) organized and processed in writing and know that such knowledge must be cultivated as part of the personal praxis which constitutes their scholarly identity; and in its narrow definition, as the group of poets, *al-šuʿarāʾ*, or *payṭanim* (*ibid.*:154, l. 68), who might have an interest in a work such as the *Egron* and derive practical benefit from. The projected audience in the Arabic introduction is, in the first place, a milieu of scholars. Only secondarily, and indeed quite vaguely (in a few offhand mentions), does "the nation" exist as the reference group, or "the public," which however is not explicitly identified as the "Jewish public." Saʿadya Gaon refers to this entity as *al-nās*, "the people," and finally also as *al-umma*, "the nation" (*ibid.*:154, l. 76), without emphasizing its Jewish identity. The book is obviously intended, in its Arabic edition, as a handbook for poets and perhaps also as a tool for understanding the Bible; in other words, as a professional work which is designed primarily for scholars and only secondarily for educated laymen, but certainly not for the entire nation.

The image of time projected in the Arabic introduction is homogeneous and unconcrete, that is, lacking specifying details on the one hand, but personal and close on the other hand. Even though basically perceived as a process which occurs in time, the particular forgetting of knowledge discussed here lacks any temporal context. From the philosophical explanation of the nature of the universe a certain relation between the individual and his knowledge is derived, which can be realized either "rightly" or "wrongly." While cultivation of knowledge is the "right" realization of this relation, its neglect is obviously a "wrong" realization of it and one should aspire to set this right as part of the correct conduct of the mind. Thus forgetting of knowledge is discussed here as a moral issue, not as a process that takes place in certain historical conditions. On the other hand, the scholarly consciousness of the author constructs a concept of time which is both short-ranged and private: the author's span of life together with the history of the dictionary,[18]

[18] *ṯumma raʾaytu fī al-ğuzʾ min al-zamān allaḏī šāʾa al-bārī ibtidāʾī fihi* [*ibid.*:150, ll. 25-26]; *fawalaftu ḏālika ʿalā mā waṣaftu waqad maḍā ilayya k̇ sanna* [*ibid.*:152, l. 47].

and a professional span of time which builds the historical consciousness of his scholarly occupation. He speaks of treatises and fields of scholarly knowledge which have been lost, presents professional—not religious, or ethnic—periodization of the generations of Jewish poets, in which he distinguishes between the early paitanim (*al-šuʿarāʾ al-awwalīn*) who are mentioned by names and are beyond literary judgment, and the later ones who, although still not of his generation (*al-šuʿarāʾ al-aqrabīn*), are not mentioned by names and whom he allows himself to put to literary judgment.[19]

The *conceptual framework* through which the argument concerning the forgetting of knowledge is put forward is, as noted, the philosophical-theological framework of scholarly discussion familiar in the contemporary Arab culture. There is nothing specifically Jewish about this knowledge which is being neglected according to Saʿadya Gaon, and its forgetting is by no means presented as having to do with the Jewish situation in the past or the present. It is first and foremost the knowledge of the learned individual (*al-ʿāqil*) that is at stake here, and its oblivion (*nisyān*) as result of neglect (*tark*) is discussed primarily in the personal context, as part of the individual's responsibility. It is the scholar's obligation to be diligent in preserving his knowledge and his language. By implication the same holds true for public knowledge (*ʿilm al-ǧamāʿa*), but even "public knowledge" is not defined here through its Jewish content, or as lying within the responsibility of the Jewish people.

Choosing *Biblical verses* to support and prove the argument on oblivion also fits the scholarly model of writing and emulates the Arabic custom of interspersing Koranic verses for the same purpose of supporting an argument. All the verses are from *Proverbs*, which Saʿadya Gaon entitles in his commentary *Kitāb ṭalab al-ḥikma*, "Book of the Pursue of Wisdom." They deal with "wisdom" in the most general sense of moral conduct as it is addressed in wisdom literature, which is the least national literary genre in the Bible. They are supposed to be taken as delivering "a moral lesson" (*ītibār li'l-ʿāqil*), without projecting any particularly Jewish content into the general philosophical framework of the introduction. On the contrary, connecting philosophical ideas to the biblical verses and thus interpreting them in a non-traditional philosophical spirit was

[19] For a highly refined discussion in similar theoretical assupmtions of a different case, cf. Algazi 1998.

a departure from the conventions of Rabbinic interpretation of the Bible as reflected in the Midrash.

The intellectual Arabic framework within which the lexicon was produced is expressly present in the Arabic introduction to the *Egron* and a respectful attitude toward that culture is displayed. The anecdote about how were the rules of eloquent Arabic first formulated, which Arab sources generally ascribe to Abū Aswad al-Duwalī, is brought here—albeit in a general way and with no historical details—as an exemplary model. The manner in which the anecdote is related shows clearly that Saʿadya Gaon sees himself as the counterpart in the Jewish society of the Arab scholar who, noticing that people were not fluent in correct Arabic, was grieved and eventually motivated to produce a work to rectify the situation. The comparison accords him a special status of being first among the reformers of language in the Jewish community, but it also places the Muslim society and the Jewish society on an equal footing: the "Ismaelites" and the "Israelites," almost identical names, are presented here as two communities experiencing the same linguistic oblivion. No acknowledgement of the Jewish people's distinctiveness is expressed here, nor any hostility or repugnance toward the Muslim society. Saʿadya Gaon is writing as a Judaeo-Arabic scholar. His learned discourse is that of the contemporary Arabic intellectual arena, in which the ethnic boundaries are blurred.

2.2. *The Hebrew introduction*

The earlier, Hebrew, introduction comes in the order of the *Egron* after the Arabic one, and unlike the latter it is complete.

The introduction opens with the assertion that Hebrew (referred to as "the holy tongue") is God's chosen language, in which the angels sing his praises. It was the language of humanity from the creation of Adam until the generation of the Tower of Babel, when humanity was divided into nations as punishment for trying to outsmart God. The human race was scattered to the four winds and made to speak in a confusion of tongues. Hebrew remained the possession of the Israelites alone, serving them in the Land of Israel, in Egypt (Moses received the Laws on Mount Sinai in Hebrew), and again in the Land of Israel until the Babylonian exile "for worshipping our King, for the singing of our Levities, for the playing of our priests, for our prophets' vision, [and] for our ministers to rule wisely" (*ibid.*:158, ll. 24-27). The exile led to the abandonment of Hebrew, for which Nehemiah chastised the nation. Since the second exile the Jewish people mingled even more among the nations. Everywhere the Jewish people intermixed with others and adopted their language, until finally Hebrew was completely displaced. This is the situation as Saʿadya Gaon writes, and he is unsparing in his condemnation: יחיל ליבנו על זאת וחית רוחינו כי נעדר נעדר מפינו הגות קדש מעוזינו ותהי לנו חזות כל משאותיו ונאמי דבר פיהו כדברי הספר החתום (pp. 158-159, ll. 40-43). He calls on the whole Jewish nation to return to Hebrew as a collective project: ובהקיץ מחזיון כי נלעג לשון בארצות שביינו: יאתה לנו ולכל עם אלהינו לדרוש ולבין ולחקריהו תמיד גם אנחנו גם טפינו גם נשינו ועבדינו לא יוח מפינו כי בו נבון חקי תורת צורינו אשו המה חיינו חייתינו אורנו מקדושינו למעולם ועד עולם (*ibid.*:159, ll. 44-48). The present book is meant to be part of that project. Its purpose lies within the framework of a comprehensive national program of a return to Hebrew, concluding with a vision in which Hebrew shall become the language of the whole world, the language in which all peoples shall worship the Lord. Although the book is obviously intended to serve in the composition of poetry and other literary forms, its declared contribution for Saʿadya Gaon is to bring Hebrew back to its former ideal status of national language spoken by all Jews in all circumstances, both formal and informal. Saʿadya's vision of the revival of the Hebrew language terminates with its becoming the language of all learned people who will be occupied in translating from all other languages (*ibid.*:159-160, ll.50-68). The introduction next provides a brief and original morphology of Hebrew and outlines the principles of Hebrew rhyming. Finally, the importance of the study of Hebrew is emphasized for understanding the words of the prophets and for praising God, the gateway to redemption.

2.2.1. *Comments on the Hebrew introduction*

As in Arabic, the Hebrew introduction also uses the argument of forgetting knowledge to explain why the lexicon was compiled. However, the Hebrew argument is presented within a completely different conceptual and rhetorical frameworks. Forgetting knowledge here becomes the forgetting of Hebrew by the Jewish people, which is described as sinful neglect resulting from the lengthy exile (itself a punishment of the Jewish people), a situation which must be remedied before redemption can be achieved.

Rather than a private person, the *speaker* in the programmatic part of this introduction is a representative of the Jewish people. Speaking in the first person plural, in the people's name, he relates the story of the Hebrew language and its oblivion as a function of the mythical-historical narrative of the Jewish people. When relating to the lexicon Saʿadya Gaon refers to himself, in the spirit of the Biblical third person, as *ha-ogger*, i.e., the author of the *Egron*. In the pragmatic part of the introduction which describes Hebrew morphology, the speaker uses the first person. Unlike the Arabic introduction, he never poses as a scholar, who is presenting a book in his field of learning to an audience of scholars and learned laymen. He adopts, rather, the mantle of a leader, even a prophet, who has come forth at a moment of crisis and is arousing the people to return to the straight path for the sake of God; in this case, the program for the revival of Hebrew.

The *time span* covered in the Hebrew introduction is immense, embracing past, present, and future. The range of time extends from the creation of the world to the very days of Saʿadya Gaon and further on to the time when Hebrew will again become the sole language spoken on earth. Notwithstanding, this enormous ethnic time span is organized historically through a precise periodization, which accords an image of "concreteness" for every stage of the story. For example, the time in which the lexicon was composed is defined as follows: ויהי בארבע עשרה שנה ומאתיים ואלף מיום נחתום חזון ונביא ויכתב האוגר את הספר הזה (*ibid.*:159, ll. 48-50). In effect Saʿadya Gaon draws on conventional Jewish ethnic-historical periodization here (from creation of the world until the division into nations; from the division until the Babylonian exile; from Nehemiah until the second exile; the exile which persists until the present time), with the emphasis on the history of the Hebrew language, its uses and its abandonment. This contrasts with the scholarly periodization which serves Saʿadya Gaon in the Arabic introduction.

Like the vast span of time, *the image of the audience* in the Hebrew introduction is also indistinct and unbounded. It is the entire Jewish people, or "the children of Israel," including infants, women, and even slaves (a Biblical rather than real reality item). Only secondarily does Saʿadya Gaon envisage the poets, or the scholars ("all the possessors of knowledge and perusers of science" [*ibid.*:160, ll.

61-62]), as his target audience. Even than he definitely sees the book as part of an enterprise of reviving Hebrew in which the whole nation is meant to participate.

Unlike the Arabic introduction, the *framework of discourse* in the Hebrew introduction is not the philosophical one. The forgetting of knowledge is discussed within the framework of the Biblical crime-and-punishment narrative: the Jewish people stray from the true road (that is, neglecting its language); they are punished by God (exile), and a prophet or leader comes forth who arouses the people to return to the righteous path for the sake of God. In this particular case, the return to righteousness involves a program to revive the language, which includes Hebrew speech, the study of the language, translation from foreign languages into Hebrew, and above all Hebrew poetry grounded in a new poetics which will give praise to God.

The *image of reality* projected in the Hebrew introduction is in fact Biblical rather than actual. This is the case with the "slaves," who, together with women and children (the weak groups in the social structure) are supposed to speak Hebrew. This is also the case with the description of the foreign languages which the Jewish people speak in their various diasporas: נפוצת מזרחה מספרת יוונית ושפת פרס ומצרים הגו חנסית וגם גלות בני קנז ובני ספרד ישיחו נועז גרי יתת כהם וכלשון עם ועם (*ibid.*:158, ll. 36-39).[20] This description seems to follow in the wake of the Bible or the constraints of rhymed prose, rather than giving an account of the actual facts: Aramaic and Arabic, which are vivid spoken languages among Jews, are not mentioned. Is this because they are not mentioned in the Bible, or because Saʿadya Gaon is not interested in the concrete situation?

From the national perspective, *observation of the surrounding Arab culture* seems irrelevant, and is indeed absent from the Hebrew introduction. The lesson that is drawn in the Arab introduction from the anecdote about Abū Aswad al-Duwalī relates to the organization of knowledge according to a specific scholarly model, and is therefore out of place in a discussion of the state of forgetting a language as the function of a national-religious sin.

[20] See also Allony's comments on this passage. He identifies חנסית as Coptic, according to Epstein; נועז as European languages; יפת as an epithet for Edom and hence also for European lasnguages. He notes that Saʿadya Gaon mentions neither Aramaic nor Arabic as the true competitors of Hebrew in this period (*ibid.*:158, ll. 39-42).

3. *Two languages, two virtual publics*

Choosing different languages for writing is ipso facto a choice of different cultural worlds, different strategies of persuasion, a different discourse, and different cultural rules. It is not a mere technical act of deciding for authorial convenience, or a desire to impress the reader by one means or another. It involves, above all, deciding between different cultural models, each with its own rhetorical techniques, modes of reasoning, and distinctive ways of building a narrative; models, which essentially serve the same purpose: to explain the collective forgetting of the Hebrew language, show why its knowledge should be restored, and point out how the *Egron* contributes to that goal.

The fact that both introductions were written by the same author for the same actual target audience—educated Jews with an interest in the Hebrew language, poetry, and the Bible—underscores the distinct difference between the two projections of audience and two self-images which Saʿadya Gaon creates in each introduction through the use of a different language. In one cultural pose Saʿadya Gaon is a Bible-type prophet who seeks to awaken the Jewish nation and restore it to righteous ways by means of a prodigious program of reviving the Hebrew language, as he would persuade us in the Hebrew introduction. In a second cultural pose he is a scholar of the Arab type who is presenting a new tool for Hebrew lexicography and poetics to a small audience of educated intellectuals, as he would persuade us in the Arabic introduction. By projecting these two imagined images on his readership, whatever its actual identity, Saʿadya Gaon sets in motion a process in which an actual milieu takes shape in the form he projected. As the Arabic models which he presented were eventually more successful than the Hebrew ones, so also the more realistic projection of the Arabic introduction was the one that effectively designed Jewish scholarly milieu. For if we are not able to discern who, exactly, in Saʿadya Gaon's generation took an interest in the new poetics which he formulates for the first time in the *Egron* and treats as though it were indispensable, yet we do know that within a few generations a scholarly concern with the Bible, the Hebrew language, and poetry becomes an established fact in the intellectual Jewish milieu.

CHAPTER NINE

DUNAŠ BEN LABRAṬ'S METRICAL INNOVATION IN LIGHT OF ARABIC PROSODY

Introduction

Throughout most of its history, Hebrew literature has been created within and alongside foreign cultures, with continuous contacts of varying forms and on different levels. The history of Hebrew literature is largely the history of these contacts, for their manifestation represents a regulating—sometimes prime—force in its development. One prominent example of such encounters between Hebrew and Arabic literature in medieval Spain was the adaptation of Arabic metrics to Hebrew poetry. Indeed, hardly any other instance in the history of Hebrew literature seems as clear and simple an example of adaptation as the introduction of Arabic metrics into Hebrew poetry by Dunaš ben Labraṭ in tenth-century Muslim Spain (circa 950 CE).

Metre has been an essential feature of Arabic poetry from its very inception. Since ancient Arabic poetry was composed orally, metre was a necessary tool in its creation.[1] Arabic prosodic rules, however, were only formulated about two hundred years later. With the evolution of Arabic linguistic disciplines an awareness of theory developed, which attracted scholarly attention to rule formulation, based on an analysis of existing material. By contrast, the rules of prosody for Andalusi-Hebrew poetry were formulated at the very same time that Arabic-oriented prosody was first introduced in Hebrew texts. The first metred poems had barely been composed when they were subjected to a meticulous examination and judged according to their adherence to strict rules and standards, which themselves were not yet fully formulated. The imitation of Arabic metrics by Hebrew poets was a conscious and intentional act, accompanied by enthusiastic pro and con declarations. These declarations may create the impression that this was a simple case

[1] This was demonstrated in the works on oral composition of classical Arabic poetry developed out of Parry and Lord's oral formulaic theory. See Lord 1974; Monroe 1972; Zwettler 1978.

of literary borrowing. The picture seems quite clear: Dunaš ben Labraṭ adopts Arabic metrics; the adherents of his rival, Menaḥem ben Sarūq, denounce Dunaš for his borrowing (while at the same time formulating their denunciation in "Arabic" metre); and an adherent of Dunaš, Yehudi ben Šešet, replies in defense of his teacher (Stern 1870; Robles 1986; Varela 1981).

The adoption of Arabic metrics and its adaptation to the structure of Hebrew language and poetic norms has aroused academic interest for several decades. The subject has been so extensively discussed, that today a general consensus has been reached. Dunaš's metrical borrowing has become a matter of common knowledge, which is reiterated in every general treatment of Andalusi-Hebrew poetry.[2] Having concurred on one interpretation, scholarly attention has shifted in recent years from Dunaš's metrical innovation to other, less familiar, metrical systems, which were apparently employed in Hebrew poetry during or even before the Spanish era: the stress-system and the syllable-system (see Fleischer 1977, and section 6 below). However, re-examination of this widely accepted consensus may well reveal that very little is truly conclusive regarding the Hebrew adaptation of Arabic metrics. Specifically, the act of "inventing" Hebrew equivalents for the basic Arabic metrical units, is not at all obvious.

[2] See Brody 1895:17-22; Halper 1913-14:159-65; Yelin 1972[2] :13-18, 44-57; Allony 1951:27, 35; Schirmann 1961[2] :4, 719-33; Hrushovski 1971b: 1212-13; Pagis 1976:112-14: Fleischer 1975:341-44; 1983: 426; 1985:142-43, 158-59; Yahalom 1983:42, 46; Beeri 1985:50-51. These discussions on the adapted metrics, and mainly on its elementary units, are not, of course, homogeneous. They vary in terms and formulations according to each scholar's conception. Nonetheless, one can discern two basic lines of argumentation: the first one (reflected, for example, in the discussions of Brody, Yelin, Allony, Pagis and Hrushovski) is inclined to refer to the basic metrical units as *yated* vs. *tenuʿa*, following the medieval prosodic theory. The second (reflected, for example, in the discussions of Halper, Schirmann, Fleischer, Yahalom), tends to regard medieval theory as appropriate for its time, and chooses to refer to the basic metrical units as *long* vs. *short syllables*, following European linguistic thinking. The discussions are heterogeneous: Some, like those of Brody, Halper, Allony and Hrushovski, are original contributions. Other discussions (Yelin, Schirmann, Pagis, Fleischer, Yahalom, Beeri) have a more synoptic character, and the Spanish-Hebrew metrical system is only discussed in these as a basis for dealing with other prosodic issues, or in order to compare it with other metrical systems (Fleischer, Yahalom, Beeri).

1. *Dunaš's decision: Hebrew equivalent of the Arabic* watad

Scholars generally accept that Dunaš ben Labraṭ intended to adapt the two basic units of Arabic metre, the *watad* and the *sabab* (together with the binary-opposition between them) to Hebrew prosody by creating Hebrew equivalents for them. The adaptation is usually explained as follows: Since Arabic metre is quantitative and depends upon an alternation of long and short syllables, Dunaš had to determine an appropriate Hebrew substitute for these units. The Hebrew units he deemed the most suitable were the mobile *ševah* and the *ḥaṭaf* as substitutes for the Arabic short syllables, and the Hebrew vowels as substitutes for the long syllables.

Dunaš's choice is elucidated, in turn, by two closely related explanations. The first is based upon the prevailing *linguistic conception* of vowels: all seven vowels recognized in Hebrew were regarded as equal, yet were distinguished from the *ševahs*. Thus linguistic works discussing the rules of Bible-reading, which developed in the East out of Masoretic teaching,[3] distinguished between "kings" (i.e., the vowels) and "servants" (i.e., the *ševahs*) (see Levy 1936: 3,6-7; Eldar; Allony and Yevin 1985). At the same time in Spain, linguistic scholars developed the concept of the "concealed-quiescent," which underlies Menaḥem's disciples' criticism on Dunaš (Stern 1870: 21-29; Robles 1986: 12*-16*), and is explicitly formulated in the writings of the Spanish-Jewish grammarian Judah Ḥayyuǧ (Eldar 1984). According to this concept, one of the three quiescent letters—*alef*, *vav*, *yod*—always follows any one of the seven Hebrew vowels. The quiescent might disappear from actual pronunciation and even from writing; nevertheless, it always exists in an abstract form, independent of its concretization. In this abstract form it is called a "concealed-quiescent." The quiescent, whether concealed or not, only accompanies vowels, thus creating a clear distinction between vowels and *ševahs*. As the only phonetic distinction known at the time, the vowel-*ševah* distinction was found to be a suitable equivalent for the Arabic long/short syllable opposition.[4]

---

[3] Most probably in Tiberias (Eldar 1985; 1994; Drory 1986:34-43).Cf. ch. 5, section 3.

[4] It should be noted that only Brody, the pioneer of all the scholars mentioned in note 2, takes into consideration the "concealed-quiescent" idea when dealing with Spanish-Hebrew metrics. For him, it explains why the mobile *ševah* became the Hebrew equivalent for the "short vowel" component of the Arabic *watad*.

The second explanation of Dunaš's choice deals with the *linguistic practice* of the period. In the Spanish-Hebrew accent, it is argued, the mobile *ševah* was pronounced as a sort of half vowel; in any event it functioned more like a vowel than a quiescent *ševah* (Allony 1951: 53-55)[5]. The Arabic length-opposition, therefore, found its equivalent in a length-opposition already existing in Hebrew pronunciation.

Both explanations of Dunaš's innovation focus entirely on the linguistic aspect of sound organization. They refer to metrical units in terms of linguistic units, thus completely identifying linguistics with metrics. In my opinion, this approach is inadequate for two reasons.

The first questions the underlying supposition that, during the period in question, the only existing distinction was between the vowels and *ševahs* (with no distinction existing among the vowels). This supposition is not indisputable. From the responses of Menaḥem's disciples we learn that they do indeed distinguish between two types of /*a*/ (large *pataḥ* and large *qamatz*), of /*e*/ (small *pataḥ* and small *qamatz*), and of /*o*/ (*ḥolam*, and *ḥataf qamatz*).[6] If such distinctions did exist (even if they were not length-distinctions), then

---

According to Brody, all Hebrew vowelled consonants could hypothetically function as Arabic *sabab ḵafīf* (Hebrew *tenuʿa*), but only in a situation where (a) there could be no possible alternative to creating a *yated* according to the example of the Arabic *watad*; (b) the mobile *ševahs* and *ḥaṭafs*, which could not function as *tenūa* because they are not followed by "concealed-quiescents," would have remained outside of the metre. The solution was found by regarding the mobile *ševahs* and *ḥaṭafs* as equivalents for the Arabic "short vowel;" thus it was possible to create a Hebrew *yated*, structured on the Arabic *watad mağmūʿ*. Brody uses the "concealed-quiescent" concept to prove that Hebrew phonology made it impossible to create a Hebrew *watad* in any way other than that which was actually used. It is interesting that Menaḥem's disciples used the same "concealed-quiescent" concept in order to prove quite a contrary point. They argued that the *yated* of Dunaš contradicts—and even distorts—the structure of Hebrew phonology. Both Menaḥem's disciples and Brody discuss the Hebrew equivalent to the Arabic metric system from the perspective of the *specific phonological content* that was realized in Hebrew. The fact that the same point of departure led to two contradictory conclusions supports my contention that the adaptation of Arabic metrics into Hebrew should be examined first and foremost as the translation of an *abstract metric pattern*, rather than the translation of a *specific phonological structure* of the Arabic language.

[5] In the Babylonian accent, the difference was even more conspicuous, see Yahalom 1983: 29-32

[6] The Spanish-Hebrew philologian Judah Ḥayyuğ also distinguishes between two types of most of the vowels. See Eldar 1984.

it seems plausible that Dunaš may have had an alternative Hebrew option for the Arabic *watad* apart from the one he chose (that is, mobile *ševah* or *ḥaṭaf*, and a vowel). Any discussion therefore must consider the reasons for Dunaš's specific choice among the available options.

The second, and perhaps more important reason is that Dunaš's choice of the mobile *ševah* or *ḥaṭaf* for the Arabic *watad* (Hebrew *yated*) imposed severe restrictions on the selection of words in Hebrew poetry, because of the small distribution of mobile *ševahs* and *ḥaṭafs* in Hebrew in comparison to the other vowels. It was no simple task for the poet to "invent" *yateds*. The efforts to overcome this difficulty have produced interesting results in the Hebrew poetic vocabulary, grammar and syntax, which deserve a separate discussion.[7] It should be emphasized, however, that Dunaš's choice did not fully consider the structure of the Hebrew language, and thereby created a number of practical difficulties for the Hebrew poets. Again, we may wonder about Dunaš's insistence on the mobile *ševah* and vowels as substitutes for the Arabic *watad*, when his decision stood against the natural phonetic structure of the Hebrew language.

2. *The Arabic concept of* watad

In order to address these issues, it is necessary to abandon the European approach to Arabic metre (i.e., describing it in terms of long and short syllables) and examine Arabic metre on its own terms.[8] Dunaš did not adapt the entire Arabic metrical system to Hebrew; he borrowed what seemed to him to be its most fundamental elements: the *watad* and the *sabab* with their binary opposition. An examination of Arabic prosodic theory will help us to understand how he perceived these units.[9]

---

[7] See, for instance, Mirsky 1961:40-44.

[8] This is no new conviction. It underlies the works of pioneer scholars in the field of Spanish-Hebrew metrics; see Brody (1985:17-21), and (in another way) Halper (1913-14:58), as well as the works of some of their followers (Yelin, Allony).

[9] Zemah (1983) criticizes the conceptualization of Arabic metrics in terms of "the alternation of long and short syllables," especially as has been formulated by Weil (1960), and describes how it undermines the correct understanding of Arabic prosody. Instead, he proposes a re-examination of the terms of medieval Arabic prosodic theory, and demonstrates how they provide the key to a correct understanding of the principles of Arabic metrics. I agree both with his criticism of "the alternation of long and short syllables" and with his presentation of the

It is well known that al-K̲alīl, the eighth-century scholar who formulated Arabic prosodic theory, was primarily a linguist and a grammarian. When working out his prosodic theory, he applied whatever linguistic tools were available to him in an effort to explain Arabic metrics. As Arabic grammarians of the period were not familiar with the concept of the syllable, the only terms they had for explaining basic linguistic units were *ḥarf mutaḥarrik*, "a mobile letter," and *ḥarf sākin*, "a quiescent letter." These are the very terms that al-K̲alīl resorted to as he defined the fundamental units, which in their different combinations and orders create the entire system of Arabic metrics. He established two such units: the *watad*, which he defined as "two mobile letters and a quiescent letter," and the *sabab*, which he defined as "a mobile letter and a quiescent letter."[10] In doing so, al-K̲alīl did not dissemble the metrical unit in accordance with its phonological components. Rather, he established an elementary metrical unit (the smallest one that could not be further dissembled), which is not identical to the elementary unit of the language. Al-K̲alīl distinguished quite well between metrical and phonological units, that is, between the phonological and metrical organization of sounds.

Why, then, did al-K̲alīl decide to establish the elementary metrical unit as a complex sound unit? He could have at least dis-

Arabic *watad* as an elementary unit which cannot be divided or converted. It should be further emphasized, however, that the use of the *watad* and the *sabab* to describe Arabic metrics, rather than long and short syllables, does not merely mean the substitution of one type of metrical units for another. Their use indicates a *different metrical principle*, one that is based on the opposition between two metrical—not phonological—units. This principle maintains a necessary sequence of two distinct phonological elements: one which is fixed, the *watad*, and another which is flexible and convertible, the *sabab*.

[10] To be precise, al-K̲alīl established the following metrical units:*watad mağmūʿ* = two *ḥarf mutaḥarrik*s + one *sākin*; for example, *laqād.watad mafrūq* = *ḥarf mutaḥarrik* + *ḥarf sākin* + *ḥarf mutaḥarrik*; for example, *waqta.sabab k̲afīf* = *ḥarf mutaḥarrik* + *ḥarf sākin*; for example, *qād.sabab ṯaqīl* = *ḥarf mutaḥarrik* + *ḥarf mutaḥarrik*; for example, *laka*There are also the *fāṣila sağīra* and *fāṣila kabīra*, which are larger units based on the same principle (4 mobiles + 1 quiescent; 5 mobiles + 1 quiescent); See Zemah 1983:328-33. These units, however, are not relevant to the matter at hand; those that do pertain are the *watad* and the *sabab*.

The original work of al-K̲alīl has not survived. Some of his ideas are known to us from quotations and references in later sources; from these we are able to reconstruct his prosodic theory. The above description of Arabic metrical units is a matter of common knowledge in Arabic prosody and many studies discuss it. Therefore, I will only mention the main references: Ibn ʿAbd Rabbihi 1965:5, 424-425; Ibn Rašīq 1972:1, 138; Weil 1958; Weil 1960:670-71; Stoetzer 1989.

sembled the *watad* to show that it partially overlapped with the *sabab* in terms of its phonological components, but he did not. The reason is intrinsically connected to the distinction between the *watad* and the *sabab*, a distinction which does not involve quantity.

All prosodic organization is based upon an opposition between constant and alterable sound elements, which creates tension between the predictable and the unpredictable. A particular prosodic system may prefer either one side or the other of this opposition, but there can be no prosodic organization at all which relies upon only one side of it. With only unpredictable elements, no organization can take place; with only predictable elements, the pattern would be difficult to employ, as well as trite and void of aesthetic effect. Although always necessary, the opposition must not always reside in the same linguistic elements. For example, a rhymeme may consist of a maximum of sound repetition of all elements, identical in sound and distinguishable only on the semantic level.[11]

In Arabic metrics the opposition between the predictable and the unpredictable determines the relationship between the *watad* and the *sabab*. The *watad* is the constant, predictable element, while the *sabab* is the (relatively) alterable, unpredictable one. In practice the *sabab* is institutionalized, and its occurrence determined by specific rules. Presuming that the elementary metrical units are *ḥarf mutaḥarrik* (mobile letter, which may be called "a short syllable") and *ḥarf mutaḥarrik* + *ḥarf sākin* (a mobile + a quiescent letter, "a long syllable"), there seems to be no particular difficulty in employing these units within Arabic metres for the following reasons:

(a) Arabic morphology allows a wide variety of substitutions of short and long syllables because of their convenient distribution in the language.

(b) Arabic metre permits the substitution of a long syllable for two short ones ("heavy *sabab*" by "light *sabab*").

(c) A very large number of *ziḥāfāt* (i.e., legitimate metrical exceptions) in the *sabab* are recognized, which facilitate the substitution of long for short syllables—two shorts for one long, and two shorts for one short.

(d) Arabic poetic licence (*ḍarūrat al-šiʿr*) allows for a variety of legitimate changes in proper nouns, general nouns, and verb declensions in order to adapt them to the metre's demands.

[11] See ch. 4, section 3.3.

Were the elementary metrical units simply short and long syllables, they could have been employed with enormous flexibility in the metrical scheme, which would have practically expunged the predictable vs. unpredictable opposition, rendering it impossible to have any metre at all. A different elementary metrical unit, not identical to the elementary phonological one, therefore had to be defined. The basic metrical unit that is recognized in Arabic prosody is thus a compound unit, determined by the *sequence* of sound elements, rather than by the distinction between them. A set sequence of two distinct sound elements appears at certain positions on the line. This means that it is not the alternation of vocal units—long and short syllables—that determines Arabic metrics, but rather the alternation of pure *metrical* units: in one type of unit (the *watad*), two distinct phonological elements alternate in a set order, while in the other type (the *sabab*), no such set order controlling the alternation exists and often there is only one phonological element. Indeed the *watad* arranges long and short vocal units, but its cohesion lies upon a specific fixed sequence, not just on the quantitative difference between the syllables (cf. Zemah 1983:324-28).

3. *Dunaš's innovation: a sequence-unit*

With this understanding of the Arabic concept of the *watad* and of the distinction that Arabic prosodic theory makes between phonological and metrical units, we can now return to Dunaš ben Labraṭ's metrical innovation. Dunaš had the Arabic concept of *watad* (and *sabab*) in his mind, and it was this particular metrical concept that he intended to apply to Hebrew. When one comprehends that the *watad* is in fact a *sequence-unit*, rather than a grouping of short and long syllables, Dunaš's choice seems reasonable and even necessary, for a fixed sequence of two different elements is readily found in the Hebrew vowels and *ševahs*' relationship. In Hebrew two quiescent *ševahs* never occur in succession. Only vowels are found in succession; and a mobile *ševah* is invariably followed by a vowel. Dunaš thus had at his disposal a fixed sequence of two elements already recognized as distinct by the linguistic theory of his day. If we accept that Dunaš did not seek Hebrew equivalent for long and short units, we can also admit that how the mobile *ševah* was pronounced or exactly how it was considered different from the vowel was not particularly significant. Most relevant here was the fact that a regular, inevitable succession of two different elements already existed in the language and was available to the poets. What was actually applied to Hebrew was thus a prosodic unit based upon sequence, not a phonological unit of long or short syllables. The claim that Dunaš simply sought Hebrew equivalents for the Arabic short and long syllables is not only misleading, it fails to explain why the Arabic *watad* was realized in Hebrew as it was (mobile *ševah* + vowel). For the same reason, there is no justification for calling Dunaš's metric system "the quantitative-syllabic system" (Fleischer 1985:143). This term assigns quantity a central status, which is inappropriate in Dunaš's metrics; at the same time it implies that Dunaš's metric system and the syllabic system ("the simple syllabic system," *ibid.*:43), have a common foundation, when in fact their principles are quite remote, as Fleischer himself admits.

4. *Objection to Dunaš's innovation*

In light of these observations, it is most instructive to examine the response of Dunaš's contemporaries to his innovation in Hebrew poetry. The well known claim that Menaḥem ben Sarūq's disciples made against Dunaš was that Arabic prosody cannot conform to the Hebrew language, in the sense that if prosody is observed, it destroys the entire system of Hebrew vocalization, while if vocalization is maintained, there is no way of applying Arabic prosody. They put forth their claim as follows:

> Thus I say it is impossible to observe [the laws of] the language and the metre at the same time, but only one or the other; for in observing the rules of the language, the prosody is undermined, and you will find yourself combining two quiescents, as is the case in the above examples. But if you strictly keep to the rules of the metre and refrain from combining these two quiescents, then the vowel of these letters and the like should be *qamatz ḥaṭaf* (that is, contrary to their correct vocalization). While you think your text has been nicely metered, it has actually been distorted (Stern 1870:25; Robles 1986:14*).

More specifically, the disciples voiced two objections against Dunaš: (a) Dunaš permits himself to make the quiescent *ševah* mobile and the mobile *ševah* quiescent in order to maintain the metre; and (b) he changed vowels because of the metre: replacing the *pataḥ* for the *qamatz*, the *segol* for the *zere*, and the *ḥaṭaf* for the *ḥolam*. All of these changes were severe violations of the Hebrew vocalization system.

Why must the metre impose a change in vocalization? The reason is directly linked to the Arabic rule of *iltiqā' al-sākinayn*, the succession of two quiescents. Dunaš's opponents claim that while in Arabic two quiescent letters cannot follow consecutively, this is in fact how they normally appear in the Hebrew language. Therefore, in order for the metre to be effective in Hebrew, this usual situation must be reformed. Such a reform can only be realized in one of two ways: either by changing the vowel preceding the second quiescent (as in: זָ[א]הָ[א]ב—זָ[א]הַב; דוֹרֵ[א]שׁ—דוֹרֶשׁ; לבוֹת—לְבָוֹת), or by making the second quiescent mobile (as in: עֵינֵי—עֵינַ[א]יְ), and so on.

In other words, Dunaš's opponents claim that the employment of Dunaš's metre in Hebrew violates the language's structure, because Arabic metrics function in a language where there are no two consecutive quiescents; the Arabic system could not possibly function in a language where two consecutive quiescents appear with a rather high frequency. This claim makes sense only if we realize that it presupposes the identification of metrical units with phonological units. Menaḥem's disciples conceived of Arabic metrics in terms of Arabic phonology. Upon realizing that the Arabic phonological units (actually the phonologic representation of the metre rather than the metric scheme) could not be adapted to Hebrew because of its different phonetic structure, they concluded that Arabic metrics was not appropriate for Hebrew. Apparently they believed that when Dunaš adopted Arabic metrics, he imposed upon Hebrew the entire syllabic structure of Arabic. It has been shown above that this was not precisely the case. Dunaš did not go nearly as far as his opponents thought in his adaptation of the Arabic pattern. It is not clear whether Menaḥem's disciples really failed to distinguish between metrics and phonology, or whether they intentionally blurred the distinction in order to polemicize against Dunaš for Arabizing the Hebrew language, of which they obviously did not approve. They did, however, pursue an ideology which connected the poor state of Hebrew with the unfortunate national Jewish existence in the Diaspora. This is clearly demonstrated by the concluding words of their response to Dunaš:

> Had we not been carried into exile, and had we preserved our language as it was in ancient times when we were sitting peacefully and complacently [in our homeland], we would have been familiar by now with all its ways and details and we would have known its rules and metrics. *For every peoples' language has its own metrics and grammar*, only from us it was lost and concealed because of our sins, for our fault has indeed become very great from the day that we fell into exile. So [our knowledge of the language] became short and diminished after being large, and now we lack it (Stern 1870:27-28; Robles 1986:15*, my emphasis).[12]

It appears that Dunaš's detractors acted upon a misunderstanding similar to that of later scholars: the identification of metrical units with phonetic units. It also seems that Dunaš's disciple Yehudi ben Šešet, who rebutted the arguments of Menaḥem's school, makes precisely this point (pp. 22-24 of his response, Stern 1870; Varela 1891:17). His response consists of two parts, one pertaining to the mobilization of the quiescent and to making a mobile letter quiescent, and the other regarding the changing of the vowels. To the first issue he replies that even if a quiescent letter is made to move and a mobile letter is made quiescent solely by virtue of the Arabic borrowed licence (he is apparently referring to the idea of *ḍarūrat al-šiʿr*; see Halper 1913-14:162-63; Goldenberg 1983:127), and with no precedent for the practice in Hebrew, it is still acceptable, because the advantages of metred poetry outweigh moving the quiescent and making the mobile letter quiescent; especially when Biblical precedents exist (he provides several examples). His reply to the second issue is more relevant to our discussion. Responding to the accusation that Dunaš's metrics mandate vocalization changes that contravene Hebrew punctuation rules, he answers that (in our terms) the particular nature of the vowels is irrelevant for the metre, which allows for vocalization in either way (see Stern 1870:23-24; Varela 1981:17*). Thus he clearly distinguishes metre from phonology, as Menaḥem's disciples apparently did not.

[12] Cf. ch. 8, sections 2. 2.1.

5. *Dunaš's innovation as a manifestation of Arabic-Jewish literary contacts*

Two points regarding the adaptation of the Arabic *watad* into Hebrew as staple of the contemporary Jewish contacts with Arabic require further discussion.

The first point touches upon the evaluation of the Hebrew equivalent that was accepted for the Arabic *watad*. It must be emphasized that translating the Arabic *watad* into Hebrew vowel + mobile *ševah* or *ḥaṭaf* significantly reduced the number of potential phonological options that could function as *yated*. In fact, only one option was left. In Arabic, all the short vowels could function as part of a *watad*, while in Hebrew only the mobile *ševahs* and the *ḥaṭafs*, which are rather infrequent, could be employed. In practical terms this imposed considerable constraints on the poetic language. Theoretically, it meant that translation into Hebrew simplified and reduced the Arabic metrical concept, because the elementary metrical unit became identified with a particular vocal component.[13]

The second point deals with the evaluation of Dunaš's metrical borrowing as one symptom of the cultural dynamics of Jewish contacts with Arabic literature. As was previously mentioned, recent scholarly attention has focused on the syllabic metre. This metre is based on a fixed number of syllables, usually ten per hemistich, not counting the mobile *ševahs* which are irregularly dispersed throughout the line. Recently, syllabic metre has been the subject of debate between two leading scholars of medieval Hebrew poetry —Ezra Fleischer and Joseph Yahalom (Yahalom 1983; Fleischer 1985; Yahalom 1985). Since the contentions raised in their debate have direct implications for understanding the dynamics of contact between the two literatures (and of the place of metrics within these dynamics), the following brief remarks are in order:

(1) It is difficult to accept the argument put forth by Yahalom, which proposes that Dunaš's metre is merely another (even a tiny) step in the course of syllabic metre (Yahalom 1983: 46-55). It might have been possible to interpret the actual findings in the texts to mean that Dunaš merely established fixed positions in the line for the mobile *ševahs* and *ḥaṭafs*, which did not have fixed positions in syllabic metre. But, in fact, Dunaš's metre and the syllabic metre

[13] This process has affected other aspects of Hebrew prosody as well. See Yahalom 1983: 142.

are based upon entirely different metrical principles (as also Fleischer 1985:143, 159). In the syllabic metre only one type of element out of all the phonological elements of the language is granted a metrical status, and the metre is thus formed by counting these elements (other elements are not taken into account). Like the Arabic metre, Dunaš's metre is founded on the opposition between two distinct metrical units, organized in specific relation to one another.[14] To impose similarity on these two distinct metrical principles in order to create a seeming connection between them is a legacy of the established—although apparently misleading—conception that Arabic metrics (and thus Dunaš's) can be described in terms of short and long syllables. Understanding Dunaš's metrical units in light of the Arabic conception of metrics exposes the essential difference between the two principles, and completely annuls the association of Dunaš's metre with the syllabic one.

(2) Fleischer's critique of Yahalom's thesis also contains some disputable points. In order to disprove the claim that Dunaš's metre is a development of the syllabic metre, there is no need for Fliescher to claim that (a) the syllabic metre developed after Dunaš's metre; (b) the syllabic metre originated in Spain and not in the East; (c) it was of Romanic and not of Eastern, or at least not Arabic, origin (Fleischer 1983:427-28).

The corpus of texts in the syllabic metre that is available today does not enable us to draw any unequivocal conclusions as to the origin of this metre; all attempts to present the existing texts as clearly proving one source or another—namely that syllabic metre originated in Spain (Fleischer) or in the East (Yahalom)—are biased. The existing findings invite a number of different interpretations. There are syllabic metred texts that might point to either an Eastern origin, or a Spanish one (such as the poems of Yizḥaq Bar Levi and Yosef Ibn Abitur[15]). In any case, one very important conclusion

---

[14] I would like to thank Prof. Harai Golomb for enlightening me on the structural distinction between metrical systems based on homogeneous units, and those based on an opposition (of quantity, stress, etc.) between heterogeneous units.

[15] I am referring here to liturgical poems signed "Yizḥaq bar Levi," which Schirmann did not include in his list of yizḥaq bar Levi ben Mar Shaul the Spaniard's authentic poems, because of their Eastern character (Schirmann 1979:144-45). Fleischer, on the other hand, ascribes them with certainty to Yizḥaq ben Mar Shaul, on the basis of their syllabic metre, which he believes to be Spanish (Fleischer 1983:428-29). However, he himself points out that their other

that can be drawn from an examination of the corpus is that Hebrew literature developed an alternative to Dunaš's metre, either during his time or slightly after, and that it was used, especially in the East, for non-liturgical poetry.

Fleischer's supposition regarding the Romanic origin of the syllabic metre is also unnecessary. There seems to be much more evidence linking the syllabic metre to the East: the most important is that of the Babylonian accent on which the syllabic metre of Saʿīd ben Bābšād's wisdom poetry is based (as Yahalom has shown), as well as the fact that most of the non-liturgical poems in syllabic metre are in fact of Eastern origin. Indeed, the very existence of Romanic prosody during this period still needs to be further substantiated.

(3) Fleischer's assumption is not necessarily the only alternative to Yahalom's thesis. Since syllabic metre as a new literary trend of non-liturgical poetry first appeared in the East, it seems reasonable to compare it to other new Eastern, rather than Spanish, phenomena in the tenth and even in the eleventh century. In this period, the appearance of various new literary trends in the East is linked to Hebrew contacts with Arabic literature. A close examination of these new trends allows for a different hypothesis concerning the relationship between the syllabic metrical principle and the principle presented by Dunaš. These two metrical principles represent two different ways of adapting Arabic metrics to Hebrew poetry. Indeed, the basic concept of the syllabic metre (counting a fixed number of syllables) reflects only the general tendency of Arabic metrics to organize most of the phonologic elements of a line in a fixed succession. But in comparison to previous metrical systems known in Hebrew poetic tradition (words system, stress system), this succession was enough to create the effect of a much tighter and more solid organization of sound elements in the line. If contacts with Arabic literature really did provide the impetus to devise a metre that would be responsible for a maximum of sound

literary features are characteristic of Eastern, and not of Spanish, liturgical poems (e.g. *ibid.*:432). I am also referring to the syllabic liturgical poems of Yosef Ibn Abitur, which Fleischer believes had to have been written in Spain before the poet emigrated to the East, because they are written according to other examples that he attributes to Yizḥaq ben Mar Shaul the Spaniard, on account of their syllabic metre (Fleischer 1983:431).

elements in the line, then the syllabic metre could indeed have this effect in comparison to the other systems with which Jewish poetry was familiar at that time. In this case, not the particular Arabic metrical scheme was adapted into Hebrew; rather, a new metrical function was imposed on already-existing elements of the Hebrew language, in response to the challenge of Arabic metrics.

Dunaš's metre, however, is different. Here it was the specific principles of Arabic metrics that were transferred into Hebrew. Dunaš's search for Hebrew equivalents for the two Arabic metrical units with an opposition between them based upon sequence—*watad* and *sabab*—led him to impose the new metrical function on an opposition between two Hebrew phonological elements. Although these elements were recognized in Hebrew linguistic theory of the period,[16] they had no independent status in the Hebrew linguistic-poetic awareness, and in this respect they were "new," "invented." Dunaš's metre represents a literary appropriation that is completely different from the adaptation of the syllabic metre. It cannot be perceived as an advanced stage in a linear progression whose similar, although relatively simple, first stage was the syllabic metre.

An observation of early Jewish contacts with Arabic literature reveals that adaptation of the syllabic metre characterizes the Eastern course of contacts with Arabic. These contacts mainly consisted of borrowing new functions from Arabic literature and imposing them on items that already existed in Hebrew literature. With the new functions, existing items often underwent considerable reorganization. There are many examples of this, which cannot be fully detailed here (see Drory 1988). Saʿadya Gaon, to mention just one, borrowed functions from the poetics of ancient Arabic poetry and imposed them upon existing *piyyuṭ* models. He made almost no attempt to construct new, non-liturgical poetic models to accomodate these new functions. As a result, well-established poetic items in the *piyyuṭ* were reorganized according to new, borrowed

[16] Linguistic writings of the period refer to two units, equivalent to Dunaš's *yated* and *tenūa*, when discussing the *ševah*. According to these sources, the *ševah* has no independent status. The quiescent *ševah* is regarded as a joint part of the vowel that precedes it, and when dividing the word into its parts (*taqṭīʿ*), it is regarded as closing the unit (*maqṭaʿ*). The mobile *ševah* is regarded as joining the vowel that follows it, and when dividing the word, it is regarded as opening the unit (see Levy 1936: a-h). At any rate, there is no separate discussion dedicated to these units.

norms (Drory 1988:260-88 and ch. 5). By contrast, the Spanish course of contacts is characterized by the "invention" of new items for the functions borrowed from Arabic, as in the case of Dunaš's metre, and, in fact, as seen in the entire Spanish phenomena of constructing new poetic models for secular poetry. The adaption of metrics exemplifies the difference between the Eastern and the Spanish courses of contact with Arabic.

(4) It is particularly interesting that one of the most persuasive texts about the Eastern environment of syllabic metre, on account of the Babylonian accent it represents, is the wisdom poetry of Saʿīd ben Bābšād. Here syllabic metre is associated with another literary trend, which, in my opinion, belongs to the course of Eastern contacts with Arabic: namely, the revived interest in the genre of wisdom proverbs. Saʿīd ben Bābšād's texts of wisdom poetry join the small corpus of wisdom proverbs (*Ben Sīra's Book* and its adaptations) discovered in the Geniza and attributed to an earlier period (the ninth and tenth centuries). This corpus bears cautious witness to the revived literary activity in this genre during the period under discussion. The genre of the wisdom proverbs, especially *Ben Sīra's Book*, had an ambivalent, semi-official, status in Jewish literature in the generations that preceded this period (Drory 1988:207-15). This ambivalent status enabled wisdom proverbs to play a new role at the early stages of literary contacts with Arabic: they provided a new model for Hebrew poetry, a need that was created by the encounter with Arabic poetry. Other established poetic models prevailing in the Jewish literary system were not available for this purpose: the *piyyuṭ* models were reserved for poetic liturgical functions, and the Bible had not yet become a source for active literary models. Wisdom poetry was basically built on the Biblical poetic model (*Psalms*, *Proverbs*, *Job*), but unlike the Bible—which was "sacred" and therefore unavailable for actual composition—it could be used legitimately as a model to the new poetry. The themes of wisdom poetry were different from those of the liturgy and their structure resembled Arabic poetry (verses of one line, divided into two "hemistiches"). When the poetic model of wisdom proverbs actually began to function as a new model for Hebrew poetry, two new additional functions—the most salient in Arabic poetry—were imposed upon it: systematic metre and rhyme. Obviously, phonological Hebrew elements had to be reorganized in order to accomo-

date the new functions. But while systematic rhyme was established and noticeable in Hebrew poetry, metre, especially in its Arabic conception of organizing as many vocal elements as possible within the line, was a novelty. Syllabic metre was, in my opinion, an attempt to adapt the overall *conception* of Arabic metre, not necessarily all of its precise principles and details, into Hebrew.

CHAPTER TEN

LITERARY CONTACTS AND WHERE TO FIND THEM: ARABIC LITERARY MODELS IN MEDIEVAL JEWISH LITERATURE

Cultural contacts, particularly literary contacts, are generally assumed in traditional theories to consist of bilateral relations between two adjacent literatures, whereby one is considered to have "influence" over the other. But very often we find cultural dynamics to be much more complex and elaborate, as literary contacts and relationships are often established among more than two literatures concurrently, and in ways more subtle and intricate than can be defined as the mere "influence" of one literature over the other. Even what may appear to be a clear cut case of the inspiration of one body of literature over another can turn out, upon close examination, to be a case of multiliterary contacts. It is not always easy to trace and account for such contacts, as they are not necessarily manifested in what are conventionally regarded by students of literature as the "concrete data" of the field, namely, written texts. At times a whole cultural context has to be reconstructed in order to understand the actual circumstances that made possible the writing or production of a particular text, that is, the processes which dominated and manipulated a literary field at a given point in time, of which the written texts are only the final products. This can be particularly difficult for historians studying the past, who have virtually nothing but written texts to go by. Yet considering these final products, the written texts, as "distinct facts" without taking into account the immediate context and circumstances of their production can be quite misleading.

It is within this framework which regards the text as the product of an entire network of cultural relations, rather than as a single and discrete item, that the term "literary contacts" is most useful and acquires substantial value. It offers a far more sophisticated means of investigating cultural interference than the traditional, rather obscure concept of "influence," which is rooted in romanticist thinking. For there are undoubtedly instances in the history of all literatures when crucial segments, we feel, are dominated by what can be identified and described as "borrowings" from "another literature," as "adaptations" and "appropriations" of various kinds, which are displayed on all levels. Speaking of elements being "taken" from "another literature" in terms of "cultural contacts" or "cultural interference" implies a different concept of literature and a whole range of hypotheses about it (see Even-Zohar 1990). It also implies a different set of questions regarding the nature of the relationships obtaining between two (or more) literatures.

What, then, are "literary contacts?" An underlying assumption is that "literary material" is conveyed from a source literature to a target one by way of certain transmission procedures. But what precisely is this "literary material?" Is it a theme, a motive, an idea, a pattern, a structure, a genre? In what way can a text be regarded as the product of more than one "homogeneous" body of literature?

These are, of course, only a few of the questions that are likely to be addressed in any discussion of cultural interference. For no account of an instance of cultural interference can be regarded as complete, or even satisfactory, if it does not attempt to explain the extent to which the source repertoire is available and accessible to its borrowers, and without referring to the function fulfilled by these literary contacts in the target system. In other words, any account must be able to answer such questions as the following: What were the specific conditions in the target literature that created the need for contact with another literature (or other literatures)? In what ways precisely did the target literature exploit the source literature repertoire? How exactly have these contacts brought about a new dynamic within the target literature?

The case of medieval Jewish literary contact with Arabic literature illuminates the complex, if not tricky, nature of the problems involved in the study of cultural interference. This complexity stems from the fact that the investigation of this subject involves constantly calling into question of all our overt and implied assumptions regarding literature in particular, and culture in general, as well as many prevailing traditional views of Jewish literary history. Traditional ways of examining the nature and scope of the field in question are often unrewarding, even futile, and one would therefore do well to try to come up with more adequate hypotheses than those that have been conventionally asserted. For example, in tenth century Babylonia and Palestine cultural activities took place that have been regarded as so inherently Jewish that Arabic involvement was never considered to have played a part in their emergence. Yet their appearance at a particular moment and in a specific locale remains, for all intents and purposes, unaccounted for unless one considers the interference of an Arabic model (chs. 5 and 6). There are other instances (for example, in twelfth- and thirteenth-century northern Spain and Provence) where the presence of an Arabic model is not only well known, but is even considered a matter of common knowledge. Yet a reexamination of the previously overlooked cultural circumstances of such literary activities modeled on Arabic models soon shows that it was not the Arabic-Jewish context that was responsible for their evolution, but rather a third, local yet non-Arabic one. These cultural phenomena all testify to the fact that literary contacts may not necessarily be exhibited, as one would typically expect, in visible, readily recognizable "concrete" items, such as "themes" "motives," or even "ideas." They may in effect pull the strings invisibly, behind the scenes like stage directors (or possibly authors) rather than actors.

Let me demonstrate this by way of two medieval Jewish literary products that evolved as a direct result of the association between Jewish literature and Arabic culture. Moses Ibn Ezra's *Kitāb al-muḥāḍara wa'l-mudạ̄kara*, written in Judeo-Arabic, and Judah al-Ḥarīzī's Hebrew *Maqāmāt*, were both produced during the final phase of Jewish cultural contact with Arabic, in twelfth and thirteenth century northern Spain and Provence, respectively. Both are famous examples of Jewish works inspired by Arabic models, yet it seems that their significance as products of Arabic interference has been poorly understood and even misjudged, as too little attention has been paid to the actual cultural circumstances under which they were produced.

1. Kitāb al-Muḥāḍara wa'l-Mudạ̄kara *of Moses Ibn Ezra*

Moses Ibn Ezra (c.1055-c.1140) wrote *Kitāb al-muḥāḍara wa'l-mudạ̄kara* (*Book of Discussion and Conversation*) (Ibn Ezra 1975) in his old age (probably not before 1138 [Schirmann 1961:2, 365]), in northern Spain. He was born, reared, and educated in Muslim Granada and had to emigrate north to Christian Spain, following the

Almoravid persecutions, sometime after 1090, about twenty years before writing this book. As is well known, this book elaborates on the theory of Hebrew poetry. It intends to teach "the best way to go about composing Hebrew poetry according to Arabic views" (*ibid.*:2) and to explain certain principles and historical matters pertaining to this poetic theory, which the author explicitly declares is modeled on Arabic poetics. These matters are covered in eight chapters, each of which addresses a particular issue or question, as follows:

(1) Defending the legitimacy of the art of rhetoric (including prose writing) and the art of poetry composition (chapters one and two).

(2) "How is it that poetry is a natural aptitude of the Arabs but an affectation among the other nations?"[1] (chapter three)

(3) "Did the Israelites have rhymed, metrical poetry during their monarchic period, and when did they begin to compose poetry?" (chapter four).

(4) "Why are the Andalusi Jews more diligent and successful at composing poetry than any other Jewish community?" (chapter five)

(5) A selection of opinions on this subject (chapter six [This chapter consists in fact of a complaint against the local Jews, who, in their lack of proper culture do not understand Ibn Ezra's poetry, and consequently fail to respect him as they should]).

(6) "Is there any truth to the claim made by some people that poetry can be composed in a dream?" (chapter seven).

(7) Practical advice for those wishing to compose Hebrew poetry in accordance with Arabic taste, including a reference to dealing with the audience and a survey of rhetorical figures (chapter eight).

The first five chapters are logically arranged to form a single argument, complete in itself: Eloquence in general and poetry in particular are legitimate practices; the gift of poetry was bestowed upon those best qualified to receive it, namely, the Arabs, who surpass other nations in the practice of poetry, while such nations as the Indians, Persians, and Greeks were granted faculties conducive to the study and preservation of the sciences. The Arabs' superb gift of eloquence, due in part to their geographical loca-

[1] Here, as in several other places in this discussion of *Kitāb al-muḥāḍara*, I quote Raymond Scheindlin's excellent translations of the original Arabic phrasings from his article on this book (Scheindlin 1976:101-102).

tion in the middle *iqlīm*, is best expressed in their poetry.[2] As descendants of the Jerusalemite expatriates of the first exile, Andalusi Jews were inherently eloquent; thus, after mastering Arabic and perceiving the beauty of Arabic poetry, they naturally adopted Arabic poetic practices, developed the Hebrew language, and gained pride of place among the Jews where eloquence was concerned, particularly in the composition of poetry. Next follows a survey of Andalusi Jewish poets, which in fact comprises a list of their merits (*faḍā'il*) rather than a mere historical account, of the kind also found in Arabic literature (e.g., *Faḍā'il 'ulamā' al-andalus* of Ibn Ḥazm, cited in *Nafḥ al-ṭīb*[3]). This survey is clearly intended to support the claim that the true and correct knowledge of poetry reposes in the Andalusi Jews.

Hebrew poetry is thus openly acknowledged in this treatise as having an Arabic model. Explaining Arabic poetics to Hebrew poets is the very raison d'être of this treatise, so it seems only natural, if not self-evident, to view it as a typical product of the Hebrew-Arabic cultural context. But is the Hebrew-Arabic culture its only context?

Scholarly interest in this book during recent decades (see, for instance, Pagis 1970) may have created an impression that the first six chapters of *Kitāb al-muḥāḍara* (which actually comprise its core) are but a collection of preliminary remarks on matters related to poetry, intended to pave the way for its main subject, namely, the survey of Arabic rhetorical figures. A careful reading of the argument developed throughout these chapters proves this impression to be misleading. It contains a series of ideological claims which, over and above their comprising a defense of poetry (Scheindlin 1976), seek primarily to convince the reader that the Arabic method of composing poetry is the right one and that Jewish Andalusi poets are its best practitioners. A vital question to be posed here is: What public was this ideology actually intended to address? If this book was indeed written in a Hebrew-Arabic context, that is, for an audience already familiar with and appreciative of Arabic poetics,

---

[2] Ibn Ezra does mention the Muslim idea that the eloquent style of the Koran is proof of its divine nature and truth, but he does so with great reserve (see Ibn Ezra 1975:36-38).

[3] See al-Maqqarī (1968:4, 150-212, particularly 156-79). Lists of *faḍāi'l* concerning poets and written in rhymed prose are to be found in the *maqāmāt* literature; see, for instance, the first of al-Hamaḏānī's (1962:10-17) *Maqāmāt* (*al-Qarīḍiyya*);see also Ibn Šaraf al-Qayrawānī (1983).

and the Hebrew poetry written accordingly, and for whom this was to be no more than a handbook of poetry composition, why go to so much trouble to preach to the converted, explaining basic ideas in such great detail? Wouldn't these ideological tenets be self-evident to such an audience? They would most likely have already formed part of what Clifford Geertz (1983) calls "the local knowledge" of the community, that is the ideas and opinions shared by all members of the community, held to be commonplace and taken for granted, and would not need to be committed to writing unless they were for some reason undergoing a change in status.

If Ibn Ezra felt the need to formulate these ideas in writing, one might rightly wonder whether there had been such a change in their status. The fact that the book was written in northern Spain rather than in al-Andalus is highly significant in this respect. Ibn Ezra wrote it not for the benefit of a Jewish audience living in the midst of Arabic culture, but for a Jewish audience that lived outside its domain, in a different cultural atmosphere. There are indications pointing to the fact that, unlike the Andalusi Jews, this audience probably did not hold poetry in high regard, nor were its members perceived by Ibn Ezra as connoisseurs of good (i.e., Arabic-style) poetry; this is apparent from the sixth chapter of the book as well as from several of Ibn Ezra's Hebrew poems in which he refers to the local Jews as ignorant and barbaric (see, e.g., Ibn Ezra 1935:I, 19, 20, 101, 102; 1975:104). The poet often complains of a sense of cultural isolation and detachment from his civilized homeland, al-Andalus. It is apparent that Ibn Ezra regards himself as the representative of a high culture among "savages" (*peraim*, which also means "wild asses") who do not acknowledge his superior position as an agent of the "correct" culture.[4] He wrote his book out of a conviction that the Jewish Andalusi culture was in danger of oblivion in the foreign regions of *Edom* and that he must do his best to preserve it, while at the same time enlightening the local "savages" on the "right way" to compose poetry.

Ibn Ezra's sense of isolation from his native culture and familiar milieu can also be noted in the introduction to his other well-known composition in Judeo-Arabic, *Maqālat al-ḥadīqa fī maʿnā al-mağāz wa'l-ḥaqīqa* (or *ʿArugat ha-bosem*, as he himself entitled it in

[4] Cf. for a similar stance of Saʿadya Gaon ch. 7, section 3.

Hebrew), which is a philosophical *adab* compilation.[5] Here, Ibn Ezra addresses an audience with whom he obviously identifies, whose members he regards as his cultural peers and who share his fate of being Jewish Andalusi emigrants in Christian Spain. He addresses them as "the remaining noble men and the last of the faithful connoisseurs of *ādāb* (letters), even if your numbers are scarce and your status unrecognized, and you are foreigners among ignorants." He urges them, in the name of the "affection created by the common origin and the affinity caused by the shared cultural bias," to take an interest in his book. From these words, as well as from similar phrasing in the introduction to *Kitāb al-muḥāḍara wa'l-mudākara* (Ibn Ezra 1975:2-7), it is clear that Ibn Ezra saw himself as a true representative of a heritage whose status was declining.

Confronting in Christian Spain a Jewish cultural atmosphere so different from that of Muslim Spain was what prompted Ibn Ezra to write this book. It caused him to examine his own cultural identity and formulate it in a way as to define it in opposition to the local Jewish one. Regarding his own cultural identity as Andalusi meant viewing it as composed of two components—a Jewish component and an Arabic one. Had he written a document of this nature back in Granada, Ibn Ezra would most probably have dwelt solely on the Jewish component, the Arabic one being self-evident and virtually unmarked. Representing "the Andalusi cause" within the Jewish community of northern Spain made the Arabic component a marked part of Ibn Ezra's Jewish identity, defining it as distinctly different from the northern-Spanish Jewish identity. This accounts for his openly (more so than any other Jewish Andalusi author) declared acceptance of the exemplary status of the Arabic model: following an Arabic model was no problem for him, as it was for the later Jewish authors of northern Spain and Provence; as an heir of the Andalusi legacy, Ibn Ezra had absorbed that model as an integral part of his cultural world.

In order to create a text so Arabic-Hebrew in spirit, another, non-Arabic cultural context was needed. It was the emergence of a new Jewish literature in northern Spain and Provence, which would ultimately be built upon a different paradigm than that of

[5] Hebrew National Library MS No. 5701 (formerly Sassoon MS No. 412), p. 12. I would like to sincerely thank Professor Joseph Fenton, who first drew my attention to this introduction.

Muslim Spain, that paved the way for the only formulation now extant of a theory of Hebrew poetry inspired by Arabic poetics.

Regarding the reception of *Kitāb al-muḥāḍara wa'l-mudākara* by the Jewish community in Christian Spain, it should be noted that the book was not translated into Hebrew at the time, despite a massive wave of contemporary interest in Arabic-Hebrew translations. The book's translation occurred only with the renewed interest in Judeo-Arabic literature that arose in the modern period (see Ibn Ezra 1924). By contrast, Ibn Ezra's philosophical treatise *Maqālat al-ḥadīqa* was translated at the time into Hebrew by Judah al-Ḥarīzī (Idel 1975-76; Abramson 1975-76) and is known to have influenced the Kabbalah in its initial stages. Ibn Ezra's liturgical poems were also well received and widely distributed. This means that Ibn Ezra was far from being a controversial literary figure and suggests that the literary ideology promoted by this particular treatise may have been losing its appeal for the Jewish community in Christian Spain. The very act of summoning up this Arabic-biased literary ideology in writing indicates that its cultural status had changed and that it had begun to be marked as a "museum piece" in need of preservation, maybe even restoration, rather than as a viable way of perceiving one's own poetry.

2. *Al-Ḥarīzī's* Maqāmāt

A similar case, in a way, is that of the famous Hebrew *Maqāmāt* by the Jewish author Judah al-Ḥarīzī (1170-1225) composed on the model of the Arabic *Maqāmāt* by al-Qāsim b. ʿAlī al-Ḥarīrī (1054-1122). This work is traditionally regarded by scholars as a highly typical (perhaps *the* most typical) example of Arabic influence over Hebrew literature: the Arabic *Maqāmāt* were first translated by al-Ḥarīzī into Hebrew, and his own *Maqāmāt* were later composed on the same model. Moreover, he openly declared that he had been inspired by al-Ḥarīrī's *Maqāmāt*, discussing this in his preface. Yet an examination of the cultural circumstances within which this work was composed reveals that it cannot be understood solely in light of the Arabic-Hebrew context. Again, one must consider contacts with another cultural context, albeit one introduced into the *Maqāmāt* in a far from simple way, but without which the very act of composing this work cannot be explained.

Al-Ḥarīzī, who was born in Toledo, was living in northern Spain during the second half of the twelfth century when an interest in Arabic texts began to flourish in Jewish as well as Christian circles. He became an Arabic-Hebrew translator and translated several Arabic and Judeo-Arabic works, usually at the invitation of distinguished patrons or scholars of the Jewish communities of northern Spain and Provence, although he sometimes produced translations on his own initiative. Among his known translations are:

Moses ibn Ezra's above mentioned *Maqālat al-ḥadīqa fī maʿnā al-maǧāz wa'l-ḥaqīqa* (*The Treatise of the Garden on Figurative and Literal Expressions*), entitled *'Arugat ha-bosem* in Hebrew (Idel 1975-76; Abramson 1975-76).

Maimonides' *Guide for the Perplexed* (*Moreh nebukhim* [Maimonides 1904]), his *Introduction to the Mishnah* (*Hakdamot le-perush ha-mishnaa* [Maimonides 1960]), his commentary on the first five tractates of the *Mishna order Ẓeraʿim*[6] and his *Epistle on Resurrection* (*Ma'mar teḥiyat ha-metim* [Maimonides 1989]);

ʿAli ibn Ruḏwān's *Epistle on Morals* (*Igeret ʿalī ha-išmeʿelī* [Ibn Ruḏwān 1900]);

Ḥunayn ibn Isḥāq's *Adab al-falāsifa* (*Dicta of the Philosophers*), entitled *Musere ha-filosofim* in Hebrew (Ibn Iṣḥāq 1896);

Galen's *Dialogue on the Soul* (Galenus 1852).

Between 1205 and 1215 (Schirmann 1961:III, 98), or between 1213 and 1216 (Habermann 1952:113), while still in northern Spain or in Provence, al-Ḥarīzī translated al-Ḥarīrī's *Maqāmāt.*[7] He then traveled to the East, where, sometime after 1216, he composed his own Hebrew *Maqāmāt*, entitled *Sefer taḥkemoni* and modeled on al-Ḥarīrī's Arabic *Maqāmāt.*[8] There, he also composed a Judeo-Arabic *Maqāma*, describing his journey to the East (Hirschfeld 1903; Stern 1964a, 1964b, 1969; Ratzaby 1980, 1988).

As mentioned earlier, this work is considered by any standard of the comparative literature approach to represent the most salient example of "Arabic influence" over Hebrew literature in its Andalusi "golden era."[9] Its Arabic-Hebrew context has generally

---

[6] According to al-Ḥarīzī's own testimony (see al-Ḥarīzī 1952:406).

[7] The work, only part of which has survived, is called *Maḥberot itiel* (see al-Ḥarīrī 1872, 1951. cf. Stern 1964a:186).

[8] for modern editions, see al-Ḥarīzī (1845), 1924 [1883], 1899, 1952); for an English translation see al-Ḥarīzī (1965-1973).

[9] This thesis is most prominently exemplified in Goitein (1951).

been regarded as so self-evident that it has been taken as plain fact, obvious enough to be passed by as common knowledge. The focus of literary research has thus been concentrated on the specific ways in which al-Ḥarīrī's *Maqāmāt* inspired *Sefer taḥkemoni*,[10] rather than on the cultural circumstances of its production. Yet it seems that a reexamination of those overlooked, or sometimes taken for granted, particular circumstances may reveal that viewing this work exclusively from a general, un-specified "Arabic-Hebrew" perspective (cf. Halkin 1963:234-35) misses important evidence for the reconstruction of Hebrew literature in northern Spain and Provence by means of a new paradigm, quite different from the Arabic-Hebrew one of al-Andalus mentioned above.

The particular circumstances that led to the composition of *Sefer taḥkemoni* will be clarified if we try to reconstruct al-Ḥarīzī's literary awareness and his attitude toward cultural trends in Jewish society at the time. It is al-Ḥarīzī himself who gives us the key to this reconstruction, as he tends to present quite lengthy explanations of his motives for writing in the several introductions, or rather the dedications of this work to different patrons, and in the introductions to some of his Hebrew translations from the Arabic.

Following the contemporary custom among scholars to seek the patronage of distinguished figures in the community and support themselves by dedicating their written works to these figures (the same composition would often be dedicated to different patrons with only the dedication changed), al-Ḥarīzī dedicated his compilation of Hebrew *maqāmāt* to several different Jewish figures during the course of his travels in the Orient.[11] We can thus draw on more than one dedication of *Sefer Taḥkemonī* in which al-Ḥarīzī takes great pains to explain—this too according to contemporary writing norms—how and why he decided to compose this work.

Al-Ḥarīzī addresses this subject in the work's two Hebrew dedications: one, to Samuel ben al-Barqūlī, forms the introduction to the printed edition of *Sefer taḥkemoni* (al-Ḥarīzī 1952:4-18); the other,

---

[10] See, for example, Schirmann (1930, 1979), Percikowitsch (1932), Stern (1946), Lavi (1984) Dishon (1979), Dana (1975, 1984) and Ratzaby (1957).

[11] In the Hebrew dedications of *Sefer taḥkemoni* the following names are mentioned: Samuel ben al-Barqūlī and his brothers, Joseph and Ezra, of Wāsiṭ, Yoshiyahu ben Yishai of Damascus, Samuel ben Nissim of Aleppo and Shemaryah ben David of Yemen. In the Arabic dedication Sadīd al-Dawla ʿAbd al-Q̄ādir of Aleppo and his son, Abū Naṣr, are named (see Habermann 1952:114; 1953).

to Yoshiyahu ben Yishai, forms the first *maqāma* in the edition (*ibid.*:19-30). The same issue is also addressed in the Arabic dedication to Sadīd al-Dawla ʿAbd al-Qādir of Aleppo and his son Abū Naṣr (Drory 1991:18-20).[12] The Hebrew dedications are extended and written in a highly stylized rhymed prose that closely resembles the literary style of allegory (the first one in particular) or of the *maqāmāt* genre (the second one). The Arabic dedication is far more concise, and although it employs a rhetorical style reminiscent of Arabic-rhymed prose, it is still far clearer and more concrete than the rhetoric used in the Hebrew dedications.[13]

2.1. *The first Hebrew dedication*

In the first dedication (al-Ḥarīzī 1952:4-18; al-Ḥarīzī 1965-73:23-43), al-Ḥarīzī describes his state when he was prompted to compose the Hebrew *Maqāmāt* as a state of ordination. Intellect woke him from his sleep of folly and assigned him the task of reviving the Hebrew language. The holy tongue, he was informed, was fast deteriorating, having been abandoned by its people, who now favored Arabic:

> They have enslaved the tongue of the Israelites to the tongue of Kedar [i.e., Arabic] and they said: "Come and let us sell her to the Ishmaelites." And they said to her: "Bow down, that we may go over." And they took her and cast her into the pit until she perished among them. And the tongue of Kedar blackened her, and like a lion, tore her. An evil beast devoured her. All of them spurned the Hebrew tongue and made love to the tongue of Hagar [i.e., Arabic]. They embraced the bosom of an alien. They desired the wife of a stranger. They kissed her bosom, for stolen waters were sweet to them. Their hearts were seduced when they saw how excellent was the poetry that Hagar, Sarai's Egyptian handmaiden had borne. And Sarai was barren! (al-Ḥarīzī 1965-73:32 [Hebrew: al-Ḥarīzī 1952:9-10]).

Bestirring himself, al-Ḥarīzī went to the fount of the Hebrew language to draw water from its sources of wisdom and awaited a sign of inspiration and instruction from God in the form of a young maiden who was to appear before him, rinsing him with drinking

[12] Only recently it was discovered that Al-Ḥarīzī died in Aleppo in 1225 (Sadan 1996).

[13] Cf. on this issue chs. 7 and 8.

water from the flow of her sweet speech. A young maiden then indeed came forth, refreshed him with the honey of her lips, and identified herself as "your mistress, the Holy Tongue." He then "betroth[ed] her unto him in righteousness and reverence without a [marriage]-contract or intercourse" (al-Ḥarīzī 1965-73:34), and she later conceived and gave birth to their offspring, a literary composition. al-Ḥarīzī then goes on to explain that the urge to compose his work had indeed come from al-Ḥarīrī's Arabic *Maqāmāt*, which was, to his mind, a fine illustration of the fact that there do exist other peoples who cherish their language and preserve it with care, unlike the people of Israel, who abandoned their native tongue and neglected it, at times even to the point of despising it. This, by the way, does not prevent al-Ḥarīzī from boasting that everything of real value and quality in this Arabic book is borrowed from the Hebrew. In composing the Hebrew *Maqāmāt* he wishes to show the people of Israel the beauty and resourcefulness of the Hebrew language and to convince them that it is appropriate for all types of literary expression, which he then lists. He stresses that many before him had tried to translate this work into Hebrew, but none had done so with much success. He himself had translated it at the request of "some generous men [nobles] of Spain (Sefarad)"; but after traveling to the East he had realized that it was inappropriate, or even sinful, "to translate a book of another people's goodly words as though the words of the living God were not among us" and that one would do best to write in one's native tongue.

2.2. *The second Hebrew dedication*

The second Hebrew dedication (al-Ḥarīzī 1952:19-30; 1965-73:44-58) is actually the first *maqāma* in the collection, which means that it draws on the narrative rather than the methodological discourse. Yet it serves the same purpose of elaborating on al-Ḥarīzī's reasons for composing the Hebrew *Maqāmāt*. In it the author, or rather his protagonist, finds himself in a literary encounter of Jewish literati (literally, "of the children of the Hebrews," [which Reichert translates as "of Jewish lineage"]). Among them is a "Hebrew lad," who advances the argument that Arabic is the most beautiful of all languages and that it would be virtually impossible to write a book such as al-Ḥarīrī's in a language other than Arabic. At this the author rises to the defense of the Hebrew language, stating that Arabic is indeed superior to all languages—except for Hebrew; unfortunately, since the Jews were exiled and began adopting the languages of their host nations, Hebrew has been gradually deteriorating; forsaken and forgotten, it has slowly wasted away.

Yet, he continues, even the little Hebrew that has survived is adequately equipped to ensure the composition of some splendid literary works; this, in its own right, attests to the language's superiority. Why then, asks the young lad, have none of the children of Israel written any praiseworthy literary works in Hebrew that equal those written in Arabic, thereby highlighting the qualities of the Hebrew language? The author replies that, as for himself, he would find no difficulty in writing a praiseworthy book in Hebrew, but the real problem is that, with the lack of demand by the Eastern Jewish public for books of this nature, there is little point in producing them:

> But the author, for whom shall he compose, and to the ears of whom shall he speak, while the ears are deaf and the hands are tight, and the times have shut up the eyes of creatures who are imprisoned in the house of passion, and have smitten the men that were at the door of the house with blindness? And there is not among them one who sees or who hears and no one takes it to heart and no one cares. And if you should search the communities of the world, from Egypt unto Babylon—you will not find one who loves wisdom or who honors its possessor or who requites it with good reward. And you know that as for precious books, their pearls are not composed except for those who understand them or for those who requite them with good reward. For they are not made for fools who deride them and scoff at them.
>
> Now the secret of all delightful wisdom is laid bare through three conditions: when she finds a patron, or a sage, or a nobleman who longs for her. Then wisdom sells herself to him as a hand-maid and her light shines and is not withdrawn. And if one of these circumstances does not happen to her, then she goes out for nothing, without money.
>
> Therefore, in our generation the hallowed stones are poured out and the most fine gold is changed, and poetry and rhetoric sell themselves for bondmen and for bondwomen and there is none to buy them. And the generosity of patrons is like a staff of reed—upon tongues there is response to it, but in hearts there is no shelter for it. And in every place where I encamp, I call out: "Ho! For a man of intellect!" But there is none who answers. And behold, the place is a place for cattle. And in city after city we see every one of them asleep in the bosom of ignorance. And behold, there is no man there,

> neither voice of man, but a tied horse and a tied ass, tied and bound by the yoke of lust. And in this circumstance, how can the spirit be stirred up or the intellect soul long to compose any word of wisdom, or to speak of any theme of edification, or to set forth a lovely letter? Lo! Wisdom in the eyes of the children of our people is as one who puts a precious stone in a sling or as one who casts pearls at the feet of cattle. (Al-Ḥarīzī 1965-73:49-50 [Hebrew: al-Ḥarīzī 1952:22-23])

The young man agrees, but swayed by the author's valorization of the Hebrew language, he nevertheless urges him to ignore the folly of this generation and to write a book which will convince everyone (including other nations) of Hebrew's superiority. Promising to attend in every *maqāma*, and instruct the author as to what he should say, the "Hebrew lad" also suggests that the book be dedicated to Yoshiyahu ben Yishai and to his two sons, David and Shelomo. The author accepts this suggestion and promptly composes fifty Hebrew *maqāmāt* which stylistically embody the beauty of the Hebrew language, yet are not too academic and are intended for a wide readership. The young man blesses the author, identifies himself as Ḥeber the Kenite—the hero common to all the *maqāmāt*—and promises to join the author in all his future *maqāmāt*.

2.3. *The Arabic dedication*

Apart from the two Hebrew dedications, an Arabic one also appears in some of the manuscripts of *Sefer taḥkemoni*.[14] As it was not included in the printed editions of the book, it seems to have escaped scholarly attention altogether. I think it would be worthwhile, therefore, to present the dedication in its entirety and in translation here:

> [And so] I have noticed that most of the Israelite community in these lands of the East are devoid of the Hebrew language and denuded of its beautiful garments. If one of them were asked about a Hebrew word, it would seem as if he were being addressed in a for-

[14] This dedication was first published by Blau (1953:47-49) as an appendix to Habermann (1953) from Bodley MS Poc. 192 (Neubauer 1886:no. 1977), with a Hebrew translation. For a revised publication and Hebrew translation, see Drory (1991:18-20). Part of it is also to be found in Bodley MS Opp. Add. 4o, 156 (Neubauer 1886:no. 2517), where it is preceded by a Hebrew dedication to "our master the Nagid Shemaryah" from "the land of Yemen," and in Bodley Heb. MS d. 57 (Neubauer and Cowley 1896-1906:no. 2745).

eign language. They are like those of whom it is said: "For with stammering lips and with a strange tongue shall it be spoken to this people" (Isaiah 28:11).[15] I consider this to be one of the most terrible misfortunes to come upon our nation during our exile. This disease continues to spread among them, to the extent that most of them are never capable of putting the (Hebrew) letters together, and when they are, they are unable to understand or recognize what they have done, like those of whom it is said: "and their children spoke half in the speech of Ashdod, and could not speak in the Jews' language" (Nehemiah 13:24).

When I saw that virtue was held in the hand of contempt, and that the Holy Speech had been exchanged for ignorance and had come to be despised, I drew the swords of my determination (though their thoughts were notched) and begged the clouds of my creative imagination for rain (though they were empty of water). I then composed fifty Hebrew *maqāmāt.* I embellished them with pearls of the Prophets' words and studded them with precious stones of Biblical phrases so that they turned out like embroidered gowns or well-ordered necklaces. Their pages shine with beauty, and their perfume is so strongly diffused that if the gardens once breathe it, they cannot but try to sniff it again. When the narrator tells his graceful stories, [even] the motionless mountains shake their shoulders (in astonishment). That is because I have included [in this collection] every amusing story and piquant tale; every enjoyable witticism and good joke(?) (*lamḥa*); every exhortation that moves to tears and every entertaining anecdote; and every brilliant epistle and skillful writing such as would turn the grieving lover to consolation, and the indifferent to the folly of passion. I have embellished it with a variety of light and serious words and with panegyrics, both those of good and bad effect; and I have followed the theme of obscenity to the limit. I have expressed the virtues and nobility of every generous man, and smitten the vile with the sword of mockery, now with the flat side of its blade, and now with its point.

And so this book became one of the most useful of all written books of its kind because its amusing anecdotes and charming stories are an incentive to ignorant souls and an encouragement to distracted hearts to study the Hebrew language and penetrate its wonderful secrets and extraordinary subtleties. For I have collected in it many words that are obscure and difficult to understand so that if the reader is able to understand those opaque expressions, he will have acquired a good deal of knowledge about the Hebrew language, understood many of its meanings, and erected a massive column of its structures. If he persists in reading these *maqāmāt*, Hebrew will run smoothly off the tip of his tongue, and the bridle of his eloquence and clear

[15] All of the English translations of Biblical verses are quoted from the *Jewish Publication Society of America* (JPS) edition of the English Bible.

> expression will be slackened. And with God's will we shall explain every phrase that seems difficult or opaque in this collection. [These are the titles of the *maqāmāt*, their number and the subject-matter of each and every one of them:[16]]
>
> When the honorable head [of the community] Sadīd al-Dawla ʿAbd al-Qādir, son of the heads of the Academy and the glory of the community of Aleppo, bestowed his generosity, charity, goodness and grace upon my tongue—even if my ink flowed from the oceans and if my pen were made out of trees, I would never have been able to express my thanks for his kindness—I thought it right to adorn this compilation with his name, unique as he is in his generation, and with the name of his honorable and precious son, Abū Naṣr. May the attention of God dwell with all its intensity upon their pure house, with its distinguished virtues. These are the titles of the *maqāmāt* according to their order: (Arabic: Drory 1991:18-19)[17]

The arguments of this dedication, which are advanced here in a rather straightforward way, can be summed up as follows: the majority of Eastern Jews have such a poor command of the Hebrew language that they can hardly join the letters together to form words, let alone understand the meaning of the words. In order to combat this ignorance, says the author, he has decided to compose fifty *maqāmāt* in Hebrew, the language of the Prophets, in a variety of enchanting literary forms (Arabic, by their description) that will attract readers and encourage them to learn the Hebrew language through reading the book. There are many awkward words and difficult expressions in it, which, when studied, will contribute to a good command of the structure and eloquence of Hebrew. The author also promises to provide a glossary of the difficult words in the *maqāmāt*.

What is so striking about these dedications is the fact that no admiration for Arabic literature, the peak of Arabic eloquence (to be expected in a work inspired by Arabic as much as this one), is expressed here, but rather discontent and unhappiness at the declining condition of the Hebrew language. Admiration for Arabic eloquence is mentioned as a seemingly popular, but nevertheless

---

[16] This sentence clearly belongs at the end of the introduction, and indeed it is repeated there.

[17] This translation, like all others in this paper, unless otherwise credited, is my own. I am most grateful to Professor Raymond Scheindlin, who was kind enough to read the draft translations of both the Arabic and the Hebrew texts and was extremely helpful in finding appropriate English equivalents for many phrases which were ambiguous and difficult in the original.

incorrect, sentiment. Al-Ḥarīzī is intrigued not so much by the idea of Arabic literary or linguistic superiority as by the Jewish cultural situation in the East, of which he became aware while visiting there and which he considered to be worrisome. In the East he discovered a Jewish public who were not as familiar with Hebrew as he expected them to be, who were uninterested in Hebrew writing and probably highly taken with Arabic culture.[18] Irritated by this situation, he raised his voice in protest; he wished to redirect the Eastern Jewish public back to their forsaken language by proving that Hebrew was no less suitable for literary and eloquent writing than Arabic and, perhaps, was even more suitable.

Why should al-Ḥarīzī have been so irritated and disturbed by this situation? Was it not common among Jews living within the Muslim culture (in the East as well as in Muslim Spain) to write more in Arabic than in Hebrew? In fact, it was customary to write in both languages while maintaining a very clear-cut division of functions between the two. Arabic served for all informative purposes, that is, the referential function of communication, while Hebrew was reserved for mainly poetic and ceremonial functions (functions which were traditionally associated in Jewish literature).[19] Thus we find Jews writing (Judeo-)Arabic Biblical and Talmudic exegesis, law, theology, philosophy, linguistics, poetics, letters (official and private), but rarely poetry.[20] Poetic texts, be they liturgical or secular, in poetry or prose, were written in Hebrew, their poetic-aesthetic (and often ceremonial) intention clearly marked by their highly ornamented rhetorical style and by their intensive play among semantic and nonsemantic linguistic features. This division of functions was already established in Jewish writing by the first half of the tenth century, when Arabic models of writing first found their way into Jewish literature,[21] and was maintained practically throughout the entire Muslim period. The impact of this division

[18] Testimony to the fact that Eastern Jews read also Arabic *maqāmāt* is provided by a Geniza fragment of Ibn Buṭlān's *Risālat da'wat al-aṭṭibā'*, found in the Taylor-Schechter collection in Cambridge (Baker 1990).

[19] See on this issue ch. 7, especially 3.3.

[20] Poetry written by Jews in Arabic (using Arabic, not Hebrew, characters) was considered to be Muslim, not Jewish, literature. It thus survived mainly in Arabic literary anthologies, not in Jewish compilations (see Ch. 7 section 3.4, especially note 16).

[21] Not without Hebrew competing with Arabic over the referential function; for a full discussion of this matter, see ch. 7.

on Jewish culture was so strong and at the same time so naturalized that one could find in the same book poems written in Hebrew with introductory passages giving details of the circumstances under which each poem had been composed written in Arabic. It was therefore quite natural for Jews not to take much interest in the business of writing in Hebrew, which provided poetic registers only, when a full range of registers and literary forms was readily available in Arabic, comprising a tradition that had been viable for over two hundred years.

What was so irritating to al-Ḥarīzī, then, about such a well-established, venerable tradition of Jewish use of Arabic as the main written language? The reason for his attention will become clear only if we consider al-Ḥarīzī's cultural background and the ideological framework within which he worked during his earlier years in northern Spain and Provence. In the dedications cited above, al-Ḥarīzī addressed the poor command of Hebrew by Jews in the East. But, as already mentioned, he himself was not a native of the East but had traveled there from northern Spain, where Jewish writing was undergoing a complete revolution at the time. In northern Spain the traditional division of functions described above was in the process of breaking down, and Hebrew had begun to take over more and more functions which had traditionally been fulfilled by Arabic, gradually replacing Arabic as the major written language of Jewish literature. As a result, new literary genres were developing in Hebrew, either through translations from Arabic or in original forms of Hebrew writing.

The struggle between Hebrew and Arabic over written-language functions is clearly reflected in the prefaces added by contemporary northern Spanish Jewish authors to their Hebrew works, in which they argue that the Hebrew language is suitable for *all literary purposes*. In the preface to his *maqāmāt* collection, for example, Jacob Ben Ele'azar (late twelfth to early thirteenth century) places the argument for writing in Arabic in the mouths of "Ishmaelite sages" who mock the Jews asking:

> Is there a language more suitable for praising or cursing, or for rousing love than the language of the Arabs?
> And for recounting wars and chronicles—are any words sweeter than our words?

To which the author responds, addressing his own people:

> You speak to me in beautiful words and say: "Does not the Holy Tongue lag behind?"
> "[Not at all!]—it puts song in the mouth of the dumb, so that he can sing fluently and not stumble,
> [You can] praise or curse in it, speak in rhyme[22] or tell a tale!"

And again in the following lines:

> My people, what is it that you lack? / You can use my words to say whatever you want / and be sure that I will supply all your [literary] needs. / Speak with ease and do not fail, / "put forth a riddle, and speak a parable" (Ezechiel 17:2), / read the book of tales [lit., parables] which I have composed, / "know therefore and discern" (Daniel 9:25). (Ben Ele'azar 1992-93:13-14 [Hebrew])

Al-Ḥarīzī himself supplies, in the first dedication to *Sefer taḥkemoni*, a long list of literary forms which he included in his *maqāmāt*:

> And I gathered together in this book many parables and sweet themes. Among them various poems and striking riddles, words of instruction, songs of friendship, proverbs of right things; words of admonition, events of the time and tidings of the years. The remembrance of death and the place of the shadow of death; words of repentance, and pardoning of guilt. The delights of love and songs of love. The betrothing of women, bridal canopy and marriage, and matters of divorce; the drunkenness of drunkards; the asceticism of ascetics; wars of heroes and events of kings; the adventures of the road; songs of praise, and supplications of prayers; ethics of the sages, and associations of the upright. The passion of lovers; gardens and hamlets; words of princes; the patter of children; the hunt of hunters; the treachery of deceivers, and the folly of fools; the slandering of scorners, the blaspheming of revilers. And wonderful songs and epistles written in a marvelous way: in order that this book may be as a garden in which are all manner of dainties and pleasant plantations. And in it each seeker will find his heart's desire and will attain of his longing sufficient for his need of that which he lacks. (Al-Ḥarīzī 1965-73:36-37 [Hebrew: al-Ḥarīzī 1952:13]).

There is, of course, an element of conventionality in this list of literary materials and forms, as it was customary among Arabic authors of the *adab* genre (and the *maqāmāt* authors followed suit[23])

---

[22] Literally, "compose a riddle"; but judging by the medieval use of such phrases as *mašal ve- ḥidda* and *mašal u-melitza*, and by contemporary Biblical exegesis of such phrases, it seems that medieval Hebrew writers held the phrase to designate "a (fictional) narrative, instructive or amusing," and used it in the sense of "a tale," "an anecdote," and quite often: "a rhymed piece of prose."

[23] Cf. the introduction to al-Ḥarīrī's *Maqāmāt* (al-Ḥarīrī 1929:6).

to present such lists in the prefaces to their writings. Yet, put in this particular ideological setting, it is also meant to declare Hebrew an adequately literary language, in which one could, and should, address in writing any literary subject, using any literary form available. Declarations of this sort typically appeared at the time when Arabic was being displaced from its position as the main language for informative writing and Hebrew was taking over. In this particular case, the declaration prefaces a belletristic Hebrew text which actually signifies both the referential and the aesthetic functions of language. Such declarations, or even debates regarding Hebrew's adequacy as a scientific and informative language, are also found within texts actually written in Hebrew throughout the entire period.

But the most prominent sign of the breakdown of the traditional division of functions between Arabic and Hebrew is the abundance of translations into Hebrew that were produced in northern Spain and Provence during this period (Steinschneider 1956 [1893]; Halkin 1971). Once again, it is the introductions to the translations, especially the earlier ones, which reflect a particular awareness of "a new state" as regards the use of Hebrew for writing—an awareness different from the traditional one. The previous situation, whereby it had been customary to write virtually everything in Arabic, now seemed somewhat incomprehensible, even strange, with the result that some of the translators now felt the need to explain why previous generations of Jews had written in Arabic rather than in Hebrew. The main explanation given was that people in earlier times had failed to master Hebrew, so, if they wished to be understood, writers had no choice but to write in Arabic.

Moses Ben Ǧiqaṭilla (mid-eleventh century) says in the introduction to his translation of Judah Ḥayyūǧ's *Kitāb ḥurūf al-līn*:

> Forasmuch as a strange people bears rule over us, and we are swallowed up among nations of a deep speech and of a hard language..., for these reasons therefore Jewish grammarians were obliged to compose their works in Arabic, this being current in the mouth of a powerful people and easy of comprehension, while Hebrew was obscure; the former clear and intelligible, the latter of doubtful meaning; as it was proper to explain the obscure by the clear, the difficult by the intelligible. The men of Zarephath, however, that dwell in the dominions of our brethren the children of Esau [i.e., the Christians], do not for the most part understand Arabic, while

> they dearly love and are accustomed to speak the holy tongue. (Ḥayyūǧ 1985 [1870]:1-2 [English section]; 1 [Hebrew section])

Judah Ibn Tibbon (Granada 1120—Lunel 1190), in the introduction to his translation of *Farā'iḍ al-qulūb* (*Duties of the Hearts by*) Baḥyā Ibn Paqūda, says more bluntly:

> And after them [i.e., the sages of the Hellenistic and Byzantine periods, of the Mishnah and Talmud] most of the Geonim were in exile in the Ishmaelite kingdom [i.e., the Muslim kingdom] in Iraq, Palestine and Persia, and they spoke the Arabic language. All the Israelite communities in those places spoke that language. They composed all their commentaries on the Biblical books, the orders of the Mishnah and the Talmud, in Arabic, as they did with most of their other works and with the responses to the queries that were asked of them. This is because all the people understood that language, and also because Arabic is an ample language that is adequate to every subject and every speaker's and author's needs. Its idiom is straightforward, clear, and capable of speaking to the point better on any subject than is possible in Hebrew. For all we have of the Hebrew language is that which is found in the books of the Bible, and this does not suffice for all of a speaker's needs. Furthermore, they intended their compositions to benefit the simple people, who did not have a good command of the Holy Tongue. Therefore most of their compositions, on whatever subject they wrote, be it Biblical or other studies, were in Arabic. (Ibn Paqūda 1949 [1928]:56-57 [Hebrew]).

And in the introduction to his translation of *Sefer ha-riqma* by Ibn Ǧanāḥ, he says:

> He [Ibn Ǧanāḥ] wrote these books in Arabic, the language of the people amongst whom he was living, because so were most of the compositions of the Geonim and the sages in the Ishmaelite kingdom. This is because Arabic is ample and eloquent, and its speaker finds nothing lacking in it. But of the Holy Tongue we only have what is found in the Bible, and that would not provide for all of a speaker's needs. Also, most of the people do not understand Hebrew, but only a few, and the rest of their contemporaries are familiar with Arabic, and so they chose it for their writings. But the people of this exile of the land of the Franks, and those of the Christian territories, do not know Arabic; those works would be like a sealed book to them, and would be inaccessible unless they were translated into Hebrew (Ibn Ǧanāḥ 1964 [1929]:4 [Hebrew]).[24]

---

[24] Cf. on the same topic Joseph Qimḥi (c. 1105—c. 1170), who also explains that it was from their Muslim neighbors that the Jews learned the importance

In his translation of Maimonides' *Introduction to the Mishnah*, al-Ḥarīzī voices, in an elegantly rhymed prose style, a more radical opinion:

> When I understood what they [i.e., the Jews of Marseilles, who ordered the translation from him] said, I hurried without waiting, fulfilled their word, and translated the commentary of this master [i.e., Maimonides] from Arabic into the Holy Tongue. I turned its lights from the west (the direction of the setting sun) towards the east (the direction of the rising sun). ... I have translated it from the dark language of Kedar [i.e., Arabic] into the language of gold and glory. This is because I was jealous for the commentaries which the Torah carried, which deserve the rights of the first born, and yet were born on the knees of Hagar, Sarah's slave, while Sarah remained barren. In wonderment, I asked: "Can holiness and worldliness be joined? How can light and darkness be united?" But the sage's [i.e., Maimonides'] intention was to give wisdom to the simple, so he wrote it in Arabic for the sake of those who do not know the Holy Tongue but only Hagarite [i.e., Arabic], and their language is "half in the speech of Ashdod and [they] could not speak in the Jews' language" (Nehemiah 13:24). So I made an effort, took courage and removed foreign expressions from this holy treatise, so it left a prison to become a king; it washed in pure water, took off its [old] clothes and put on [new] ones. I translated its words into eloquent phrases and sweetened it with the sweetness of the Holy Tongue (Maimonides 1960:4 [Hebrew]).

Al-Ḥarīzī no longer wishes to be understanding, or sympathetic, toward a practice so natural to Jewish literature in the East and in Muslim Spain, that is, using Arabic to write texts which bear upon the sacred scriptures or the Jewish codes of law. For him this practice is unacceptable, impossible, and obsolete and must be modified and corrected. By translating into Hebrew Jewish works originally written in Arabic al-Ḥarīzī feels that he is enabling these works to revert to their "true" language, thus restoring the nation's lost treasures.

Judah al-Ḥarīzī as well as Judah Ibn Tibbon and his son Samuel (Provence, c. 1160-c. 1230), were among the first translators into Hebrew, as were also Abraham Bar Ḥiyya, Moses Ben Ǧiqaṭilla, Joseph Qimḥi, Jacob Ben Ele'azar, almost all of whom were emigrants to northern Spain and Provence. They translated mainly

of being aware of one's own language and taking measures to preserve and cultivate it (J. Kimhi 1887:3; cf. D. Kimhi 1952 [1862]:1).

Jewish Arabic works, and sometimes the same work would be translated by more than one translator, as in the case of Maimonides' *Guide for the Perplexed*, which was translated by both al-Ḥarīzī and Samuel Ibn Tibbon. It may be typical of the vanguard to feel an (almost compulsive) need to comment frequently on their profession, thereby legitimizing it over and over again. Both al-Ḥarīzī and Judah Ibn Tibbon did so, as did Judah Ibn Tibbon's son Samuel, while at the same time they contested and criticized each other's work. We are thus afforded a fairly well-rounded view of how the translators themselves perceived the task of translating from Arabic into Hebrew at the time. These comments reveals that al-Ḥarīzī and the Tibbons each viewed their mission quite differently: al-Ḥarīzī's overall attitude was one of unequivocal acceptance of the Hebrew-for-writing ideology, and he was in full accord with his mission. He seemed happy to convert into Hebrew any text he may have been asked to, convinced that by so doing he was simply reclaiming what had originally been there to begin with, but which had, over the ages, been lost or even "stolen." He sought to prove that the Hebrew language could be appropriately used in a wide range of written forms, so over and above translating, he also wrote his own *maqāmāt*, comprising a handbook of Hebrew styles intended to encourage Eastern Jews to use Hebrew as a written language. This is why he declares his intention to provide the reader of the *maqāmāt* with a glossary.

The Tibbons, on the other hand, regarded their work very differently. Judah Ibn Tibbon, for instance, expresses explicit doubts about the very possibility of translating into Hebrew and is skeptical about the quality of such translations (Ibn Paqūda 1949 [1928]:58). He addresses the difficulties facing the translator, discussing the fact that Arabic is an "ample" language, while Hebrew is "short" (i.e., limited) and sparse. His attitude movingly attests to the harsh difficulties facing an Andalusi newcomer to northern Spain who was accustomed to writing in Arabic and was forced to switch to Hebrew, undertaking to transform it into a language capable of accommodating topics for which in fact it had no working registers (cf. Halkin 1963:239-241).

Debates and discussions concerning the functions of Hebrew, its ability to supply a full range of literary modes of expression, and specific modes of translation, were all part of a single overall process: the creation of a new Jewish literature. Since Arabic literature still retained its high status in northern Spain and Provence, the construction of this new Jewish literature was accomplished mainly by borrowing from the Arabic literature. This is why northern Spanish Jewish literature resembles Andalusi literature up to a point and is usually regarded as a direct extension of it. But in fact the paradigm on which the new Jewish literature in Christian Spain was based, was quite different from the dominant paradigm of Jewish literature during the Muslim period. The foremost innovation was the production of the new literature mainly (indeed, almost exclusively) in Hebrew. Writing in Hebrew was accompanied by ideological declarations which assigned to Hebrew writing the role of marking a particular collective or ethnic identity, that could be called "national."

What were the reasons for imposing this new role on Hebrew at this specific point in time and place? To what extent did the local environment motivate the use of vernacular languages (such as Castilian and Romance) in writing or the renaissance in Arabic-Latin translations introduced new literary practices into Jewish society, practices to be performed in Hebrew? These questions are still open and remain to be answered. Yet one thing does seem clear: if not for the prevailing cultural climate in northern Spain and Provence at the time, al-Ḥarīzī would most probably never have written his Hebrew *maqāmāt*. For although they seem so Arabic in character, as products of the Jewish-Arabic culture they would have been most unlikely, particularly in the East.[25] There would have been no reason to disturb the traditional Arabic-Hebrew division of functions prevalent during the Muslim period, thereby bringing about new forms of writing in Hebrew.[26] In other words, it took

[25] The different attitudes toward Hebrew writing found in northern Spain and the East are best illustrated by al-Ḥarīzī himself, who, in the preface to *Sefer taḥkemoni* describes how he was asked while still in Spain to translate al-Ḥarīrī's work into Hebrew: "For the nobles of Spain, when they heard the words of the Arab's book [al-Ḥarīrī's *Maqāmāt*], marvelled at them. And they sought of me while I was still among them to translate this book for them and I was not able to turn them away" (al-Ḥarizi 1965-73:39). But when he composed his own Hebrew *Maqāmāt* in the East, he had to "seek of the patrons of the world, from Egypt to Babylon, [for] one with whose name I might adorn the book and it would be sealed with his seal. I searched him among the leaders of the time, and sought for him but found him not, and no one answered me when I called" (*ibid.*:41), until at last a patron was found.

[26] The fact that while still in the East, but apparently after he had composed

a non-Muslim and non-Arabic cultural atmosphere, that of Christian Spain, to produce a literary work so notably Arabic-Hebrew in nature.

Sefer taḥkemoni (Stern 1964a:199), al-Ḥarīzī also wrote a Judeo-Arabic *Maqāma*, seems to indicate that he himself realized that there was no great public for Hebrew writing there and that he would have to write in Arabic in order to make his voice heard. Explaining why he wrote in Arabic, he notes, "When I visited Baghdad the Jewish community there turned its back on me and treated me rudely. I have therefore decided to compose a *Maqāma* in Arabic about them, in which I will expose some of their hidden feats ...; let me quote here from this *Maqāma*, so that it serve to commemorate what they have done ..." (Stern 1964b:150-151). His explanation clearly echoes the argument used about two hundered years earlier, when Arabic first began competing with Hebrew for the referential function of Jewish writing, namely that one should write in Arabic if one wants the message to be clearly conveyed and understood by all (cf. ch. 7, 2.3). Such an argument would accompany, needless to say, a refutation or a piece of satirical writing.

BIBLIOGRAPHY

Abbot, N., 1949. "A Ninth-Century Fragment of the 'Thousand Nights'." *Journal of Near Eastern Studies* 3: 129-64

'Abd al-Ǧabbār, b. Aḥmad, 1960. *al-Muġnī fī abwāb al-tawḥīd wa'l-'adl.* ed. al-Ḵūlī, A.. Cairo

Abermann, Abraham M., 1953. "*Sefer Taḥkemoni*'s Dedications and its List of Contents," *Maḥbarot le-Sifrut* 5(2-3): 39-46. (in Hebrew)

Abū Dā'ūd, Sulaymān b. al-Aš'at, 1950-51. *Sunan Abī Dā'ūd.* ed. Muḥammad Muḥī al-Dīn 'Abd al-Ḥamīd. Cairo

Abū Nuwās, al-Ḥasan b. Hānī, 1861. *Diwan des Abū Nuwās.* ed. Ahlwardt, Wilhelm. I. Die Weinlieder. Greifswald

1898. *Dīwān.* ed. Wāṣif, Maḥmūd. Cairo

1932. *Dīwān.* ed. Farīd, Maḥmūd Kāmil. Cairo

1953. *Dīwān.* ed. al-Ġazālī, Aḥmad 'Abd al-Ḥamīd. Cairo

1958-88. *Dīwān.* ed. Ewald Wagner and Gregor Schoeler. Wiesbaden, Stuttgart and Cairo

1962. *Dīwān.* ed., al-Ġazālī, Aḥmad 'Abd al-Maǧīd. Beirut

1980. *Dīwān Abī Nuwās biriwāyat al-Ṣūlī.* ed. Bahǧat 'Abd al-Ġafūr al- Ḥadīṯī. Baghdad

1992. *Dīwān.* ed. Iskandar Āṣāf. Cairo

Abū al-Ṭayyib al-Luġawī, 'Abd al-Wāḥid b. 'Alī, 1974. *Marātib al-naḥawiyyīn.* ed. Muḥammad Abū al-Faḍl Ibrāhīm. Kuwait

Abramson, Sheraga, 1965. *Centres and Peripheries in the Gaonic Period.* Jerusalem (in Hebrew)

1975-76. "A Note on the Article by M. Idel (*Leshonenu* 34: 484)." *Qiryat Sefer* 51: 712 (in Hebrew)

Abū Tammām, Ḥabīb b. Aws, 1972. *Dīwān al-ḥamāsa ma'a muḵtaṣar šarḥ al-Tibrīzī.* Cairo

Abū Ya'lā, Aḥmad b. 'Alī, 1986. *Musnad.* ed. Ḥ.S. Asad, Damascus

al-'Aǧlūnī, Ismā'īl b. Muḥammad, 1974. *Kašf al-ḵafā' wa muzīl al-ilbās 'ammā 'štahara mina al-aḥādīṯ 'alā alsinat al-nās.* ed. A. al-Qalāš. Aleppo

al-Aḥdab, Ibrāhīm al-Ṭarābulsī, 195?. *Kašf al-ma'ānī wa'l-bayān 'an rasā'il Badī' al-Zamān.* ed. Yūsuf al-Fakhūrī. Beirut

Ahlwardt, A., 1895. *Die Handschriftenverzeichnisse der Königlichen Bibliothek zu Berlin.* Berlin

Algazi, Gadi, 1998. "Ein gelehrter Blick ins lebendige Archiv: Umgangsweisen mit der Vergangenheit im 15. Jahrhundert." *Historische Zeitschrift.* 266: 317-357

Allony, Nehemia, 1951. *The Scansion of Medieval Hebrew Poetry.* Jerusalem. (in Hebrew)

Allony, Nehemia, ed., 1969. *Ha'egron, Kitāb uṣūl al-šīr al-'ibrānī by Rav Se'adya Ga'on.* Jerusalem (in Hebrew)

Allony, Nehemia, 1970. "'Alī ben Yehūda ha-Nazīr and His Treatise *Yesodot ha-Lashon ha -'Ivrīt.*" *Leshonenu* 34, 75-105, 187-209 (in Hebrew)

Allony, Nehemia & Yevin, I., 1985. "Four Texts from the *Muṣawwitāt* Literature" *Leshonenu* 48-9: 85-117 (in Hebrew)

al-Anbārī, Kamāl al-Dīn, 1956. "Kitāb al-mūǧaz fī 'ilm al-qawāfī." ed. 'Abd al-Hādī, Hāšim. *Revue de l'Academie Arabe de Damas* 31: 51-8

Arazi, Albert, 1979. "Abū Nuwās: fut-il Šuʿubite?," *Arabica* 26: 1-61
1989. *La Réalité et la Fiction dans la Poésie arabe ancienne.* Paris
Arkoun, M., Le Goff, J., Fahd, T., Rodinson, M. eds., 1978. *L'étrange et le merveilleux dans l'Islam médiéval.* Colloque organisé par l'Association pour l'Avancement des Etudes Islamiques en mars 1974 à Paris. Paris
al-Aʿšā, Maymūn b. Qays, 1983. *Dīwān al-Aʿšā al-Kabīr.* ed. Muḥammad Ḥusayn. Beirut
al-ʿAskarī, al-Ḥasan b. ʿAbd Allāh Abū Hilāl, 1952. *Kitāb al-ṣināʿatayn, al-kitāba wa'l-šīr.* eds. ʿAlī Muḥammad al-Bağāwī and Muḥammad Abū al- Faḍl Ibrāhīm. Cairo
1988. *Ğamharat al-amṯāl.* ed. Ibrāhīm, Muḥammad Abū al-Faḍl and ʿAdb al-Mağīd Qaṭāmiš. Beirut
al-Aṣmaʿī, ʿAbd Allāh b. Qurayb, n.d. *al-Aṣmaʿiyyāt.* eds. Aḥmad Muḥammad Šākir and ʿAbd al-Salām Hārūn. Cairo
al-Akfaš, Saʿīd b. Maṣada, 1970. *Kitāb al-qawāfī.* ed. ʿIzzat, Ḥasan. Damascus
Baker, Colin F., 1990. "Medical Examination at the Dinner Table," *Geniza Fragments* 20, 2-3
al-Bāqillānī, Muḥammad b. al-Ṭayyib, 1981. *Iʿğāz al-qur'ān.* ed. Aḥmad Ṣaqr. Cairo
al-Bayhaqī, Ibrāhīm b. Muḥammad, 1902. *Kitāb al-maḥāsin wa'l-masāwi'.* ed. Friedrich Schwally. Giessen
1970. *al-Maḥāsin wa'l-masāwi'.* Beirut
Beeri, Tova, 1985. "The phonetical-syllabic meter in medieval Hebrew" *Jerusalem Studies in Hebrew Literature.* 8: 50-70 (in Hebrew)
Beeston, A. F. L., 1971. "The Genesis of the *Maqāmāt* Genre." *Journal of Arabic Literature* 2, 1-12
1990. "Al-Hamaḏānī, al-Ḥarīrī and the *maqāmāt* genre." *ʿAbbasid Belles-Lettres.* eds. Julia Ashtiany et al. Cambridge. 125-35
Bell, Richard, 1953. *Introduction to the Qur'ān.* Edinburgh
Bencheikh, Jamel, 1963-64. "Poésies bachiques d'Abū Nuwās, thémes et personnages." *Bulletins d'Etudes Orientales* 17: 1-84
Ben Eleʿazar, Jacob, 1992-93. *The Love Stories.* ed. Yonah David. Tel Aviv
1939. See Schirmann 1939.
Ben Labraṭ, Dunaš 1980. *Tešubot.* ed. Angel Sáenz-Badillos. Granada
Blachère, R., 1950. "Les savants iraquiens et leur informateurs bédouins aux IIe-IVe siècles de l'hégire." *Mélanges William Marçais.* Paris. 37-48
Blachère, R. et Masnou, P., 1957. *Al-Hamadānī, Maqāmāt (Séances): Choisies et traduites de l'arabe avec une étude sur le genre.* Paris
Blau, Joshua, 1953. "The Arabic Introduction of *Sefer Taḥkemoni* and Its Hebrew Translation," *Maḥbarot le-Sifrut* 5: 47-56. (in Hebrew)
1962. "On the status of Hebrew and Arabic among Arabic-speaking Jews in the first centuries of Islam". *Leshonenu* 26: 281-84 (in Hebrew)
1981². *The Emergence and Linguistic Background of Judaeo-Arabic.* Jerusalem
Bloch, Alfred, 1946. *Vers und Sprache im Altarabischen.* Basel
Bogatyrëv, P., 1976. "Costume as a Sign." *Semiotics of Art.* eds. L. Matejka and I.R. Titunik. Cambridge Mass. 12-20
Bohas, G., 1974. "La Métrique arabe classique." *Linguistics* 140: 59-68
Bonebakker, Seger Adrianus. "*Ḳāfiya.*" *EI²*. Leiden. vol. 4, 411-414
1992. "Nihil obstat in story telling?" *Mededelingen van de Afdeling Letterkunde* 55(8): 289-307
Bornstein , Hayyim Y., 1904. *The Polemics of Saadia Gaon and Ben Meir.* Warsaw
Bosworth, C.E., 1976. *The Medieval Islamic Underworld: The Banū Sāsān in Arabic Society and Literature.* Leiden

Brockelmann, Carl, 1909. *Geschichte der arabischen Literatur*. Leipzig. Supplementband: Leiden 1937

Brody, H., 1895. *Studien zu den Dichtungen Jehuda ha-Levi's*. 1. Über Metra der Versgedichte. Berlin

al-Buḥturī, Aḥmad b. Muḥammad, 1910. *Kitāb al-ḥamāsa*. ed. Louis Cheikho. Beirut

Chapira, B., 1914. "Fragments inédits du sefer haggaloui de Saadia Gaon." *Revue des Etudes Juives* 68: 1-14

Bürgel, J.C., 1974. "Die beste Bedeutung: eines literarischen Streites des arabischen Mittelalters im Lichte komparatistischer Betrachtung." *Oriens* 22-24: 7-102

Cohen, Mark, 1976. "New Light on the Conflict over the Palestinian Gaonate, 1038-1042, and on Daniel b. ʿAzarya: A Pair of Letters to the Nagid of Qayrawan." *AJS Review* 1: 1-40

al-Damanhūrī, Muḥammad, n.d. *al-Ḥāšiya al-kubrā ʿalā matn al-kāfī fī al-ʿarūḍ wa'l-qawāfī*. Cairo

Dana, Joseph, 1975. "Concerning the Source of Taḥkemoni," *Tarbiz* 44: 172-181 (in Hebrew)

1984. "Al-Hamaḏānī as a Source for Rabbi Judah al-Ḥarīzī," *Dappim (Research in Literature)* 1: 79-89. (in Hebrew)

Davidson, Israel, ed., 1934. *The Book of the Wars of the Lord Containing the Polemics of the Karaite Salmon ben Yeruhim Against Saadia Gaon*. New York

Derenbourg, H., 1884. *Les manuscrits arabes de l'Escorial*. Paris

Derenbourg, J., ed., 1886. *Le livre des parterres fleuries. Grammatique hébraïque en arabe d'Abou'l-Walid Merwan ibn Djanah de Cordoue*. Paris

De Sacy, Silvestre, 1826. *Chrestomathie arabe*. vol. 3. Paris

1831. *Grammaire arabe*. Paris

Dishon, Judith, 1979. "On the Source of Judah al-Ḥarīzī's Twenty-First *Maqāma* in the *Tahkemoni*." *Criticism and Interpretation* 13-14: 9-26 (in Hebrew)

Drory, Rina, 1988. *The Emergence of Jewish-Arabic Literary Contacts at the Beginning of the Tenth Century*. Tel Aviv. (in Hebrew)

1991. "The hidden context: on literary products of tri- cultural contacts in the middle ages." *Peʿamim (Studies in Oriental Jewery)* 46-47: 277-302

1998. "*maqāma*". *Encyclopedia of Arabic Literature*. ed. Julie Scott Meisami and Paul Starkey. London and New York. 2, 507-508

Ḏū al-Rumma, Ġaylān b. ʿUqba, 1919. *Dīwān*. ed. Carlile Henry Hayes MaCartney. Cambridge

al-Du'alī, Abū Aswad, 1954. *Dīwān*. ed. ʿAbd al-Karīm al-Duǧaylī. Baghdad

Eldar, Ilan, 1984. "The wandering of the concept 'al-sākin al-layyin' ('weak quiescent') from Spain to Palestine." *Miscelanea de Estudios Arabes y Hebraicos* 33/2: 1-9. (in Hebrew; English and Spanish summaries)

1985. "Biblical Orthöepy." *Tarbitz* 54: 225-43 (in Hebrew)

1988. "The Treatise on the Shewa and 'Seder ha-Simanim—Two Parts of a Whole." *Teʿuda* 6 (Studies in Hebrew and Arabic in memory of Dov Eron): 127-138 (in Hebrew)

1994. *The Study of the Art of Correct Reading as Reflected in the Medieval Treatise Hidāyat al-Qāri (=Guidance of the Reader)*. Jerusalem (in Hebrew)

Even-Zohar, Itamar, 1970. "The Nature and Functionalization of the Language of Literature under Diglossia." *Hasifrut* 2/2: 286-302. (in Hebrew)

Even-Zohar, Itamar, 1976. "What did Gitl Cook and What did Cicikov Eat?: On the Status of Denotation in Hebrew Literary Language Since the Revival Period." *Hasifrut* 23: 1-6. (in Hebrew)

1978. *Papers in Historical Poetics*. Tel Aviv

1986. "System, literary; Interference, literary; Dynamics, literary." *Encyclopedic Dictionary of Semiotics*. ed. Thomas A. Sebeok. Indiana

1990. "Polysystem Studies." Poetics Today 11/1

1994. "Culture Planning and the Market: Making and Maintaining Socio-Semiotic Entities." *http://www.tau.ac.il/itamarez/papers/plan_clt.html*

1997. "Culture Planning and Cultural Persistence in the Making and Maintaining of Entities." *http://www.tau.ac.il/itamarez/papers/plan_res.html*

Farūk̲, ʿUmar, 1946. *Abū Nuwās, šāʿir Hārūn al-Rašīd wa-Muḥammad al-Amīn*. Beirut

Fleischer, Ezra, 1975. *Hebrew Liturgical Poetry in the Middle Ages*. Jerusalem (in Hebrew)

1977. "Remarks Concerning the Metric System of Ancient Hebrew Liturgic Poetry." *Ha-Sifrut* 24: 70-83 (in Hebrew)

1982. "A Fragment from Ḥīvī al-Balkhī's Criticism of the Bible." *Tarbiz* 51: 49-58 (in Hebrew)

1983. "New Information on Rabbi Yitzḥaq Bar Levi's Works." *Hebrew Language Studies Presented to Professor Zeev Ben-Hayyim*. ed. E. Bar-Asher et al. Jerusalem. 425-450 (in Hebrew)

1984. *The Yozer: Its Emergence and Development*. Jerusalem (in Hebrew)

1985. "The ascendance of exact metres in Hebrew poetry." *Leshonenu*. 48-9: 143-62 (in Hebrew)

Freytag, Georg Wilhelm, 1830. *Darstellung der arabischen Verskunst*. Bonn

Gabrieli, F., 1953. "Abū Nuwās, Poeta ʿAbbāside." *Oriente Moderno* 33: 279-296

al-Ǧāḥiẓ, ʿAmr b. Baḥr Abū ʿUt̲mān, 1932. *Kitāb al-bayān wa-'l-tabyīn*. ed. Ḥasan al-Sandūbī. Cairo

1938. *Kitāb al-buk̲alāʾ*. ed. al-ʿAwāmirī et al. Cairo

1990[5]. *Al-Buk̲alāʾ*. ed. Ṭāha al-Ḥāǧirī. Cairo

1943. *Kitāb al-ḥayawān*. ed. ʿAbd al- Salām Hārūn. Cairo

1968. *Kitāb al-ḥayawān*. ed. Fawzī ʿAtawī. Beirut and Damascus

(pseudo-)al-Ǧāḥiẓ, ʿAmr b. Baḥr Abū ʿUt̲mān, 1991. *al-Maḥāsin wa-'l-aḍdād*. ed. ʿAlī Fāʿūr et al. Beirut

(psuedo-)Galenus, 1852. *Dialog über die Seele*. trans. Judah al-Ḥarīzī. ed. Adolph Jellinek. Leipzig

Geertz, Clifford, 1983. *Local Knowledge*. New York

Ghazi, M.F., 1957. "La littérature d'imagination en arabe du IIe /VIIIe au Ve/XIe siècles." *Arabica* 4: 164-178

Ginzberg, L. 1929. *Geniza Studies in Memory of Dr. S. Schechter*. New York

Goitein, Shlomo Dov, 1951. "The *maqāma* and the *maḥberet*," *Maḥbarot le-Sifrut* 5 (1): 26-40 (in Hebrew)

1962. *Jewish Education in Muslim Countries*. Jerusalem. (in Hebrew)

Goldenberg, Esther, 1973-74. "On the Egron of Seʿadya Ga'on." *Leshonenu* 37: 117-36, 275-89; 38 (1974), 78-90 (in Hebrew)

1983. "*Doḥaq ha-šir* (poetic license) in medieval Hebrew linguistic theory." *Hebrew language studies presented to Professor Zeev Ben-Hayyim*. Jerusalem. 117-41 (in Hebrew)

Goldziher, Ignaz, 1971. *Muslim Studies*. London

Gottheil, R., 1905. "Some Hebrew Manuscripts in Cairo." *Jewish Quarterly Review* 17: 609-55

Grangeret de Lagrange, Jean Baptiste André, 1828. *Anthologie arabe*. Paris

al-Ǧurǧānī, ʿAbd al-Qāhir b. ʿAbd al-Raḥmān, 1968. *al-Risāla al-šāfiyya*. In: K̲alafallah and Sallām, 1968

Habermann, Abraham M., 1952. "*Sefer Taḥkemoni* of Rabbi Jehuda al-Ḥarīzī," *Sinai* 31: 112-27 (in Hebrew)
Halkin, Abraham S., 1963. "The Medieval Jewish Attitude Towards Hebrew." In: *Biblical And Other Studies.* ed. Alexander Altmann. Cambridge Mass. 233-48
1971. "Translation and Translators (Medieval)." In: *Encyclopaedia Judaica.* Jerusalem. 15: 1318-29
Halper, B., 1913-14. "The Scansion of Medieval Hebrew Poetry." *Jewish Quarterly Review* N.S. 4: 153-224
Hamori, Andras, 1969. "Examples of convention in the poetry of Abū Nuwās." *Studia Islamica* 30: 5-26
al-Hamaḏānī, Aḥmad b. Ḥusayn Abū al-Faḍl Badī' al-Zamān, 1880. *Maqāmāt.* ed. Yūsuf al-Nabhānī, Constantinople
1908. *Maqāmāt.* ed. Muḥammad 'Abduh. Beirut
1962. *Maqāmāt.* ed. Muḥammad Muḥī al-Dīn 'Abd al-Ḥamīd. Cairo
al-Ḥanafī, Abū al-'Alā' Aḥmad b. Abī Bakr al-Rāzī, 1912. *Maqāmāt al-Ḥanafī.* Constantinople. 1-116
al-Ḥarīrī, al-Qāsim b. 'Alī Abū Muḥammad, 1847. *Maqāmāt.* ed. Silvestre De Sacy. Paris
1929. *Maqāmāt.* Cairo
1872. *Maḥberot itiel.* trans. Judah al-Ḥarīzī. ed. Thomas Chenery. London
1951. *Maḥberot itiel.* trans. al-Ḥarīzī, Judah. ed. Yitzḥaq Peretz. Tel Aviv
al-Ḥarīzī, Judah, 1845. *Die ersten Makamen aus dem Tahkemoni oder Divan des Charisi nebst dessen Vorrede / nach einem authentischen Manuskript aus dem Jahre 1281 hrsg.* ed. S.I. Kaempf. Berlin
1899. *Taḥkemoni.* ed. A. Kaminka. Warsaw
1924. *Taḥkemoni.* ed. P. De Lagarde. Hannover [Göttingen 1883]
1952. *Taḥkemoni.* ed. Y. Toporowsky. Tel Aviv
1965-73. *The Taḥkemoni of Judah al-Ḥarīzī.* trans. Victor Emanuel Reichert. Jerusalem
Harkavy, A.A., 1970 [1878-80]. *Me'assef niddaḥim.* Jerusalem
Harkavy, A. E., 1892. *Ha-sarid veha-paliṭ misefer ha-egron umisefer ha-galuy. Zikaron larishonim vegam laakharonim* 1/5. Peterburg
Ḥāwī, Īlyā Salīm, 1970. *Fann al-ši'r al-ḵamrī wataṭawwuruhu 'inda al-'arab.* Beirut
al-Hayṯamī, 'Alī b. Abī Bakr Nūr al-Dīn, 1967. *Mağma' al-zawāi'd wa-manba' al-fawāi'd.* Beirut
Ḥayyūğ, Judah, 1985 [1870]. *Two Treatises on Verbs Containing Feeble and Double Letters by R. Jehuda Hayug of Fez, translated into Hebrew from the Original Arabic by R. Moses Gikatilia of Cordova; to which is added the Treatise on Punctuation by the same author, translated by Aben Ezra.* ed. John William Nutt. Jerusalem [London and Berlin]
al-Ḥillī: see Hoenerbach
al-Ḥimyarī, Abū Sa'īd Nišwān, 1948. *al-Ḥūr al-'ayn.* ed. Muṣṭafā Kamāl. Cairo
1984. *Al-Qawāfī.* ed. Muḥammad Abū al-Futūḥ Šarīf. Cairo
Hirschfeld, Hartwig, 1903. "Fragment of an Unknown Work by Judah al-Ḥarīzī." *Jewish Quarterly Review* 16: 683-88, 693-97
Hoenerbach, Wilhelm, 1956. *Die Vulgärarabische Poetik: al-Kitāb al-'āṭil al-ḥālī wa'l-murakhkhaṣ al-ğālī des Ṣafīyaddīn Ḥillī.* Wiesbaden
Hrushovski, Benjamin, 1971a. "The Major Systems of Hebrew Rhyme from the Piyyuṭ to the Present Day (500 A.D.-1970): An Essay on Basic Concepts." *Hasifrut* 2/4: 721-79 (in Hebrew)
1971b. "Prosody, Hebrew." *Encyclopedia Judaica.* Jerusalem. 13: 1195-240

Huart, Cl. 1908. "Les séance d'Ibn Nāqiyā." *Journal Asiatique*, 10 (12): 435-54
Ḥāǧī Kalīfa, Muṣṭafā b. ʿAbd Allah, 1941-43. *Kašf al-ẓunūn ʿan asmāʾ al-kutub waʾl-funūn*. ed. Muhammad Šaraf al-Dīn Yāltaqāyā et al. Constantinople
al-Ḥuṣrī, Abū Isḥāq al-Qayrawānī, 1953. *Ẓahr al-ādāb wa-ṯimār al-albāb*. ed. ʿAlī Muḥammad al-Baǧāwī. Cairo
al-Ḥuṭayʾa, Ǧarwal b. Aws, 1957. *Dīwān*. Ṭaha, Nuʿmān Amīn, ed. Cairo
Ibn ʿAbd Rabbihi, Aḥmad b. Muḥammad, 1965. *Kitāb al-ʿiqd al-farīd*. eds. Aḥmad Amīn, Aḥmad al-Zay and Ibrāhīm al-Ibyārī. Cairo
Ibn al-Anbārī, Muḥammad b. al-Qāsim, 1963. *Šarḥ al-qaṣāʾid al-sabʿ al-ṭiwāl al-ǧāhiliyyāt*. Cairo
Ibn al-Aṯīr, al-Mubārak b. Muḥammad, 1963. *al-Nihāya fī ġarīb al-ḥadīṯ wa-ʾl-aṯar*. eds. Ṭ.A. al-Zāwī and M.M. al-Ṭanāǧī. Cairo
Ibn Bassām, Abū al-Ḥasan ʿAlī al-Šantarīnī, 1979. *al-Daḵīra fī maḥāsin ahl al-ǧazīra*. ed. Iḥsān ʿAbbās. Beirut
Ibn Buṭlān, al-Muḵtār b. al-Ḥasan Abū al-Ḥasan, 1985. *The Physicians' dinner party (Risālat daʿwat al-aṭibbāʾ)*. ed. Felix Klein-Franke. Wiesbaden
Ibn Ezra, Moses, 1924. *Sefer širat yisrael (Kitāb al-muḥāḍara waʾl-muḏākara)*. trans. Ben-Zion Halper. Leipzig
Ibn Ezra, Moses, 1935. *Šire ha-ḥol*. ed. Ḥayyim Brody. Berlin
1975. *Kitāb al-mūḥāḍara waʾl-muḏākara*. ed. Abraham Halkin. Jerusalem
Ibn Fāris, Aḥmad b. al-Ḥusayn, 1963. *al-Ṣāḥibī fī fiqh al-luġa wasunan al-ʿarab fī kalāmihā*. ed. M. al-Šuwaymī. Beirut
Ibn Ǧanāḥ, Jonah, 1964 [1929]. *Sefer ha-riqma*. trans. Judah Ibn Tibbon. ed. M. Vilenski. Jerusalem [Berlin])
Ibn al-Ǧawzī, ʿAbd al-Raḥmān b. ʿAlī Abū al-Farağ, 1940. *Al-Muntaẓam fī taʾrīḵ al-mulūk waʾl-umam*. Haydarābād
Ibn al-Ǧawzī, ʿAbd al-Raḥmān b. ʿAlī Abū al-Farağ, 1980. *Maqāmāt*. ed. Muḥammad Naġš. Cairo
Ibn Ḥabīb, Muḥammad, 1942. *Kitāb al-muḥabbar*. ed. Ilse Lichtenstaedter. Haydrabad
Ibn Ḥaǧar al-ʿAsqalānī, 1972. *al-Iṣāba fī maʿrifat al-ṣaḥābā*. ed. ʿAlī Muḥammad al-Baǧāwī. Cairo
Ibn Ḥamdīs, ʿAbd al-Ǧabbār b. Abī Bakr, 1879. *Dīwān*. ed. Celestino Schiaparelli. Roma
Ibn Ḥanbal, Aḥmad b. Muḥammad, 1969. *Musnad*. Beirut
Ibn Hārūn, Sahl, 1973. *Kitāb al-nimr waʾl-ṯaʿlab*. ed. ʿAbd al-Qādir al-Mahīrī. Tunis
Ibn Ḥazm, ʿAlī b. Aḥmad, 1992. *Ṭawq al-ḥamāma fī al-ulfa waʾl-ullāf*. ed. Iḥsān ʿAbbās. Tunis
Ibn Hišām, ʿAbd al-Malik, 1859. *Sīrat sayyidinā Muḥammad*. ed. Ferdinand Wüstenfeld. Göttingen
Ibn Isḥāq, Ḥunayn, 1896. *Sefer musre haphilosophim* ("Sinnsprüche der Philosophen"). trans. Judah al-Ḥarīzī. ed. Abraham Loewenthal. Frankfurt a/M
Ibn al-Kalbī, Hišām b. Muḥammad, 1924. *Kitāb al-aṣnām*. ed. Aḥmad Zakī Bāšā. Cairo
Ibn Kaṯīr, Ismāʿīl b. ʿUmar, 1932-37. *Al-Bidāya waʾl-nihāya*. Cairo
1966. *Tafsīr al-Qurʾān al-ʿaẓīm*. Beirut
Ibn Kaysān, Muḥammad b. Aḥmad, 1859. "Kitāb talqīb al-qawāfī watalqīb ḥarakātihā." In: *Opuscula Arabica*. ed. William Wright. Leyden
Ibn Kalikān, Aḥmad b. Muḥammad, 1968-71. *Wafayāt al-aʿyān*. ed. Iḥsān ʿAbbās. Beirut
Ibn al-Kaššāb, ʿAbd Allah b. Aḥmad Abū Muḥammad al-Baġdādī, 1929. *Al-Iʿtirād ʿalā al-Ḥarīrī fī Maqāmātihi wamaʿahu al-Intiṣār lil-Ḥarīrī liAbī Muḥammad ʿAbd Allah b. Barrī al-Muqaddasī al-Misrī*. In: al-Ḥarīrī 1929

Ibn Manẓūr, Muḥammad b. Mukrim, 1955-65. *Lisān al-ʿarab*. Beirut
1992. *Akbār Abī Nuwās*. in: al-Iṣbahānī 1992, vol. 25
Ibn al-Muʿtazz, ʿAbd Allah, 1989. *Fuṣūl al-tamāṯīl fī tabāšīr al-surūr*. ed. George Qunāziʿ and Fahd Abū Kadra. Damascus
Ibn al-Muqaffaʿ, ʿAbd Allah, 1913. *Kitāb al-adab al-kabīr*; *Kitāb al-adab al-ṣaġīr*. In: *Rasāʾil al-bulaġāʾ*. ed. Muḥammad Kurd ʿAlī. Cairo
Ibn al-Nadīm, Muḥammad b. Isḥāq, 1872. *Kitāb al-Fihrist*. ed. Gustav Flügel. Leipzig
1964. *al-Fihrist*. Beirut
Ibn Nāqiyā, ʿAbd Allah b. Muḥammad Abū al-Qāsim, 1912. *Maqāmāt*. In: al-Ḥanafī, *Maqāmāt*. [Rescher, O., 1914. *Beiträge zur Maqāmen-Literatur*. Constantinople
1988. *Maqāmāt Ibn Nāqiyā*. ed. Ḥasan ʿAbbās. Alexandria
Ibn Paqūda, Baḥya, 1949 [1928]. *Sefer ḥobot ha-lebabot (Farāʾiḍ al-qulūb)*. trans. Judah Ibn Tibbon. ed. A. Zifroni. Tel Aviv [Jerusalem]
Ibn al-Qifṭī, ʿAlī b. Yūsuf, 1955. *Inbāh al-ruwāt ʿalā anbāʾ al-nuḥāt*. ed. Muḥammad Abū al-Faḍl Ibrāhīm. Cairo
Ibn Qutayba, ʿAbd Allah b. Muslim Abū Muḥammad, 1904. *Kitāb al-šiʿr wa-ʾl-šuʿarāʾ*. ed. M.J. De Goeje. Leiden
1963a. *Adab al-kātib*. ed. Muḥiyy al-Dīn ʿAbd al-Ḥamīd. Cairo
1963b. *Kitāb ʿuyūn al-akhbār*. Cairo
Ibn Qutayba, ʿAbd Allah b. Muslim Abū Muḥammad, 1970. *Kitāb al-maʿārif*. ed. M.I.A. al-Ṣāwī. Beirut
Ibn Rudwān, ʿAli, 1900. *Igeret ʿali ha-ishmeeli*. trans. Judah al-Ḥarīzī. ed. Menasseh Grossberg. London
Ibn al-Sarrāǧ, Muḥammad b. ʿAbd al-Malik al-Šantarīnī, 1968. *Al-Miʿyār fī awzān al-Šiʿr wa'l-kāfī fī ʿilm al-qawāfī*. ed. Muḥammad Riḍwān al-Dāya. Beirut
Ibn Šaraf al-Qayrawānī, 1953. *Masāʾil al-intiqād (Questions de critique littéraire)*. ed. Charles Pellat. Alger
1983². *Rasāʾil al-intiqād (fī naqd al-šiʿr wa-ʾl-šuʿarāʾ)*. ed. Ḥasan Ḥusnī ʿAbd al-Wahhāb. Beirut
Idel, Moshe, 1975-76. "Who was the translator of R. Moses ibn Ezra's *ʿArugat ha-bosem?*," *Qiryat Sefer* 51: 484-87 (in Hebrew)
Ingrams, W.H., 1933. *Abū Nuwās in life and legend*. Mauritius
al-Iṣbahānī, ʿAlī b. al-Ḥusayn Abū al-Faraǧ, 1963. *Kitāb al-aġānī*. ed. A.Z. al-ʿAdawī. Cairo
1992. *Kitāb al-aġānī*. ed. ʿAbd Allah ʿAlī Muhannā and Samīr Ǧābir. Beirut
al-Iṣbahānī, Ḥamza b. al-Ḥasan, 1971. *al-Durra al-fāḵira fī al-amṯāl al-sāʾira*. ed. ʿAbd al-Maǧīd Qaṭāmiš. Cairo
al-Iṣbahānī, Muḥammad b. Muḥammad ʿImād al-Dīn, 1955. *Karīdat al-qaṣr wağarīdat al-ʿaṣr. al-Qism al-ʿIrāqī*. ed. Muḥammad Bahǧa al-Aṯarī et al. Baghdad
Jacobi, Renate, 1972. "Dichtung und Lüge in der arabischen Literaturtheorie." *Der Islam* 49: 85-99
Jakobson, Roman, 1956. "Two Aspects of Language and Two Types of Aphasic Disturbances." In: Roman Jakobson and Morris Halle, *Fundamentals of Language*. The Hague. 69-96
1981. "Linguistics and Poetics," in: *Selected Writings*. The Hague. 3: 18-51
Kahle, Paul, 1913. *Masoreten des Osten*. Leipzig
1927-30. *Masoreten des Westens*. Stuttgart
1966 [1902]. *Der masoretische Text des alten Testaments nach der Uberlieferung der babylonischen Juden*. Hildesheim [Leipzig].

al-Kalāʿī, Muḥammad b.ʿAbd al-Ġafūr, 1985. *Iḥkām ṣanʿat al-kalām.* Beirut

Karahan, Abdülkadir, 1955. "Aperçu sur les 'Quarante Hadiths' dans la littérature islamique." *Studia Islamica* 4: 39-55

Kennedy, Philip F., 1997. *The Wine Song in Classical Arabic Poetry.* Oxford

K̲alafallah, Aḥmad and Sallām, M. Zaġlūl, eds., 1968. *T̲alāt̲ rasāʾil fī iʿǧāz al-Qurʾān.* Cairo

al-K̲aṭṭābī, Ḥamd b. Muḥammad Abū Sulaymān, 1968. *Bayān iʿǧāz al-Qurʾān.* In: K̲alafallah and Salām, 1968

Khawam, René, Trans., 1981. *Le fantastique et le quotidien. Kitāb al-nawādir* de Aḥmad al-Qalyūbī. Paris

Kilito, Abdelfatthah, 1976. "Le genre 'séance': une introduction." *Studia Islamica* 43: 25-51

1983. *Les séances, récits et codes culturels chez Hamadanī et Ḥarīrī.* Paris

Kimhi, David, 1952 [1862]. *Sefer mik̲lol.* ed. Y. Rittenberg. Jerusalem [Lyck]. English translation and annotations: Chomsky, W. *David Kimhi's Hebrew Grammar 'Mikhlol'.* New york

Kimhi (Kimchi), Joseph, 1887. *Sefer ha-galuj.* ed. H.J. Mathews. Berlin. (in Hebrew)

Kister, Meir. J., 1975. "Call Yourselves by Graceful Names." In: *Lectures in Memory of Professor Martin M. Plessner.* Institute of Asian and African Studies at the Hebrew University. Jerusalem. 3-25

al-Kišwān, Muḥammad Ḥusayn al-Qazwīnī, 1968. *Tuḥfat al-k̲alīl fī al-ʿarūḍ wa'l-qāfiya.* ed. ʿAbd al-Ḥamīd al-Rāḍī. Baghdad

Klar, B., 1954. *Meḥqarim vediyyunim.* Tel Aviv (in Hebrew)

Kutscher, Y., 1972. "Some problems of Mishnaic lexicography... ." in: *Darke hamilon heḥadaš lesifrut Ḥazal.* Ramat Gan. 29-82 (in Hebrew)

Lambert, M., 1900. "Un fragment polémique de Saadia." *Revue des Études Juives* 40, 84-86, 260

Lavi, Abraham, 1984. *A Comparative Study of al-Ḥarīrī's Maqāmāt and Their Hebrew Translation by al-Ḥarīzī.* Ph.D. diss., University of Michigan, Ann Arbor

Levin, B. M., 1932. "Esa Meshali of Rav Saʿadya Gaon." *Tarbiz* 3: 147-160 (in Hebrew)

Levin, Israel, 1968. "The War Poems of Samuel ha-Nagid on the Background of the Ancient Arabic Hero Poetry." *Ha-Sifrut* 1: 343-367 (in Hebrew)

1977. "The Pen and the Rider (on the Kasida)." in: *Shay le-Heiman, A.M. Habermann Jubilee Volume.* ed. Zvi Malachi. Jerusalem. 143-73 (in Hebrew)

Levy, K. ed., 1936. *Zur masoretischen Grammatik.* Stuttgart

Lewin, B.M., 1943. "Esa Meshali of Rav Saʿadya Gaon." in: *Rav Saadia Gaon.* ed. J.L. Fischmann. Jerusalem. 481-532. (Hebrew; also published separately)

Lord, Albert B., 1974. *The Singer of Tales.* New York

Lotman, Jurij. M., 1976. "The Content and Structure of the Concept of Literature." *Poetics & Theory of Literature* 1: 356-399

1976. "Un Modèle dynamique du système semiotique." in: *Travaux sur les systèmes de signes: Ecole de Tartu.* Bruxelles. 77-93

Lotman, Jurij N. and Uspenskij, Boris A. 1978 [1971]. "On the Semiotics Mechanism of Culture." *New Literary History* 9:2, 211-32

Lotman, Jurij N. & Uspenskij, B.A., Ivanov, V.V., Toporov, V.N. & Pjatigorskij A.M. 1975. "Theses on the Semiotic Study of Cultures (as Applied to Slavic Texts)." in: *The Tell-Tale Sign.* ed. Thomas A. Sebeok. Lisse. 57-84

al-Maʿarrī, Abū al-ʿAlāʾ, 1971. *Luzūm mā lā yalzam.* Beirut

MacDonald, Duncan Black., 1924. "The Earlier History of the Arabian Nights." *Journal of the Royal Asiatic Society.* 353-97

MacKay, Pierre A., 1971. *Certificates of Transmission on a Manuscript of the Maqāmāt of Ḥarīrī (Ms. Cairo, Adab 105)*. Transaction of the American Philosophical Society 61, Philadelphia

Maimonides, Moses, 1904 [1851]. *Moreh nebukhim*. trans. Judah al-Ḥarīzī. ed. L. Schlossberg and S. Scheyero. Warsaw [London]

1960. *Hakdamot le-perush ha-mishna*. trans. Judah al-Ḥarīzī. ed. M.D. Rabinovitz. Jerusalem

1989. *Ma'amar teḥiyat ha-metim*. trans. Judah al-Ḥarīzī. ed. A.S. Halkin. *Kobez Al Yad (Minora Manuscripta Hebraica)* 9: 129-50

Malter, H., 1912. "Saadia Studies." *Jewish Quarterly Review*. NS 3: 487-99

1921. *Saadia Gaon: his life and his work*. New York

Malti-Douglas, Fedwa, 1985. "*Maqāmāt* and *adab*: *al-maqāma al-Maḍīriyya* of al-Hamaḏānī." *Journal of the American Oriental Society* 105: 247-58

Mann, J., 1972 [1931]. *Texts and studies in Jewish history and literature*. New York [Philadelphia]

Mannā', Hāšim Ṣāliḥ, 1989. *Al-Šāfī fī al-'arūḍ wa'l-qawāfī*. Beirut

al-Maqqarī, Aḥmad b. Muḥammad, 1968. *Nafḥ al-ṭīb min ġuṣn al-Andalus al-raṭīb*. ed. Iḥsān 'Abbās. Beirut

Margoliouth, D.S., 1927. "Hamaḏānī." *EI²*. Leiden. 2: 242-43

Markon, I.D., ed.,1957. *Commentarius in librum duodecim prophetarum quem composuit Daniel al-Kumissi*. Jerusalem (in Hebrew)

al-Marzubānī, Muḥammad b. 'Imrān, 1965. *al-Muwaššaḥ*. ed. Muḥammad 'Alī al-Bağāwī. Cairo

al-Mas'udī, 'Ali b. al-Ḥusayn, 1964. *Murūğ al-ḏahab wa-ma'ādin al-ğawhar*. ed. Muḥammad Muḥiyy al-Dīn 'Abd al-Ḥamīd. Cairo

1978. *Akbār al-zamān*. ed. 'Abd Allah al-Ṣāwī. Beirut

Mattock, John N., 1987-8. "Description and genre in Abū Nuwās." *Quaderni di Studi Arabi* 5-6: 528-40

al-Maydānī, Aḥmad b. Muḥammad, 1955. *Mağma' al-amṯāl*. ed. Muḥammad Muḥiyy al-Dīn 'Abd al-Ḥamīd. Cairo.

McDonald, M.V., 1978. "Orally transmitted poetry in pre-Islamic Arabia and other pre-literate societies." *Journal of Arabic Literature* 9: 14-31.

Mez, Adam, 1937. *The Renaissance of Islam*. trans. S.Kh. Bukhsh and D.S. Margoliouth. London

Mirsky, A., ed. 1961. *Itzhak Ibn Kalfun, Poems*. Jerusalem. (in Hebrew)

al-Mīkālī, 'Ubayd Allāh b. Aḥmad, 1908. *Darğ al-ġurar wadurğ al-durar*. ed. A. Mober. Leipzig

Monroe, James T., 1972. "Oral Composition in Pre-Islamic Poetry." *Journal of Arabic Literature* 3: 1-53

1983. *The art of Badī' az-Zamān al-Hamadhānī as picaresque narrative*. Beirut

Morag, Shlomo, 1960. "Ševa' kefulot bg"d kfr"t." in: *H. Tur-Sinai Jubilee Volume*. ed. Menahem Haran and Ben-Zion Luria. Jerusalem. 207-42 (in Hebrew)

al-Mubarrad, Abū al-'Abbās, 1973. "al-Qawāfī wamā 'štaqqat alqābuhā minhu." ed. 'Abd al-Tawāb, Ramaḍān. *Annals of the Faculty of Arts, Ain Shams University* 13: 1-18

Mubārak, Zaki, 1931. *La Prose arabe au IVe siècle de l'Hégire (Xe siècle)*. Paris

1934. *al-Naṯr al-fanni fī al-qarn al-rābī'*. Cairo

al-Mufaḍḍal b. Muḥammad al-Ḍabbī, 1964. *al-Mufaḍḍaliyyāt*. ed. Aḥmad Muḥammad Šākir and 'Abd al-Salām Hārūn. Cairo

al-Mufaḍḍal b. Salama, 1960. *Al-Fākhir*. ed. 'Abd al-'Alīm al-Ṭaḥāwī and Muḥammad 'Alī al-Nağār. Saudi Arabia

Muḥammad al-Baġdādī, 1942. *Kitāb al-muḥabbar*. Ḥaydarābād

al-Nahrawānī, Muʿāfā b. Zakariyyā Abū al-Farağ, 1981. *al-Ğalīs al-ṣāliḥ al-kāfī wa'l-anīs al-nāṣiḥ al-šāfī*. ed. Muḥammad Mursī al-Kūlī. Beirut
Naṣṣār, Ḥusayn, 1980. *Al-Qāfiya fī al-ʿarūḍ wa'l-adab*. Cairo
Nemoy, Leon, 1939-43. See al-Qirqisānī 1939-43
1972. "The Epistle of Sahl ben Maṣliaḥ." *Proceedings of the American Academy for Jewish Research* 38-9: 145-77
Neubauer, Adolf, 1866. *Aus der Petersburger Bibliothek*. Leipzig
1886. *Catalogue of the Hebrew Manuscripts in the Bodleian Library and in the College Libraries of Oxford*. Oxford
Neubauer, Adolf and Cowley, Arthur E., 1896-1906. *Catalogue of the Hebrew Manuscripts in the Bodleian Library and in the College Libraries of Oxford*. Oxford
Nöldeke, Theodor, 1899. *Fünf Moʿallaqāt*. Wien
Pagis, Dan, 1970. *Secular poetry and poetic theory: Moses Ibn Ezra and his contemporaries*. Jerusalem. (in Hebrew)
1976. *Change and tradition in the secular poetry: Spain and Italy*. Jerusalem. (in Hebrew)
Pellat, Charles, 1986. *Maḳāma*. EI². Leiden. 4: 107-15
Percikowitsch, Aisik, 1932. *al-Ḥarīzī als Übersetzer der Makamen al-Ḥarīrīs*. Munich
Perry, B. E., 1960. *The origin of the book of Sindbad*. Berlin. (offprint from *Fabula* 3,2 [1959])
Pinsker, Simhah, 1968 [1860]. *Liqqutei qadmoniyyot. zur Geschichte des Karaismus und der karaischen Literatur*. Jerusalem [Wien]
Poznanski, S., 1897. "Meswi al-Okbari, chef d'une secte juive au IXe siècle." *Revue des Etudes Juives* 34: 161-91
Prendergast, W. J., 1915 (1973²). *The Maqāmāt of Badīʿ al-Zamān al-Hamadhānī*. London and Dublin
al-Qalqašandī, Aḥmad b. ʿAlī Abū al-ʿAbbās, 1913-19. *Ṣubḥ al-aʿšā fī ṣināʿat al-inšā'*. Cairo
al-Qirqisānī, Yaʿqūb, 1939-1943. *Kitāb al-anwār wa'l-marāqib*. ed. Leon Nemoy. New York
al-Qurašī, Muḥammad b. Abī al-Kaṭṭāb, 1963. *Ğamharat ašʿār al-ʿarab*. Beirut
Rabin, Chaim, 1981. "What Constitutes a Jewish Language?." *International Journal of the Sociology of Language* 30: 19-28
1985. "Massorah and 'Ad Litteras'." *Hebrew Studies* 27: 81-91
Ratzaby, Yehuda, 1957. "On the Source of Yehuda al-Ḥarīzī's Taḥkemoni." *Tarbiz* 26: 424-39 (in Hebrew)
1980. "An Arabic *Maqāma* by al-Ḥarīzī." *Criticism and Interpretation* 15: 5-51 (in Hebrew)
1988. "An Arabic *Maqāma* by al-Ḥarīzī." *Criticism and Interpretation* 23: 51-5 (in Hebrew)
Rescher, O., 1912. "Über arabische Handschriften der Aja Sofia." *Wiener Zeitschrift fur die Kunde des Morgenlandes* 26: 63-95
1913. "Über arabischen Manuskripte der Lālelī-moschee." *Le Monde Oriental* 7: 97-137
Revell, Dov, 1923. "A letter of Saʿadya Gaon." *Devir* 1: 180-90 (in Hebrew)
Rice, David S., 1958. "Deacon or drink: some paintings from Samarra re-examined." *Arabica* 5: 15-33
Richards, D.S., 1991. "The *Maqāmāt* of al-Hamaḏānī: general remarks and a consideration of the manuscripts." *Journal of Arabic Literature* 12: 89-99
Robles, Santiaga Benavente, 1986. *Tšubot de los discipulos de Mnaḥem contra Dunaš Ben Labraṭ*. Granada
al-Rumānī, ʿAlī b. ʿIsā, 1968. *al-Nukat fī iʿǧāz al-Qur'ān*. In: Kalafallah and Sallām, 1968

Sa'adya Gaon, *Ha'egron*. See Allony 1969
1970. *Siddur R. Saadja Gaon (Kitāb ǧāmī aṣ-ṣalawāt wa'l-tasābīḥ)*. ed. I. Davidson, S. Asaf, B.I. Joel. Jerusalem
Sadan, Joseph, 1975. *Artistic Prose: Some Annotated Texts*. The Hebrew University of Jerusalem (in Hebrew)
1977. "Vin—fait de civilisation." in M. Rosen-Ayalon, ed. *Studies in Memory of Gaston Wiet*. Jerusalem
1983. *al-Adab al-'arabi al-hāzil wanawādir al-tuqalā'*. Tel Aviv and Acre
1996. "Rabbi Judah al-Ḥarīzī as cultural junction." *Pe'amim* 68: 16-67 (in Hebrew)
(forthcoming). *From margin to core: the eve of the emergence of modern Arabic literature*
Ṣafwat, Aḥmad Zakī, 1937. *Ǧamharat rasā'il al-a'rāb fī 'uṣūr al-'arabiyya al-ẓāhira*. Cairo
al-Sakākī, Yūsuf b. Abī Bakr, 1938. *Talḵīṣ al-miftāḥ fī al-ma'ānī wa'l-bayān wa'l-badī'*. Cairo
al-Saraqusṭī, Muḥammd b. Yūsuf Ibn al-Ištarkūnī, 1982. *al-Maqāmāt al-luzūmiyya*. ed. Badr Aḥmad Ḍayf. Alexandria
1995. *al-Maqāmāt al-luzūmiyya*. ed. Ḥasan al-Warāklī. Tetuan
al-Šarīšī, Aḥmad b. 'Abd al-Mu'min Abū al-'Abbās, 1952. *Šarḥ maqāmāt al-Ḥarīrī*. ed. Muḥammad 'Abd al-Mu'min Ḵafāǧī. Cairo
al-Sarī al-Raffā', 1936. *Dīwān*. Cairo
al-Sayyid, Riḍwān, ed., 1978. *al-Asad wa-'l-ġawwāṣ*. Beirut
Schechter, S., 1902. "Geniza Specimens." *Jewish Quarterly Review* 14: 37-63
1903 [1967]. *Saadyana, Geniza Fragments of Writings of R. Saadia Gaon and Others*. Cambridge [Jerusalem]
Scheindlin, Raymond, 1976. "Rabbi Moshe Ibn Ezra on the Legitimacy of Poetry." *Medievalia et Humanistica* 7: 101-15
Schirmann, Jefim (Ḥayyim), 1930. *Die hebräische Übersetzung der Maqamen des Ḥariri*. Frankfurt a/M
1939. "The Love Stories of Ja'aqob Ben El'eazar." *Yedīot ha-Maḵon le-Ḥeqer ha-Šira ha-'Ivrit (Studies of the Research Institute for Hebrew Poetry in Jerusalem)* 5: 209-266 (in Hebrew)
1961². *Hebrew Poetry in Spain and Provence*. Jerusalem & Tel Aviv. (in Hebrew)
1965. *New Hebrew Poems from the Genizah*. Jerusalem. (in Hebrew)
1979. *Studies in the History of Hebrew Poetry and Drama*. Jerusalem. (in Hebrew)
1979. "Yitzhaq Ben Mar Shaul, the poet from Lucena". in: Schirmann 1979. 1: 136-48 (in Hebrew)
1979. "On the sources of *Sefer taḥkemoni* of Judah al-Ḥarizi." in: Schirmann 1979. 1: 369-74 (in Hebrew).
Schoeler, G., 1990. "Bashshār b. Burd, Abū 'l-'Atāhiyah and Abū Nuwās." in: *'Abbasid belles-lettres*, ed. T.M. Ashtiany et al. Cambridge. 275-99
Semah, David, 1983. "The Rhythmical Function of the *Watid* and the *Fāṣila*." *Journal of Semitic Studies*. 28/2: 321-35
Sībawayhi, 'Amr b. 'Uṯmān, 1881. *Le Livre de Sibawaihi*, ed. Hartwig Derenbourg. Paris
al-Sīrafī, al-Ḥasan b. 'Abd Allāh, 1985. *Aḵbār al-naḥawiyyīn al-baṣriyyīn*. ed. Muḥammad Ibrāhīm al-Bannā. Cairo
Skoss, S., ed., 1936. *The Hebrew-Arabic Dictionary of the Bible Known as the Kitāb Jāmī' al-Alfāẓ (Agron) of David ben Abraham al-Fāsī, the Karaite (Tenth Century)*. New Haven.
Somekh, Sasson, 1981. "The concept of 'third language' and its impact on modern Arabic poetry." *Journal of Arabic Literature* 12: 74-86

Steinschneider, Moritz, 1902. *Die arabische Literatur der Juden*. Frankfurt a/M
1956 [1893]. *Die hebräischen Übersetzungen des Mittelalter und die Juden als Dolmetscher*. Graz [Berlin]
Stern, Samuel M., 1946. "The Arabic source of *The Rooster Maqāma*." *Tarbiz* 17: 87-100 (in Hebrew)
1955. "A New Fragment from the *Sepher Hagaluy* of R. Sa'adya Gaon." *Melila* 5: 133-147. (in Hebrew)
1963. "Arabic Poems by Spanish-Hebrew Poets." *Romanica et Occidentalia*. ed. Moše Lazar. Jerusalem. 254-63
1964a. "An unpublished *maqāma* by al-Ḥarīzī." *Papers of the Institute of Jewish Studies, London*. ed. J.G. Weiss. Jerusalem. 1: 186-201
1964b. "A New Description by Judah al-Ḥarīzī of His Tour to Iraq." *Sefunot, Annual for Research on the Jewish Communities in the East* 8: 145-56 (in Hebrew)
1969. "Rabbi Judah al-Ḥarīzī in praise of Maimonides." *Hagut ivrit be'eyropa (Studies on Jewish Themes by Contemporary European Scholars)*. ed. M. Zohori and A. Tartakover. Tel Aviv. 91-103 (in Hebrew)
Stern, S. G. ed., 1870. *Liber Responsionum*. I. Responsiones discipulorum R. Menahem b. Saruk. II.Responsiones discipuli Dunasch b. Labrat. Wien
Stoetzer, W.F.G.J, 1989. *Theory and Practice in Arabic Metrics*. Leiden
al-Suyūṭī, 'Abd al-Raḥmān b. Abī Bakr Ǧalāl al-Dīn, 1275(H). *al-Maqāmāt al-suyūṭiyya*. Cairo
1986. *Maqāmāt al-Suyūṭī*. ed. 'Abd al-Ġaffār Sulaymān al-Bandārī and Muḥammad al-Sa'īd Basyūnī Zaġlūl. Beirut
1988. *Maqāmāt al-Suyūṭī*. ed. Aḥmad al-Ṭawīlī. Tunis and Constantinople
al-Suyūṭī, 'Abd al-Raḥmān b. Abī Bakr Ǧalāl al-Dīn, 1970. *Mu'tarak al-aqrān fī i'ǧāz al-Qur'ān*. ed. 'A.M. al-Bağāwī. Cairo
1951. *Al-Itqān fī 'ulūm al-Qur'ān*. Cairo
T̲a'lab, Aḥmad b. Yaḥya, 1966. *Qawā'id al-ši'r*. ed. Ramaḍan 'Abd al-Tawwāb. Cairo
al-T̲a'ālibī, 'Abd al-Malik b. Muḥammad, 1956. *Yatīmat al-dahr fī maḥāsin ahl al-'aṣr*. ed. Muḥammad Muḥī al-Dīn 'Abd al-Ḥamīd. Cairo
al-T̲a'ālibī, 'Abd al-Malik b. Muḥammad, 1965. *T̲imār al-qulūb fī al-muḍāf wa-'l-mansūb*. ed. Muḥammad Abū al-Faḍl Ibrāhīm. Cairo
al-Ṭabarī, Muḥammad b. Ǧarīr, 1957-60. *Ǧāmi' al-bayān 'an ta'wīl al-Qur'ān*. ed. M. Šākir and A. Šākir. Cairo
al-Tanūk̲ī, 'Abd al-Bāqī b. al-Ḥasan, 1970. *Kitāb al-qawāfī*. ed. 'Umar al-As'ad and Muḥī al-Dīn Ramaḍān. Beirut
al-Tanūk̲ī, al-Muḥassin b. 'Alī Abū 'Alī, 1930. *Kitāb ǧawāmi' al-tawārīk̲ al-mussamā bikitāb nišwār al-muḥāḍara wa'akhbār al-mud̲ākara*. vol. 8. ed. D.S. Margoliouth. Damascus
1971. *Nišwār al-muḥāḍara wa'akhbār al-mud̲ākara*. vols 1 & 2. ed. 'Abūd al-Šāliğī. Beirut
al-Tawḥīdī, Abū Ḥayyān, 1953. *Kitāb al-imtā' wa-'l-mu'ānasa*. ed. Aḥmad Amīn et al. Beirut
al-Tibrīzī, Yaḥya b. 'Alī al-K̲aṭīb, 1966. "Kitāb al-kāfī fī al-'arūḍ wa'l-qawāfī." ed. Ḥasan 'Abd Allāh al-Hasānī. *Mağallat Ma'had al-Mak̲ṭūṭāt al-'Arabiyya* 12: 146-68
1988. *Al-Wāfī fī al-'arūḍ wa'l-qawāfī*. ed. Fak̲r al-Dīn Qabāwa. Damascus. 193-227
1894. *Kitāb šarḥ al-mu'allaqāt al-'ašr*. ed. Charles James Lyall. Calcutta
al-Tirmid̲ī, Muḥammad b. 'Īsā, 1925. *Ḥāšiyat Ibrāhīm al-Bāǧūrī 'alā matn al-Šamā'il al-muḥammadiyya*. Cairo

Tynjanov, Jurij N., 1971 [1929]. "On Literary Evolution." in: *Readings in Russian Poetics*. ed. L. Matejka and K. Pomorska. Cambridge, Mass. 66-8
1971. "Problems in the Study of Literature and Language." in: *Readings in Russian Poetics*. eds. L. Matejka and K. Pomorska. Cambridge, Mass. 29-81
ʿUmar b. Abī Rabīʿa, 1901. *Dīwān*. ed. Paul Schwarz. Leipzig.
Vadet, Jean Claude, 1968. *L'ésprit courtois en Orient dans les premiers siècles de l'hégire*. Paris
Vajda, George, 1957. "Quarante Arbaʿūn peu remarqués ou inconnus." *Arabica* 4: 34-41
Varela, M. E. ed., 1981. *Tešubot de Yehudi ben Šešet*. Granada
Wagner, Ewald, 1965. *Abū Nuwās: Eine Studie zur arabischen Literatur der frühen ʿAbbāsidenzeit*. Wiesbaden
al-Waššāʾ, Muḥammad b. Aḥmad Abū al-Ṭayyib, 1991. *Kitāb al-fāḍil fī ṣifat al-adab al-kāmil*. ed. Yaḥyā Wahīb al-Ǧabūrī. Beirut
Weil, Gotthold., 1958. *Grundriss und System der altarabischen Metren*. Wiesbaden.
1960. "ʿArūḍ." *EI*². Leiden and London. 1: 667-77
Wellhausen, Julius, 1884-99. *Skizzen und Vorarbeiten*. Berlin
Wertheimer, Sh. A., 1925. *Sefer geon ha-gaonim*. Jerusalem
Wieder, N., 1962. *The Judean Scrolls and Karaism*. London
Wright, William, 1967 [1862]. *A Grammar of the Arabic Language*. Cambridge
Yahalom, Joseph, 1983. "The Beginning of exact Metre in Hebrew Poetry." *Lešonenu* 47: 25-61 (in Hebrew)
1985. "A response." *Lešonenu* 48-9: 163-66 (in Hebrew)
Yahalom, Shelly, 1979. "Problèmes d'interférence de système sémiotiques." *Paper presented to the 2nd International IASS Congress*. Vienna, 2-6 July
1980. "Du non-littéraire au littéraire." *Poetique* 44: 406-421
Yelin, D., 1972². *Introduction to the Hebrew Poetry of the Spanish Period*. Jerusalem (in Hebrew)
Yāqūt, b. ʿAbd Allah al-Rūmī, 1923. *Kitāb iršād al-arīb ilā maʿrifat al-adīb al-maʿrūf bimuʿǧam al-udabāʾ*. ed. D.S. Margoliouth. London
1936-38. *Muʿǧam al-udabāʾ*. Cairo
al-Yūsī, al-Ḥasan b. Masʿūd, 1981. *Zahr al-akam fī al-amṯāl wa-'l-ḥikam*. ed. Muḥammad Ḥaǧǧī and Muḥammad al-Akḏar. Casablanca
Zakharia, Katia, 1994. "Norme et fiction dans la genèse des *Maqāmāt* d'al-Ḥarīrī." *Bulletin d'Études Orientales* 46: 217-31
al-Zamakšarī, Maḥmūd b. ʿUmar, 1987. *al-Mustaqṣā fī amṯāl al-ʿarab*. Beirut
al-Zubaydī, Muḥammad b. al-Ḥasan, 1984. *Ṭabaqāt al-naḥawiyyīn wa'l-luġawiyyīn*. ed. Muḥammad Abū al-Faḍl Ibrāhīm. Cairo
Zucker, M., 1959. *Rav Saʿadya Gaon's Translation of the Torah*. New York. (in Hebrew)
Zwettler, M., 1978. *The Oral Tradition of Classical Arabic Poetry*. Columbus

INDEX

BRILL'S SERIES IN JEWISH STUDIES

1. Cohen, R. *Jews in Another Environment.* Surinam in the Second Half of the Eighteenth Century. 1991. ISBN 90 04 09373 7
2. Prawer, S.S. *Israel at Vanity Fair.* Jews and Judaism in the Writings of W.M. Thackeray. 1992. ISBN 90 04 09403 2
3. Price, J.J. *Jerusalem under Siege.* The Collapse of the Jewish State 66-70 C.E. 1992. ISBN 90 04 09471 7
4. Zinguer, I. *L'hébreu au temps de la Renaissance.* 1992. ISBN 90 04 09557 8
5. Gutwein, D. *The Divided Elite.* Economics, Politics and Anglo-Jewry, 1882-1917. 1992. ISBN 90 04 09447 4
6. Eraqi Klorman, B.-Z. *The Jews of Yemen in the Nineteenth Century.* A Portrait of a Messianic Community. 1993. ISBN 90 04 09684 1
7. Ben-Dov, N. *Agnon's Art of Indirection.* Uncovering Latent Content in the Fiction of S.Y. Agnon. 1993. ISBN 90 04 09863 1
8. Gera, D. *Judaea and Mediterranean Politics,* 219-161 B.C.E. 1998. ISBN 90 04 09441 5
9. Coudert, A.P. *The Impact of the Kabbalah in the Seventeenth Century.* The Life and Thought of Francis Mercury van Helmont (1614-1698). 1999. ISBN 90 04 09844 5
10. Gross, A. *Iberian Jewry from Twilight to Dawn.* The World of Rabbi Abraham Saba. 1995. ISBN 90 04 10053 9
12. Ahroni, R. *The Jews of the British Crown Colony of Aden.* History, Culture, and Ethnic Relations. 1994. ISBN 90 04 10110 1
13. Deutsch, N. *The Gnostic Imagination.* Gnosticism, Mandaeism and Merkabah Mysticism. 1995. ISBN 90 04 10264 7
14. Arbel, B. *Trading Nations.* Jews and Venetians in the Early Modern Eastern Mediterranean. 1995. ISBN 90 04 10057 1
15. Levenson, D. *Julian and Jerusalem.* The Sources and Tradition. 1996. ISBN 90 04 105441
16. Menache, S. (ed.). *Communication in the Jewish Diaspora.* The Pre-Modern World. 1996. ISBN 90 04 10189 6
17. Parfitt, T. *The Road to Redemption.* The Jews of the Yemen 1900-1950. 1996. ISBN 90 04 10544 1
18. Assis, Y.T. *Jewish Economy in the Medieval Crown of Aragon, 1213-1327.* Money and Power. 1997. ISBN 90 04 10615 4
19. Stillman, Y.K. & Stillman, N.A. (eds.). *From Iberia to Diaspora.* Studies in Sephardic History and Culture. 1999. ISBN 90 04 10720 7
20. Barkai, R. *A History of Jewish Gynaecological Texts in the Middle Ages.* 1998. ISBN 90 04 10995 1
21. Heller, M.J. *Printing the Talmud.* A History of the Individual Treatises Printed from 1700 to 1750. 1999. ISBN 90 04 11293 6
22. Deutsch, N. *Guardians of the Gate.* Angelic Vice Regency in Late Antiquity. 1999. ISBN 90 04 10909 9
23. Ratzabi, S. *Between Zionism and Judaism.* The Radical Circle in Brith Shalom 1925–1933. 2000. ISBN 90 04 11507 2

24. Brasz, C. & Kaplan, Y. (eds.). *Dutch Jews as Perceived by Themselves and by Others.* Proceedings of the Eighth International Symposium on the History of the Jews in the Netherlands, 22–25 November 1998. 2000. ISBN 90 04 11705 9
25. Drory, R. *Models and Contacts.* Arabic Literature and its Impact on Medieval Jewish Culture. 2000. ISBN 90 04 11738 5
26. Lamdan, R. *A Separate People.* Jewish Women in Palestine, Syria and Egypt in the Sixteenth Century. 2000. ISBN 90 04 11747 4